GEORGE MOORE DUBLIN, PARIS, HOLLYWOOD

Edited by
Conor Montague and Adrian Frazier

IRISH ACADEMIC PRESS
DUBLIN • PORTLAND, OR

First published in 2012 by Irish Academic Press

8 Chapel Lane,
Sallins,
Co. Kidare, Ireland

920 NE 58th Avenue, Suite 300
Portland, Oregon,
97213-3786, USA

www.iap.ie

British Library Cataloguing in Publication Data

George Moore : Dublin, Paris, Hollywood.
1. Moore, George, 1852-1933—Criticism and interpretation.
2. Moore, George, 1852-1933—Political and social views.
I. Montague, Conor. II. Frazier, Adrian Woods.
823.8-dc23

ISBN 978 0 7165 3147 0 (cloth)
ISBN 978 0 7165 3165 4 (paper)
ISBN 978 0 7165 3199 9 (Ebook)

Library of Congress Cataloging-in-Publication Data
An entry can be found on request

Printed and bound by CPI Group (UK) Ltd, Croydon, CR0 4YY

Contents

Acknowledgements

The idea for this collection of essays originated during an extremely pleasant evening spent in the company of an eclectic group of scholars outside a seaside restaurant in Almeria, Spain. It was April 2010, the final evening of the Fourth International George Moore Conference, organised by Elena Jaime de Pablos of the University of Almeria. The sunset, together with wonderful Spanish hospitality and perhaps a little too much – or just enough – Spanish wine, lent a warm glow to the evening. At some stage, among the countless servings of tapas and the relentless stomps and wails of flamenco, it was proposed that the next Moore conference should take place in Galway, at the institute that bears the Moore name. That this event took place just fourteen months later, the fruits of which are compiled in this collection, is thanks to the vision, cooperation and efforts of many.

We owe a debt of gratitude to the following: Elena Jaime de Pablos, for providing a template for how a Moore conference, or indeed, any conference, should be hosted; Mary Pierse of University College Cork, for sharing her experience and humour throughout the organisational process; Elizabeth Grubgeld of Oklahoma State University and Ann Heilmann of the University of Hull for their advice and suggestions; the keynote speakers, Professor Mark Llewellyn (University of Strathclyde), Professor Lucy McDiarmid (Montclair State University) and Professor James Pethica (Williams College); from the Moore Institute, Professor Nicholas Canny and Professor Nicholas Allen, development manager, Martha Shaughnessy and administrative assistant, Kate Thornhill; local historian Art Ó Súilleabháin for sharing his wealth of knowledge concerning Moore Hall and the area around Lough Carra; playwright Thomas Kilroy, for allowing us to stage his two-hander, *The Dreaming House*, about George Moore and his manservant; Mephisto Theatre for bringing it to life. We are similarly indebted to Head of English at NUI Galway, Professor Sean Ryder, Head of History, Professor Stephen Ellis, Head of Humanities, Dr. Lionel Pilkington, Acting Director of Irish Studies, Dr. Nessa Cronin; Professor Gearoid O'Tuathaigh, Marie Boran and Brigid Clesham of the Irish Landed

Estates Project; John Kenny, Muireann O'Cinneide, Fiona Bateman, Vinnie Browne, Mary Montague, Dearbhla Mooney, Geraldine Jeffers, Mark Corcoran-Kelly; and Hilda at the Coole Park visitor centre.

Valuable assistance was received from Irish Research Council for Humanities and Social Sciences (IRCHSS); Fáilte Ireland; Texts, Contexts, Cultures, Moore Institute, NUI Galway; Irish Landed Estates Project.

We would like to especially thank Glenn Close, who shares her experience in bringing *Albert Nobbs* to the big screen as an afterword to this volume.

Last, but by no means least, we wish to thank Lisa Hyde of Irish Academic Press, for her encouragement and guidance throughout.

Conor Montague & Adrian Frazier

Notes on Contributors

Mark Llewellyn joined the University of Strathclyde as Professor in English Studies under the John Anderson Research Leadership (JARL) scheme in 2011. Previous to this, Mark worked at the University of Liverpool as an AHRC Postdoctoral Researcher (2006–07), then Lecturer and Senior Lecturer in English (2007–11); he also served as Liverpool's Director of Postgraduate Research in Humanities and Social Sciences (2008–11). In 2012, Mark was appointed Director of Research at the Arts and Humanities Research Council. He has published widely on Victorian literature and culture in relation to gender, family relations and society, and on the enduring presence of the nineteenth century in contemporary culture.

Fiona White is a native of Galway. She was educated at National University of Ireland, Galway, where she received a BA in History and Archaeology and an MA in Archaeology. She lectures on the Heritage Studies programme at the Galway–Mayo Institute of Technology, Castlebar Campus, Co. Mayo. She recently commenced a PhD entitled: 'Moore Hall Estate, 1845–1870: Perspectives on its History and Heritage'.

Haim Goren, a historical-geographer, is an Associate Prof. in the Department of Multidisciplinary Studies and Vice President for academic affairs at the Tel-Hai Academic College. His main fields of interest include Holy Land pilgrim's and traveller's literature, European activity in Ottoman Palestine and the Near East, and history of the modern scientific study of these regions.

Margaretta D'Arcy is a prolific playwright, writer, film maker, broadcaster, felon and agitator and is a member of *Aosdana*. Much of her work has been produced in collaboration with John Arden. In 2011 Margaretta and John produced 'Tea at four with George Moore', where they performed excerpts from Moore's *Hail and Farewell*. Margaretta lives in Galway.

Lucy McDiarmid is Marie Frazee-Baldassarre Professor of English at Montclair State University and a former fellow of the Guggenheim

Foundation and of the Cullman Center for Scholars and Writers at the New York Public Library. Her scholarly interest in cultural politics is exemplified by her most recent book, *The Irish Art of Controversy*, and her forthcoming book, *Poets and the Peacock Dinner: the literary history of a meal*, which features Lady Gregory among the poets (Wilfrid Blunt, W. B. Yeats, and Ezra Pound). She is co-editor of the Penguin *Selected Writings of Lady Gregory* and the author and editor of several other books.

Michel Brunet is a Senior Lecturer in English at the University of Valenciennes and Hainaut-Cambrésis, France. A graduate of the Universities of Paris and Lille, he wrote his doctoral thesis on William Trevor's short stories. His main areas of research lie in Irish literature, with a particular focus on Anglo-Irish writing. He also has a strong interest in Irish minorities and issues related to identity. His forthcoming publications include essays on George Moore and on contemporary Irish fiction.

Mary Pierse teaches Irish feminisms and feminist theory for the Women's Studies M.A. UCC. She compiled the 5-volume *Irish Feminisms 1810–1930* (Routledge 2010). Editor of *George Moore: Artistic Visions and Literary Worlds* (2006), she has published on the writings of Kate Chopin, Arthur Conan Doyle, Antonio Fogazzarro, and the poets Dennis O'Driscoll and Cathal Ó Searcaigh. She is a board member at National Centre for Franco-Irish Studies, and on editorial boards/ scientific committees for publications in France and Spain.

Mª Elena Jaime de Pablos is a Senior Lecturer at the University of Almería, Spain, where she teaches Feminist Literary Criticism and English Literature. Her doctoral thesis was on the representation of women in Moore's narrative. She has recently co-edited: *Amor y matrimonio: Entre lo ideal y lo real* (2008), *Identidades femeninas en un mundo plural* (2009), *Distancias cortas. El relato breve en Gran Bretaña, Irlanda y Estados Unidos (1995–2005)*(2010), and *Epistemología feminista: Mujeres e identidades* (2011). She is currently working on the fiction of Mary O'Donnell.

Mark Corcoran-Kelly is a postgraduate researcher at the Moore Institute, National University of Ireland Galway. His research concerns the representation of marriage in Irish Literature 1850–1930.

Conor Montague is a postgraduate researcher at the National University of Ireland, Galway. A graduate of the NUI Galway MA in Writing, Conor was awarded a four-year fellowship in 2008 as part of the IRCHSS funded, Texts, Contexts, Cultures programme. His research concerns epistolary networks among cultural elites during the Irish revival.

Stoddard Martin has taught at Harvard, Oxford, Lodz and Warsaw Universities and is an associate fellow of the Institute of English Studies, University of London. His books include *Wagner to the Waste Land* and *The Great Expatriate Writers* as well as several anthologies. He is a reviewer and essayist and is on the board of *Quarterly Review*. He writes short fiction under the name Chip Martin and manages his own small press, Starhaven.

Melanie Grundmann is a cultural scientist who lives and works in Berlin, Germany. Her research interests include dandyism, taboo, and celebrity culture. Most recently, Melanie Grundmann published a German translation of Théophile Gautiers *Les Jeunes-France*(1833) in 2011. 2012 will see the release of her dandyism-inspired cookbook.

Elizabeth Grubgeld is Professor of English at Oklahoma State University. In addition to publishing many articles on Irish literature, autobiography, and disability studies, she is author of *George Moore and the Autogenous Self: The Autobiography and Fiction* (Syracuse UP, 1994), *Anglo-Irish Autobiography: Class, Gender, and the Forms of Narrative* (Syracuse UP, 2004), both of which won the American Conference for Irish Studies prize for best book of literary and cultural criticism in their respective years.

Jayne Thomas is a postgraduate researcher at Cardiff University. Her current research project focuses on the development of the romantic visionary moment, or epiphany, in the Victorian period, and includes an analysis of George Moore's use of the Wordsworthian 'spot of time'.

Adrian Frazier is a professor in the English Department, National University of Ireland, Galway, director of its MA in Writing, and a member of the Royal Irish Academy. He is the author of *Behind the Scenes: Yeats, Horniman, and the Struggle for the Abbey Theatre* (1990), *George Moore 1852–1933* (2000), and *Hollywood Irish: John Ford, Abbey Actors, and the Irish Revival in Hollywood* (2011).

Preface

On 3 June 2011, some fifty delegates arrived at the Moore Institute, NUI Galway, for the Fifth International George Moore Conference. It truly was an international conference. Representatives from Spain, Germany, Israel, France, Switzerland, Italy, Japan, England, Wales and the US joined those who had travelled from all over Ireland to participate in this event dedicated to the work of George Moore. Added to the academic rigour that accompanies any such gathering, there was also a sense of pilgrimage. For many delegates, it was their first visit to the west of Ireland, a region with strong connections to the Moore family, and which had a profound influence on the Irish literary revival. The River Corrib passes some twenty metres to the rear of the Moore Institute. It originates at Lough Carra, enters Lough Mask through the River Keel, then disappears underground before emerging into Lough Corrib. It passes by the Moore Institute before flowing through the city to enter Galway Bay at the Claddagh. It was here, following the Gaelic League *Feis* in 1902, that Moore left Lady Gregory and Douglas Hyde at St Pat's Temperance Hall, and, accompanied by W.B. Yeats and Edward Martyn, walked by the river to the end of the Claddagh Pier and watched three girls, their skirts kilted up, wading into a tidal pool:

> As if desiring my appreciation, one girl walked across the pool, lifting her red petticoat to her waist, and forgetting to drop it as the water shallowed, she showed me thigh whiter and rounder than any I have ever seen, their country coarseness heightening the temptation.

Moore would only have had to look a short distance across the estuary, to the end of the Long Walk, to see the point from which, just over a century earlier, his great grandfather exported the seaweed harvested along Ireland's western seaboard to Alicante, Spain to be processed for iodine. It was the profit from this enterprise, coupled with proceeds from his wine business, which enabled this George Moore (of Alicante) to purchase the land overlooking Lough Carra at Carnacon, Co Mayo and build Moore Hall. His son John, the author's great uncle, joined the United Irishmen's ill-fated rebellion of 1798, becoming briefly the first, and indeed the last, president of the Republic of Connacht. As they walked from the Claddagh that day in August 1902, Yeats, Moore and Martyn made their way over the cobblestones of Quay St., passing the townhouse of 'Dear Edward's' distant cousin Humanity Dick Martin at Kirwin's Lane. It was in this house that Wolfe Tone finalised plans for the events of 1798. History, geography and ancestry are importantly and inextricably linked.

Moore had many connections to Galway. His tribal pedigree – Athy, Lynch, Browne and Blake – no doubt lent a swagger to his gait as he passed through its thoroughfares in August 1902. The Boer War had ended, which allowed his brother Maurice to return to Ireland. The Gaelic League was enjoying unparalleled success. The Irish Literary Theatre had evolved into the Irish National Theatre Society, an organisation in which Moore still felt he had an important role to play. In some ways, though George Moore was unaware of it at the time, this visit to Galway signalled the end of his storyteller's holiday. Soon after, the controversy over authorship of *Where There is Nothing* soured Moore's relations with the Coole circle, a conflict Michel Brunet explores in 'George Moore's Dana Controversy Revisited'. Added to this, the Gaelic League distanced themselves from theauthor, despite his ambitions for *An tÚr Gort*. George Moore would never again feel that same affinity with those who had enticed him to return to Ireland.

Galway is a vastly different place in 2012, but its narrow streets still resonate with stories, its hinterland remains alive with folklore. Lady Gregory's townhouse – where she stayed when visiting Galway Gaol, or on folklore gathering trips to the city workhouse – is now the Galway Arts Centre. Queen's College Galway is now National University of Ireland, Galway, with the Moore Institute, named after the Moore family, its flagship institution for humanities. The often strained relationship between George Moore and Lady Gregory, and the cultural dynamics involved in her collection of folklore are given fascinating treatment by Lucy McDiarmid in 'Lady Gregory, George Moore and Gathering Folklore'.

Early in 2011, some 130 miles east of Galway, another international cast had gathered in celebration of George Moore, albeit a gathering conducted in a different fashion. *Albert Nobbs*, an adaptation of Moore's story of the same name, was shot on location in Dublin in January. The project had come about due to the efforts of two very different women: the French feminist and playwright Simone Benmussa, and the American actor Glenn Close. The release of *Albert*

Nobbs signalled the end of a prolonged labour of love. Not for the first time, Moore's writing had seduced women from afar. Simone Benmussa, of the Théâtre du Rond-Point in Paris, had successfully mounted a stage adaptation of Moore's story in Paris and London and was in New York to direct a production of the play at The Manhattan Theater Club in 1982. Glenn Close auditioned for Benmussa and was cast in the title role. In Chapter 16, Glenn Close speaks of the intense connection she felt with Moore's creation, and the long-lasting relationship she shared with the character over the thirty years it took to bring it to the screen. In the penultimate chapter of this collection, Adrian Frazier re-visits 'Albert Nobbs' and tells us why it qualifies as one of the greatest short stories in twentieth-century English literature.

With these two very different gatherings taking place on opposite coasts of Ireland in 2011, one could be forgiven for thinking that George Moore's moment had arrived, that he was finally getting the recognition that had long been due. Moore's literary reputation took some time to revive following the misrepresentation and vindictive criticism to which he had been subjected by W.B. Yeats and others following his death in 1933. The characteristics that made Moore fascinating, both as man and author – his incessant experimentation with style and form, his knack for controversy, his unwillingness to conform to convention, his independence of mind and spirit – are the same traits that led to the decline in Moore's literary repute. With no direct descendants to prolong his legacy, and few contemporaries willing to do so, it seemed as if Moore belonged to nobody.

There were also, no doubt, underlying factors – social, historical, literary and personal – for the posthumous decline in Moore's reputation. He didn't fit into any of the neat categories favoured by literary critics and academics. Though an important figure in the Irish literary revival, Moore was not a nationalist, and most of his work has little obviously to do with the revival. He did not, and does not, fit into the confines of any country's literary pantheon. Moore's artistic awakening occurred in the Paris of the 1870s. His friendship with the Impressionists and his championing of Zola and literary naturalism, marked him as a European artist. To the English, he was a French writer living in England; to the French, he was an English writer living in France; to the Irish, he was the absentee author of *Parnell and His Island*. In a literary echo of his alleged ancestor, Sir Thomas More, George Moore became stranded in a no-place of his own creation.

Over the past twenty years, thanks to the work of scholars such as

Richard Allen Cave, Elizabeth Grubgeld and Adrian Frazier, this imbalance has been gradually redressed, and Moore's work has been afforded the opportunity to speak for itself. There are sixty-five titles by Moore listed in Edwin Gilcher's *Bibliography of George Moore*, many of them, such as *Confessions of a Young Man* and *Esther Waters*, recognised masterpieces that have made their way onto university curricula across the globe. His role in introducing French modernism to English literature, his critique of late-Victorian fiction, his willingness to take on the monopoly of the circulating libraries, the sheer volume and quality of an oeuvre that influenced James Joyce, Virginia Woolf, Arnold Bennett, Ernest Hemingway and John McGahern to name but a few. These are all reasons explaining Moore's recent return to vogue, and why there are an ever-increasing number of scholarly articles, of dissertations, of collections such as this, all of which explore the continued relevance of Moore's writings.

As Mark Llewellyn illustrates in the opening chapter of this collection, the writings of George Moore seem prophetic. Moore recognised the danger posed by the Irish Catholic church as it took advantage of the power vacuum created by the demise of the Anglo-Irish Ascendancy. He recognised the threat posed to individual freedom by nationalism, to individual sexuality by rigid convention, and utilised the novel in highly original ways to expose such dangers. With Moore, the novel could be philosophical enquiry, personal odyssey, and an experiment in form and function. His innovations with autobiographical narrative foreshadowed what is today the most rapidly expanding section of the book market. He espoused a pan-European mindset while nations obsessed about borders. In short, George Moore matters, as much if not more than ever.

This collection goes some way towards reinforcing this viewpoint. The variety of topics reflects the sheer diversity of Moore's oeuvre, the eclecticism of the man's interests. The theme of female vocation in Moore's fiction, explored by Elena Jaime de Pablos, coexists comfortably with Jayne Thomas's discussion of how Moore utilised romantic epiphany in his novels. We gain a sense of Moore's pedigree in Haim Goren's account of George Henry Moore's adventures in the Middle East. Fiona White expands on our knowledge of George Henry (MP) by taking us back to Moore Hall during the Famine, to Coranna's legendary Chester Gold Cup win in 1847, and through turbulent times for the Moore estate in the years leading up to the author's birth.

Moore Hall was built by Moore of Alicante in the 1790s. The once proud mansion stands ruined in the woods by Lough Carra, Co Mayo. George and his brother Maurice roamed this countryside as children with Oscar and Willie Wilde. Champion racehorses galloped around the now overgrown track that circled the property in the days of George Henry. George Moore's final resting place, Castle Island, lies low in the middle distance, a ten-minute boat ride across the lake that 'lay like a mirror that somebody had breathed upon'. The island is overgrown with hazel, birch and larch, inhabited by wildfowl, and visited only by otters and occasionally by anglers seeking shelter from the sudden winds that rise out on the lake. The modest stone that marks Moore's grave is overgrown by brambles, thorns appropriate for the self-proclaimed messiah who travelled over land and sea to save Ireland. The contrast with the resting place of his childhood playmate couldn't be greater. Castle Island is a long way from the Père Lachaise cemetery. It is a fitting resting place for a perpetual outsider who put art before companionship, and whose finest prose describes the countryside around this lake.

The paths of Moore and Wilde diverged following those childhood adventures in south Mayo, but, as Melanie Grundmann points out in 'The Dandyism of George Moore', the two shared a flamboyant eccentricity that led to their self-stylising into marginalised and fascinating works of art. Elizabeth Grubgeld has published important work on Moore's 'autogenous self' and builds on that here as she draws on epistolary theory to reveal new depths to Moore's correspondence. George Moore belonged on the margins. Self-educated in the cafe culture of 1870s Paris, he learned that on the outside is where the true artist resides. Like his younger contemporary, Groucho Marx, George Moore was naturally suspicious of any club that would have him as a member. Anytime it seemed as if he was in danger of *belonging*, to family, city, nation or cultural movement, a bridge-burning would serve to realign his compass and return him to his own unique course.

Moore's reaction to the Boer War while living in England is one such example, and this turbulent period in Moore's life is explored by Margaretta D'Arcy in 'The Metamorphosis of George Moore'. At the turn of the twentieth century, Moore arrived in an Ireland that was 'interesting because it is in the process of making, but at present ignorance is everywhere, and intellectually the country is unwashed, that is why it is interesting; green fruit is more interesting than red, though not so sweet to the taste.'

Though GM drifted from the Coole circle at this time, he positioned himself at the centre of his own influential network in Dublin. During the decade he resided there the correspondents and callers to 4 Upper Ely Place were a veritable who's who of contemporary artistic and professional elites. George Moore revelled in the cultural maelstrom that was Dublin at the turn of the century – 'as full of accidents as a fire is full of sparks'. He thrived on the energy generated by the frictions that typified the period. Those who called regularly to 4 Upper Ely Place to converse on art, literature, politics, religion and contemporaries at various stages of GM's residence included: George Russell (AE), John Butler Yeats, W.K. Magee, Richard Best, Oliver St. John Gogarty, Maurice Moore, Tom Rutledge, Walter Osbourne, Thornley Stoker, W.B. Yeats, Fr. Finlay, Clara Christian, Susan Mitchell, Frank Fay, Lady Gregory, Douglas Hyde, Horace Plunkett, Hugh Lane, Edward Martyn, Arthur Griffith, Edith Oldham, William Orphen, John Hughes, George Coffey, Kuno Meyer, T.P. Gill and Fr. Jeremiah O'Donovan. In 'George Moore and his Dublin Contemporaries: Reputations and Realities', Mary Pierse reveals hitherto unexplored relationships with Pádraic Ó Conaire, James Stephens and others. Mark Corcoran-Kelly and Conor Montague unearth fresh connections with James Joyce, while Stoddard Martin makes a case for Moore's influence on Ernest Hemingway. The ideas that inspired and informed Moore's work were mined from the relationships that attached him to numerous social networks. Friends, family, lovers, colleagues, correspondents and rivals were all exploited for use in Moore's writing. His extensive oeuvre is primarily a literary interpretation of the diverse cultural milieux in which he practised his craft over a lengthy career.

This is not to diminish GM's originality. Rather it is a recognition of what Samuel Taylor Coleridge referred to as the 'parallelisms' – the co-existence of several texts, voices and narratives within a single structure of ideas and the accompanying fear of their irretrievable loss – that facilitates the creation of any work of literature. When George Moore said that ideas are the most important things we possess, it was a strong affirmation of any individual's position at the centre of his or her own unique maelstrom of coexisting texts, voices, and narratives. It was the concomitant fear of their irretrievable loss that fuelled George Moore's prodigious literary output. A criticism often levelled at George Moore is his lack of consistency, that he has no definitive style or allegiance that allows his work to be easily categorised. This is true, and reinforces the above analysis. In keeping with the ethos of naturalism, Moore was very much a product of his environment, or to be more accurate, a constantly evolving product of the many diverse environments in which he practised his trade. It was in his ability to articulate the cultural stimuli of a given time and place that Moore's talent resided. He exploited this sensibility with artistic integrity, and with an acerbic personality that itself served as a counter-stimulus to those individuals unwittingly coaxed into the complex ecosystem of texts, voices and narratives that animated his writing.

The eclectic nature of this collection reflects the multiple narratives of a life well-lived, the sensibilities of an ever-evolving artist, and the complexities of a self in a constant process of re-invention. In an era where globalisation and capitalism, or to use Mark Llewellyn's phrase, cultural economics, has led to marketability superseding originality as the goal of artistic endeavour, there are valuable lessons to be taken from George Moore's life and work. The past decade has seen a paradigm shift in how artistic endeavour is valued and exchanged. Thanks to new technologies, middlemen who for too long profiteered from music, literature and film are losing absolute control. Artist and audience can increasingly enjoy a direct relationship, a symbiotic partnership of which Moore would have approved. The success of *Albert Nobbs* has raised the profile of George Moore, introduced him to a public previously unaware of his existence. This exposure means that screenwriters and film producers are examining Moore's back catalogue as we speak, in the hope of unearthing new gems. There are many. There will be aberrations and misrepresentations, successes and failures, but, for the first time since his death, Moore's profile will expand outside of academia and lovers of fine literature.

Albert Nobbs, upon opening in January 2012 at 245 locations across the US and Canada, received a positive critical response. Nominated for Golden Globes, Academy Awards, and Screen Actors Guild awards in the categories of Best Actress in a Leading Role, Best Actress in a Supporting Role, Best Make-up, and Best Original Song, the film was critically acclaimed for its delicate and moving portrayal of Albert, and for its recreation of nineteenth-century Dublin. George Moore, in his most unlikely collaborative venture since *Diarmid and Grania*, was nominated for a Satellite Award, together with Glenn Close, John Banville and Gabriella Prekop, for best screenplay. Two films dominated the awards in 2012, relegating Albert Nobbs to third place in most of the categories in which it was nominated. *The Artist*, directed by Michel Hazanavicius, and starring Jean Dujardin and Bérénice Bejo, and *The*

Iron Lady, directed by Phyllida Lloyd and starring Meryl Streep got most of the attention. It was not the first time that Moore had fallen between the cracks of French Flair and British Realism.

There will be no return to the silent movie, and certainly no regression to Thatcherite politics. However, George Moore is relevant as never before. His individuality, his iconoclastic nature, his candour and most importantly, his shamelessness, can inspire a new generation. Moore's refusal to conform to the conventions of his time contributed to the posthumous demise in his literary reputation. The post-war twentieth century was a period of rules, of control, of neat categories into which all human beings were placed. It was natural that Moore would be neglected. A product of the equally restrictive and judgmental nineteenth century, George Moore quickly outgrew both literary and social conventions of his time. His innovative approach to his art had a profound effect on twentieth-century literature but younger contemporaries, such as Joyce and Woolf, cast a longer shadow and his star faded as theirs soared. George Moore didn't belong to the nineteenth century. He didn't belong to the twentieth century. If anything has become clear over the period of the past five International George Moore Conferences, underlined by the 2012 success of *Albert Nobbs*, it is that George Moore belongs to the twenty-first century. It is just a matter of claiming him.

Conor Montague
September 2012

CHAPTER ONE

George Moore, the Credit Crunch and Cultural Economics

MARK LLEWELLYN

In her 2011 novel *The Forgotten Waltz*, the Dublin-based Booker Prize-winning writer Anne Enright explores the nature of an adulterous affair taking place during the years 2008 and 2009. The setting is Ireland, predominantly Dublin, with interludes in European business capitals such as Switzerland or the increasingly open eastern European frontier. Although not explicitly about the credit crunch, the reflections of the female narrator, Gina Moynihan, the other woman of the affair, take place in the financially fateful month of December 2009, and the narrative bristles with its sense of the intensely personal, emotional and in some ways everyday nature of family, sex, relationships with an astute awareness of and occasional nod to the global and the capitalist sentiments of the marketplace beyond. The most telling conjunction of these two pathways of living occurs in the chapter midway through the book entitled 'Money (That's What I Want)'; like all the chapters in the book its title is derived from a popular song. Gina has to sell her dead mother's house, the home of her childhood, in the Terenure suburb of Dublin. At the time of her mother's death the property was valued at 'two and bit' but now, in the narrative timeframe of late 2009, that valuation is off the mark:

> Outside in the snow, the For Sale sign looks fresh as the day it was hammered home. No one knows what the house is worth now. No one will buy it, so that's how much it is worth. Nothing. Despite which, we will owe tax based on that 'two and a bit'. For a house that is currently worth whistling for. I can't figure out the fake money from the real. I walk around this magic box, this trap, with its frost-flowered windows, weeping condensation as the morning proceeds. I gather my briefcase from the console

table in the hall. I open the same door I have opened since I
could reach the latch. And I head out to earn some money.[1]

The average price of a Dublin house increased by 500 per cent
between 1994 and 2006,[2] as every good credit crunch commentator
knows, and the expense of property in some districts challenges faith
in the rationality of markets: one needs only think of the French
ambassador's residence up for sale in January 2008 for €60 million
(£45 million) making it the most expensive property in Ireland, all 10
bedrooms, 11.5 thousand square feet and 1.75 acres of it in Ballsbridge.
Built in 1900 and owned by the French since 1930 it is, according to
Senator David Norris, 'very grand but in a rather pushy late Victorian
way'.[3] Later in the scene from Enright's novel, it is this very artificiality of the money-driven world in which the passion and intensity
of the protagonist's affair takes place which begins to seep into
consciousness: 'we listen to it for a moment; the rumour of money
withering out of the walls and floors and out of the granite kitchen
countertops, turning them back to bricks and rubble and stone.'[4]

You may wonder why one begins a chapter on George Moore with
a comment about a French-owned mansion in Dublin in 2008 and
quotations from a novel by the contemporary novelist Enright, a
writer whose presence will recur throughout this chapter, along with
John Banville and other current literary Irish voices. The reason
resides in the fact that this chapter derives from the conjunction of a
series of thoughts and traces I have been following in my work, not
on Moore but on other things, in recent years. In 2010 Ann Heilmann
and I published a book on the theme of neo-Victorianism[5] which,
broadly conceived, is about the turn in recent historical fiction to the
nineteenth century and the ways in which the Victorians have been
adapted, (mis)appropriated and re-presented at the start of the twenty-
first century. While our joint focus has been on cultural revisions in
literature and film, my own interest in the subject has, since late 2009,
looked towards the wider cultural, social, political and economic
reverberations of the nineteenth century in contemporary discourse.
For example, the fiscal crisis, the partial nationalisation of the banks
and the invocation of a nostalgic age when bankers were good,
honest men (an age that never was) has led to work on public
appropriations of a Victorian legacy in English political discourse
around monetary policy, prisons, welfare and education alongside
the celebrations of the Darwin, Tennyson and Dickens bicentenaries
in 2009 and 2012.[6] I use the term 'English' here deliberately. I'm a born

Welshman, I work at a Scottish university and the paper on which this chapter is based was delivered as a keynote at a conference in Ireland. But part of what I want to reflect on is precisely this conjunction of identities, histories and pasts, presents and futures within a national context. I'm not going to use the term 'neo-Victorianism' to describe what this chapter is about because this causes problems in the Scottish context (where 'neo-Enlightenment' might be preferred) let alone in the Irish context. Heritage studies doesn't do it either and while I might have a leaning towards 'legacy studies', it does rather make me sound like a specialist in probate law. So although it sounds less than ideal I'm going to settle on 'neo-Moorism'. What I want to explore is the continuing relevance of Moore as a writer and commentator on Ireland to the contemporary, the ways in which that relevance seems to be rather obvious in its absence, and the hope we Moorites might take from the potential for Moore to re-enter a critical and cultural place at an important moment.

As a way into the topic one need only consider Moore's explicit negotiation of issues around money, society and the individual in *Parnell and His Island* (1887). It is a book that Moore wrote in response to the Land League, his sense of threat as a landowner and the growing demands of what he considered to be a financially illiterate public, or in his term 'peasants'. *Parnell and His Island* is a strange hybrid text. A mixture of social commentary, narrative sketches, parody and caricature, it nevertheless continues to carry something of the immediacy of its original form as a series of short outlines and letters written for its earliest readers in *Le Figaro* in July, August and September 1886. The disarmingly romanticised vision of Dublin in the opening pages is sharply undercut by an image of decadence and decay:

> No town in the world has more beautiful surroundings than Dublin. Seeing Dalkey one dreams of Monte Carlo, or better still of the hanging gardens of Babylon, of marble balustrades, of white fountains, of innumerable yachts, of courts of love, and of sumptuous pleasure palaces; but alas, all that meets the eye are some broken-down villas! The white walls shine in the sun and deceive you, but if you approach you will find a front-door where the paint is peeling, and a ruined garden.
>
> And in such ruin life languishes here! The inhabitants of the villas are, for the most part, landlords whom circumstances have

forced to shut up their houses and to come here to economise; or, they may belong to the second class of landlords: widows living on jointures paid by the eldest sons, or mortgagees upon money placed by them or by their ancestors upon the land. For in Ireland there is nothing but the land; with the exception of a few distillers and brewers in Dublin, who live upon the drunkenness of the people, there is no way in Ireland of getting money except through the peasant.[7]

Moore's imagery reveals, as Brendan Fleming terms it, a 'perfect reflection of the present condition of Ireland and prediction of the country's future'.[8] Moore declares a few pages later that 'Dublin is a town of officials',[9] and it is this sense of Dublin as a central point in the pages of the text and in the institutionalised administrative and bureaucratic model which provides the hub of the opening and closing sections of the book. In between, we are taken with Moore's narrative voice outside of the city into the landscape in reflections on, among others, 'The House of An Irish Poet', 'The Landlord', 'The Tenant-Farmer', 'The Priest', 'The Patriot' and 'A Hunting Breakfast'. These aspects of Moore's projection of Irish conflict, controversy and debates over the land as opposed to the nation have been well covered elsewhere. What I am interested in thinking about here, however, is the highly-fused 'Conclusion', which Carla King in the most recent edition of *Parnell and His Island*, published in 2004, terms 'the angriest part of an angry book'.[10] It is vicious, angry, embittered and dangerously febrile in its imaginative projection of the dystopian vision Moore presents before his readers and, indeed, his enemies. But it is a brave proclamation of Moore's characteristic stance on 'morality' in writing:

> The scenes in the pages of this book point to no moral – at least to no moral that I am conscious of. … Where the facts seemed to contradict, I let them contradict. Nevertheless, it does not strike me as wholly foreign to, and incompatible with, my method to look upon that which the world terms the serious side of things. The serious side of things I take to mean: first, the direct pecuniary loss or gain; secondly, the indirect, or in other words, the moral loss or gain.[11]

Moore's Whitmanesque comfort in contradictions is one thing, but the conjunction of moral value and financial value is another, and it is at the core of what I want to consider here. Moore's representation of a view of the 'serious' that must necessarily negotiate the Scylla and Charybdis of gain and loss has been overlooked not only in consideration of *Parnell and His Island* but in Moore's work more widely.

Put simply, one must pay attention to the different levels of economic function in Moore's work as part of his humanistic inter-pretation of character, events, nation and identity. There is an important level of imaginative economy at play in the book. The Parnell that Moore conjures up is an imagined figure. Specific refer-ences to Parnell himself are very small in number. Instead Parnellian ideas do battle with Moore's own perspectives on events and their consequences. Although Moore is writing in the 'Conclusion' of the specificities of the Land Act of 1881, his presentation of permissive-ness, moral value, financial jeopardy, and human interaction is relevant to much of his subsequent fiction. Moore writes – or rather proclaims – that the Irish 'peasant' has not really been liberated through part-ownership of the property that he formerly just rented. He thought he was buying land; in fact, he himself has been bought by a bank:

> Since he has become part-proprietor of his holding he has borrowed money at the bank. The bills fall due; they are renewed; the interest keeps running on. In the past he was rendered improvident and thriftless by the uncertainty of his tenure, and the certainty that if he made any improvements they would be confiscated – (I remember when they would not thatch their houses for fear of being evicted) – now having passed from servitude through land meetings and murder, plans to murder and mutilate, he is at once afforded facilities for borrowing of all kinds. Is it possible to conceive a state of things more calculated to destroy whatever remnant of morality political agitation may have left to him? His passions are awakened – but for food, for drink, for dress. … He spends his share of the money in the public-house, his wife and daughters spend theirs on hideous millinery – dreadful hats with ostrich feathers and shapeless mantles, and tea and eggs for breakfast. Dissoluteness, subscriptions to the Land League, and borrowing money at the banks, have in five years reduced the tenantry to the verge of bankruptcy, and headed by Parnell they again come to their landlords and demand large reductions. And this will occur again and again until the landlords are ruined and the tenants become sole proprietors of their holdings. Nor will it then cease;

the banks will insist upon payment of their bills, and worse than the banks, there will be the county usurers (a class of men that Balzac has more than once depicted with terrible eloquence), and several generations will pass before the Irish peasant[,] will be able to hold his own against these men and the temptations they will hold out to him; and were an Irish Parliament sitting in Dublin, unless, indeed property were abolished and a Commune established, I am convinced that in five years' time there would be more evictions carried out by order of the banker and the usurer than there are by the landlords to-day. The Irish peasant has been left a little behind in the march of civilisation: he will have to first conquer the landlords, then he will find himself outdone by banks, usurers, and centuries of inherited idleness and filth, supplemented by ten years of the most infamous moral teaching possible to conceive. When he has overcome these dangers and difficulties he may then be able to take his place as an equal by the side of his Saxon neighbour.

But this is looking very far ahead: let us confine ourselves to considering the issues of to-day's combat.[12]

Thus endeth the lesson from economic prophet Moore.

There is a serious point here: while I am not arguing that Moore predicted the credit crunch, the financial meltdown, the global fiscal crisis or whatever other name we select for the events of the past four years, I am suggesting that Moore's attention to the combination of moral cost at two levels, characterological and commercial, personality and pecuniary, have often been neglected in considerations of his endurance and legacy as a writer. An exception to this comes in Mary Pierse's essay in the collection she edited arising from the first George Moore conference in Cork in 2005. She comments on *Parnell and His Island* and Moore's 'familiarity with the theses of Marx and Engels' as 'not merely a passing use of terminology since it is apparent from his depiction of the centrality of property and money in several texts that one of his core political messages has a Marxist flavour',[13] and there is of course Adrian Frazier's comment on the 'Marxian edge of lampoon' to Moore's representation of the 'cash nexus in Irish social relations'.[14] Yet Moore's narratives are littered with issues of economics – be it bodily, libidinally, psychologically or financially. This is the reason I would like to suggest that Moore is very much a writer for our times and should, for example, have a much more prominent place in the UNESCO Literary Dublin tours and the

Discover Ireland marketing of culture, heritage and national narrative.

When we look at those sites, we find an abbreviated cultural presence: George Moore receives '0 results' on the Discover Ireland website, and on the Visit Dublin site there are several hundred hits for James Joyce, but the depressingly familiar '0 results' for George Moore. The Literary Dublin sub-section of the same site has features on James Joyce, W.B. Yeats, and Oscar Wilde, alongside others such as George Bernard Shaw, Bram Stoker, and Oliver Goldsmith. On the Discover Ireland literary interest search the only hit on George Moore, beside a passing citation of his name in relation to Yeats and the Irish Literary Revival, is a guide to Carrick on Shannon:

> Costello Chapel is right next to Carrick's Market Yard, which dates from 1839 but has also been restored – this time to house a restaurant, shops and farmers' market. From here, you can continue along Bridge Street to the birthplace of Susan Mitchell, the poet and so-called 'red-headed rebel' who became a biographer of George Moore.[15]

To be remembered through the hair colour of one of your more astringent biographers is a form of cultural memory no doubt, but it is a strange one.

Where does the cultural relevance of Moore lie? The frequent acknowledgements of the influence of *The Untilled Field*, his Irish short stories from the early years of the twentieth century, play a role here. Writing in the introduction to his edition of the volume in 2000, Richard Allen Cave commented that the 'stories can be viewed retrospectively not only as a personal landmark, but also as a point of major cultural change: with them modern Irish fiction came into being'.[16] Cave states that Moore's tone in *Parnell and His Island* 'preserves the lofty superiority of the cosmopolitan artist returning from cultured Europe to visit with barely concealed scorn and distaste … the work is decidedly nasty'.[17] But such nastiness, in all its hostility and edginess, could be condoned if the impertinence was pertinent in other ways. Moore gave himself license to be 'subversive', and for that he incurred penalty points in the eyes of others during the Irish renaissance and after it, as Cave explains:

> [a]ny renaissance, personal or national, is a time not only of reawakening but also of taking stock of the past; and Moore's past for many of his Irish contemporaries was that of an absentee Catholic landlord turned renegade agnostic novelist. It was not

an easy reputation to live with, especially in Nationalist circles; but to Moore himself that past and present explained his freedom to question everything and be what he thought all true revolutionaries should be: subversive.[18]

It is that revolutionary or subversive trend in Moore's work that seems much needed in contemporary literary culture, where a marked absence of such provocation has been noted, especially in the Irish context. There is in fact a sense of cultural expectation around such a traumatic event as the recent fiscal crisis. Writing in *The Economist* in February 2011 under the headline 'Haven't they noticed there's a recession on?' the commentator T.N. remarked on the lack of creative artists' engagement with the credit crunch in Ireland, stating:

> You'd expect this sorry tale to have generated a wave of films, plays and novels. After all, the Irish have never shied away from telling stories about themselves. Visual artists must have hit upon a new mode of expression. Musicians, surely, would have found a way to express the story through song, as they have done with so many of Ireland's historical traumas. Hell, this story could make an opera. ... But there is little sign of an artistic response to Ireland's crash. In Dublin, I saw a production of John B. Keane's *The Field*, a 1965 play about a land dispute in southwest Ireland. ... The play was about a very different time in Irish history, but a few lines happened to resonate with more recent events – 'There's a craze for land everywhere!', for instance. These invariably drew hearty chuckles from the audience, suggesting an appetite for some kind of dramatic interpretation of the Celtic Tiger years. But one of the producers told me that they had decided to re-stage the play before Ireland came bumping down to earth; the fact that parts of the script now sounded like a description of recent years was a (happy) coincidence.[19]

The commentator is clearly aiming to create a new form of cultural heritage tourism here – credit crunch bargain trips, anyone? – and the comment does seem rather impertinent given that there isn't much to be said for recent English artistic engagements with the fiscal event of the millennium. Even counting something like David Hare's play on Enron *The Power of Yes* (2009) there isn't much literary boom about this bust, despite calls from critics such as Boyd Tonkin of the *Independent* who, back in January 2009, asked 'Does the credit crunch have a silver lining for literature?',[20] hoping for the austerity years of the 2010s to regenerate the literary talents of the Thatcherite 1980s.

T.N. goes on to allude to the now well-known polemic by the *Irish Times* journalist, economic commentator and cultural critic Fintan O'Toole entitled *Ship of Fools: How Stupidity and Corruption Killed the Celtic Tiger* (2009) in which O'Toole suggests that it is the absence of a canon of social realist fiction that left the Celtic Tiger period without an author to chronicle it. When T.N. raised the question with Anne Enright her response harked back to the lack of an industrial heritage; 'We can't produce a George Eliot any more than we can a steam railway.'[21] I suggest we turn to another George.

O'Toole comments in his book on the way in which it is Ireland's past, specifically the past that was Moore's present, which culminated in aspects of the trauma in recent years, and also, somewhat ironically, indicate a way out. As O'Toole states it,

> In retrospect, plonking a hyper-charged globalized economy on top of such an underdeveloped system of political governance and public morality was always likely to create an unbearable strain. But only the most irredeemable pessimist would have predicted that the forces that would destroy the Celtic Tiger would be nineteenth-century revenants, come back to haunt its dreams of twenty-first century success.[22]

Those 'revenants' are poverty, financial crisis, and emigration. According to the Central Statistics Office, net outward migration stood at 34,500 during the period April 2009 and April 2010, up from 7,800 in the period April 2008–2009, which is the highest level since 1989.[23] The chart provided by the CSO shows the narrative of emigration from the mid-nineteenth century to 2006.

Moore is the writer who has best dealt with Irish migration. Narratives of the economic migrant abound in *The Untilled Field*. The passion of characters such as Ned in 'The Wild Goose' is to find a life beyond the strictures of orthodox morality:

> [Ned] was speaking on the depopulation question, and he said that this question came before every other question. Ireland was now confronted with the possibility that in five-and-twenty years the last of Ireland would have disappeared in America. There were some who attributed the Irish emigration to economic causes: that was a simple and obvious explanation,

one that could be understood by everybody; but these simple and obvious explanations are not often, if they are ever, the true ones.[24]

It is the absence of aesthetic rather than ethical economies that is the problem of life in Ireland within the narrative. The morality of the hero's experience is separate from that of the community yet deeply implicated within it. When Ned casts out for a word to describe what Ireland requires, it is a sense of 'joy' and liberation from constraint:

> The first part of Ned's speech was taken up with the examination of the economic causes, and proving that these were not the origin of the evil. The country was joyless; man's life is joyless in Ireland. In every other country there were merry-makings. ... He was the last man in the world who would say that religion was not necessary, but if he were right in saying that numbers were leaving Ireland because Ireland was joyless he was right in saying that it was the duty of every Irishman to spend his money in making Ireland a joyful country.[25]

It is boom and bust but with joy, and therefore not as we know it. The terminology employed by Moore here invokes something of that debate between the different moral gestures and gambles of the passage quoted earlier from *Parnell and His Island*. Moral hazard here is monetary hazard too, and the stakes are the odds against winning joy or losing to judgement. Yet we also see that Moore's analysis fits precisely contemporary culture as well as that of his own period. The simplicity with which Ned rationalises the move from religious constraint to economic libertarianism is not sustainable, in fact, it is not an argument that carries weight. Happiness and joy are, for Moore, not themselves the ends of creditworthiness within the sphere of Irish culture.

The danger of such purchasable joys within the present period has been starkly outlined in a melancholic piece by John Banville for *The New York Times* in November 2010. Under the openly ironic title of the Syngean 'Debtor of the Western World' Banville's critique of the balance of pleasures vs responsibilities is simple and, over one hundred years after Ned's declaration, provides an answer to the spending of money on joy:

> Throughout the 2000s there was a lot of cross-border shopping, almost all of it one-way, since usually in those years the euro was

strong and the British pound weak. Newly rich middle-class couples from the Republic, riding the broad back of the Celtic Tiger, would travel north on Saturday mornings, have a leisurely lunch at one of Belfast's fine new restaurants, spend the afternoon in the supermarkets and return at evening happy as Visigoths with their booty – liquor, cigarettes, electrical goods, designer-label clothes and, as the autumn set in, boxes and boxes of fireworks. Those were the sparkling years ...

In the months after September 2008, when the Irish government, after a night-long crisis meeting, was forced to give a guarantee of some 400 billion euros – money we had no hope of ever having – to save the Irish banks from collapse, we used to say that it would fall to our children to pay for our financial folly. Now we know that it will be our children and our children's children and our children's children's children, unto the nth generation, who will bear the burden of our debts, including the 'substantial loan' from international lenders that officials now acknowledge is necessary.[26]

Compare that to Moore's declaration in *Parnell* that 'The sins of the fathers descend on the children, and my host's property exists upon paper only.'[27] We have been here before. Such comparisons, I must emphasise again, are not about conflating present and past or undermining the very unique historical perspectives required to place the Dublin and Ireland of Moore's commentary anywhere near contemporary events. However, at a time when the legacies of the nineteenth century, and economics, are at the forefront of cultural debate, even if not quite formulated in political and social discourse, Moore's works are a much needed lens through which we can consider the lives of individuals and communities in that past that is, at the broadest level, not so differently constituted in terms of crisis, economic trauma, and social discontent, as our own. Indeed, this is the core point of this essay: Moore's works should come into their own in the present because of what they can reveal to us about the need for renaissance now that we are faced with such trauma on a regional, country-wide, and European if not global scale. This is not the past as reassurance. Who could take solace from the demonisation of nation and institutions, people and politics, found in *Parnell and His Island*? And even so there is a constructive element of antagonism in Moore's polemic, and a benefit to those unspeakable things contrarian thinkers say on our behalf and for our own good. As Susan

Mitchell put it, in a more telling phrase than she intended, 'There is no art in *Parnell and His Island*, and there is sufficient truth in it to make it a horrible exhibition of Mr. Moore's soul.'[28] The soul that gave 'Mr. Moore' gravest concern was that of his land if not his nation.[29]

One might say that Anne Enright and others are in fact providing letters on Ireland on the model of Moore's original letters from Paris. In the *London Review of Books* in January 2010 Enright's 'Sinking by Inches' was published. It is a reflection on contemporary Irish poverty that speaks within the tradition of Moore's outrage in *Parnell and His Island*, beginning as follows:

> Last year, the Society of St Vincent de Paul spent €6.1 million giving people in Ireland food. This year, it says that requests for food are up 50 per cent, that calls in general are up 35 per cent and in Dublin 50 per cent, and that 25 per cent of callers are new clients, many of whom were contributors to the charity at the church gates last year. These new clients are people who, 'like the rest of us', as one of their volunteers, John Monaghan, says, 'were living on 110 per cent of their salaries'; this year, something in the working situation has changed, and they cannot manage their usual debts, mortgage, car, credit card.
>
> This time last year the sky was falling, and then it didn't. You wake up after the credit crisis and pat yourself down, and find everything the same, more or less, as it was before. Twelve months later, you look back to see that the sky did not fall so much as sink by inches.

Enright concludes this opening passage with the words: 'I don't know if Ireland does recession differently from other countries.'[30] It may not, but it is the return here to narrative means of exploration and explication that is most reminiscent of George Moore. In the context of English literature we have the contemporary novelists Sebastian Faulks in *A Week in December* (2009) rekindling Joseph Conrad's *The Secret Agent* (1886) but this time the anarchist plot is replaced by a sub-Al Qaeda threat which looks set to blow up a banker along the way, or Justin Cartwright's sub-Trollopian Victorian realism in *Other People's Money* (2011) on the good old days when banking was a slower, more sedate, trustworthy and comforting affair. (Sub-Trollopian in the sense that Cartwright is aware of Trollope but I don't think he's quite 'got' *The Way We Live Now* (1875) and its implications.) In Ireland, however, it is not the grand realist novel of the nineteenth century but the short story of the twentieth that has come in for a renaissance. Here too Moore's influence might be perceived in what has already been done, and could indeed be of further benefit.

In 2010, Enright edited *The Granta Book of the Irish Short Story*, which doesn't include Moore because apart from a bit of a cheat on Elizabeth Bowen's date of birth, Enright has restricted her trawl to 'writers who were born in the twentieth century'.[31] But Enright's collection was hotly followed by Joseph O'Connor's edition of New Irish Short Stories (2011), not to mention the collection from Colm Tóibín *The Empty Family* (2010) which has much in common in its lonely, sexually anxious characters with Moore's own short fiction. As O'Connor comments, contemporary – or 'new' – short stories from Ireland are deeply indebted to the 'tradition[al] outposts of Irish emigration'.[32] Furthermore, '[T]he short story seems to be experiencing something of a renaissance in post-Celtic Tiger Ireland.'[33]

Writing about Moore's desire to write an 'unprecedented book' in *Hail and Farewell*, Herbert Howarth remarked on the horror with which the text was met, but also the outcome of that shock: Moore 'performs the therapy of art for Ireland.'[34] O'Connor makes a similar point about the need for artists, and writers in particular, to hold up the morality which is not morality, it is through short stories, he says, that a people can gain access to the shock of recognition, the bitterness of hindsight, and the economics of the duped: 'Old certainties are shattered. We got fooled, and we know it. But sometimes, in the Irish sentence, the greatest thing we have ever invented, we glimpse what yet might be. The arts have brought the consolation of dignity to Ireland at a time when we sorely needed it.'[35]

Before these more recent collections, there was William Trevor's *The Oxford Book of the Irish Short Story*, first issued in 1989 and reprinted several times since. Here Moore is represented by a single tale, 'Albert Nobbs'. The story was originally published in *A Story-Teller's Holiday* in 1918, and was subsequently used by Moore as the replacement narrative for 'Hugh Montfort', the aborted revision of 'John Norton', in the revised edition of *In Single Strictness* (1922, 1923) published as *Celibate Lives* in 1927.[36] In some ways it is unlike the other tales in Moore's collection because it inherits the structure of the overt narrator and his interlocutor 'Alec', which sits oddly against 'Wilfrid Holmes' or 'Sarah Gwynn' in the same volume. What connects the tales is the thread of economic necessity and the commerce of desire and longing which I mentioned earlier. Holmes, with his leech-like financial dependency on the regular payment of an allowance which disappears, is a suitable contrast to the hardworking, thrifty saver Albert Nobbs. In fact, Moore's text brings two things into distinct relation in the narrative of Albert: geographic location and the economic bodies that move within it. Morrison's Hotel becomes the locale of the libido. The shifting engagements of Nobbs with guests and with the Dublin streets beyond the lobby door that loom largest in the story. Navigating and negotiating the falsely assumed identity of male bodies – both that of Albert and Hubert Page, the painter who like Albert is a woman dressing for a man's world – it is the space beyond the narrow confines of room, bed, and structured levels of engagement – literary in the case of the dividing boundaries between the different floors of the hotel envisioned by the younger Moore's narrating character – that support and yet also destroy contentment, satisfaction, and life itself. As the narrator comments on the issue of escape, '[o]ne of the advantages of Dublin is that one can get out of it as easily as out of any other city.'[37] Yet the cartography of credit and desire presented in the narrative is highly contained and restricted: Morrison's Hotel on Dawson Street, College Green, Sackville Street, as Albert imagines the spatial dimensions of reality and dream, 'the points that had seemed so convincing in Rathmines Avenue were forgotten in Rathgar Avenue, and at Terenure she came to the conclusion that there was no use trying to think the story out beforehand.'[38] Through the course of the story, the disastrous pseudo-courtship of Helen Dawes, the aborted plans for shop and hearth, through to the death in accumulated capital, literally surrounding the walls and floors of Albert's room, it is the abject nature of the culturally economic which creates tension in Moore's narrative. As Ann Heilmann has argued, the roots of Albert's obsession with money can be traced to the payments that once connected the young girl Albert to her parents, payments that then stopped.[39] But the psychological issue also enters into a cultural economic issue at the same point. Behavioural economics tells us that there is a tension between the nature of rational choice models of consumer activity, a contradiction present in models of economic man since Max Weber and other nineteenth-century thinkers. In the story of Albert Nobbs such tensions drive narrative credit. Recognising the dangers of fantasy, Albert ponders that fleeting visions of 'the shop with two counters. … Like Lisdoonvarna, it had passed away, it had only existed in her mind – a thought, a dream. Yet it had possessed her completely.'[40] Desire is here mixed with consumerist fixations on property. In a sort of reverse fiscality, the thing bought can gain a purchase on the buyer. Ultimately, it is in a single room for a single 'man' that Albert finds a portion of solace and comfort:

> And from that moment her life expended itself in watching for tips, collecting half-crowns, crowns and half-sovereigns. … She took to counting her money in her room at night. The half-crowns were folded up in brown-paper packets, the half-sovereigns in blue, the rare sovereigns were in pink paper and all these little packets were hidden away in different corners; some were put in the chimney, some under the carpet. She often thought that these hoards would be safer in the Post Office Bank, but she who has nothing else likes to have her money with her, and a sense of almost happiness awoke in her when she discovered herself to be again as rich as she was before she met Helen.[41]

The emotional parallels are stark and clear here in a way that they are not in, for example, Anne Enright's *The Forgotten Waltz*. Where in that fiction the economic realities of environment, culture and exchange are inscribed simultaneously in national/global finance and individual relations, Moore's short story presents the pared-down version of commercial comfort and institutional suspicion. Although Enright's protagonist has that vision I quoted at the start of this chapter of the money evaporating from the walls and granite work surfaces of her upmarket kitchen units, she hasn't actually engaged in stuffing banknotes in there in the first place. Enright's upwardly mobile middle-class has not had the value factor brought into its psychology in the way that Albert has. Commenting on Moore's story, Ernest Fontana states that 'It is [the] middle-class ideal of a decent life – or an ordered, independent life – that will drive Albert to male impersonation.'[42] But it is also beyond this, an epistemological dilemma concerning reciprocity, trust and the gift. Affection that is not reciprocated becomes trust lost and gifts not given. That is the story of 'Albert Nobbs'.

Given William Trevor's selection and the comments I've made here it is fitting that the text which has been seeing something of a renaissance in recent months is 'Albert Nobbs'. This comes partly on the back of the decision, a result of several decades of negotiation and false starts, to film an adaptation of Moore's tale. The story was adapted for the stage by the French feminist playwright Simone Benmussa in the 1970s as *The Singular Life of Albert Nobbs*. In 1982 the American actress Glenn Close performed the lead role in New York, a performance praised by *The New York Times* as a transformation of 'manner, movement and sensibility'. For the last 30 years Close has been keen on making a movie of the play and for the last decade this has been an active project for her. After an aborted attempt several years ago, Close co-directed the film with Rodrigo Garcia and co-authored the screenplay with John Banville. Commenting during filming in Dublin in December 2010, Close stated: 'At one point we were thinking of filming in Hungary, eastern Germany, Montreal in Canada. ... We've been all over the place but I'm really happy that we're here [in Dublin] because this is where it should be.' Close went on to say that 'I believe in this story and its potential to take everyone on a sensuous, funny, heart-breaking, wildly unexpected ride.' The director Rodrigo supported this by commenting that 'It is the kind of script that is moving and funny with a story that is compelling. It is something about people's interior lives and their longing. It is rare for a script to bring together so many interesting themes.'[43] Thinking of Moore's story, and even Benmussa's adaptation, it is hard to see the 'funny ... wildly unexpected ride' in the tale of 'Albert Nobbs', partly because this seems to be Hollywood hype but also because in the current cultural and economic climate what was 'singular' in Nobbs's life might actually be more shared and collective than it once was. The fragility of fiscality, and the problems of credit at emotional, psychological, political and social levels has provided a new edge to Moore's tale.

At the end of my 'Introduction' to volume 5 of Ann Heilmann's and my edition of *The Collected Short Stories of George Moore* (2007) I commented in relation to 'Albert Nobbs' and the Benmussa play:

> The fact that Moore's short story was adapted fifty years after its publication in *Celibate Lives* and almost sixty years after its first appearance in *A Story-Teller's Holiday* (1918) demonstrates the timelessness of Moore's analysis of the human condition. The unusual nature of the story is inevitably an attraction, but the reinterpretation of the text in the mid-1970s suggests that Moore's identification of the performative nature of gender, sexuality and desire, and his ability to see through the emotional and psychological masks we seek to present to the world in

order to hide our weaknesses, instabilities and deepest selves, was ahead of its time and remains pertinent even in our contemporary world.[44]

That statement means more now than it did then. Moore's speaking truth to the ordinary makes him subversive to some, controversial to others, maybe even deviant or immoral to a few; like the French ambassador's mansion he might even be 'pushy in a late Victorian way'. But the continuum of awareness, perception and sharpness found in *Parnell and His Island* through to the monetary madness of Albert Nobbs in the 1920s reflect Moore's abiding willingness to see us in every shade. It also makes him human and humane. If cultural economics, like the dismal science from which part of its name stems, is purely about statistics, data, numbers, and the cash nexus, then it is writers like Moore that see its relevance. His works can contribute to how we might live now through knowing the pertinence of what he knew then.

NOTES

1. Anne Enright, *The Forgotten Waltz* (London: Jonathan Cape, 2011), p.148.
2. Michael Lewis, 'When Irish Eyes Are Crying', *Vanity Fair* (March 2011): see http://www.vanityfair.com/business/features/2011/03/michael-lewis-ireland-201103 (accessed 24 April 2012).
3. See http://uk.reuters.com/article/2008/01/18/oukoe-uk-ireland-france-house-idUKL18719 120080118 (accessed 04/07/2012).
4. See Enright, *The Forgotten Waltz*, p.185.
5. Ann Heilmann and Mark Llewellyn, *Neo-Victorianism: The Victorians in the Twenty-First Century, 1999–2009* (Basingstoke: Palgrave Macmillan, 2010).
6. See, for example, my '"Posthumous Productivity", Political Philosophy, and Neo-Victorian Style: Review of Paul Ginsborg, *Democracy: Crisis and Renewal'*, *Neo-Victorian Studies*, 2, 1 (Winter 2008/09), pp.179–186.
7. George Moore, *Parnell and His Island* (Dublin: University College Dublin Press, 2004 reprint), pp.2–3.
8. Brendan Fleming, 'French spectacles in an Irish case: from "Lettres sur l'Irlande" to *Parnell and His Island'*, in Alan A. Gillis and Aaron Kelly (eds), *Critical Ireland: New Essays in Literature and Culture* (Dublin: Four Courts, 2001), pp.69–76.
9. See Moore, *Parnell and His Island*, p.7.
10. Ibid., p.xxiii.
11. Ibid., p.89.
12. Ibid., pp.93–4.
13. Mary Pierse, 'His Father's Son: The Political Inheritance', in Mary Pierse (ed.), *George Moore: Artistic Visions and Literary Worlds* (Newcastle: Cambridge Scholars Press, 2006), pp.102–114, 110.
14. Adrian Frazier, *George Moore, 1852–1933* (New Haven and London: Yale University Press, 2000), p.126.
15. http://www.discoverireland.ie/Activities-Adventure/carrick-on-shannon-historic-town-walk/85587 (accessed 04/07/2012).
16. Richard Allen Cave, (ed.), 'Introduction', *The Untilled Field* (Gerards Cross: Colin Smythe, 2000), p.vii.
17. Ibid., p.xi.
18. Ibid., p.xx.

19. T.N., 'Haven't they noticed there's a recession on?', *The Economist*, 18 February 2011, http://www.economist.com/node/21015970 (accessed 04/07/2012).
20. Boyd Tonkin, 'Does the credit crunch have a silver lining for literature?', *Independent*, 9 January 2009: see http://www.independent.co.uk/arts-entertainment/books/features/does-the-credit-crunch-have-a-silver-lining-for-literature-1232961.html (accessed 04/07/2012).
21. Ibid.
22. Fintan O'Toole, *Ship of Fools: How Stupidity and Corruption Killed the Celtic Tiger* (London: Faber and Faber, 2009), p.214.
23. Central Statistics Office, 'Population and Migration Estimates April 2010': see http:// www.csoie/releasespublications/documents/population/current/popmig.pdf (accessed 04/07/2012).
24. Ann Heilmann and Mark Llewellyn (eds), *The Collected Short Stories of George Moore: Gender and Genre* (London: Pickering and Chatto, 2007), Vol. 3, p.270.
25. Ibid.
26. John Banville, 'The Debtor of the Western World', *The New York Times*, 19 November 2010: see http://www.nytimes.com/2010/11/19/opinion/19banville.html (accessed 04/07/2012).
27. See Moore, *Parnell and His Island*, p.15.
28. See Frazier, *George Moore, 1852–1933*, p.142.
29. Carla King, 'Introduction', *Parnell and His Island*, p.xxvii.
30. Anne Enright, 'Sinking by Inches', *London Review of Books*, (7 January 2010), pp.21–2.
31. Anne Enright (ed.), *The Granta Book of the Irish Short Story* (London: Granta, 2010), p.vxi.
32. Joseph O'Connor (ed.), *New Irish Short Stories* (London: Faber and Faber, 2011), p.xi.
33. Ibid., p.x.
34. Herbert Howarth, 'Dublin 1899–1911: The Enthusiasms of a Prodigal', in Graham Owens (ed.), *George Moore's Mind and Art* (Edinburgh: Oliver and Boyd, 1968), pp.77–98.
35. See O'Connor, *New Irish Short Stories*, p.xiv.
36. For a discussion of Moore's rewriting of these tales and the reorganisation of the collections, see Ann Heilmann and Mark Llewellyn, 'What Kitty Knew: George Moore's John Norton, Multiple Personality and the Psychopathology of Late-Victorian Sex Crime.' *Nineteenth-Century Literature*, 59, 3 (December 2004), pp.372–403.
37. George Moore, *A Story-Teller's Holiday*, 2 vols (New York: Privately printed, 1918), Vol. 1, p.302.
38. Ibid., v.1, p.302.
39. Ann Heilmann, 'Female transvestism, object relations and mourning in George Moore's "Albert Nobbs"', *Women: A Cultural Review*, 14, 3 (2003), pp.248–62.
40. See Moore, *A Story-Teller's Holiday*, Vol. 1, p.316.
41. Ibid., pp.317–318.
42. Ernest L. Fontana, 'Sexual Alienation in George Moore's "Albert Nobbs"', *International Fiction Review*, 4 (1977), pp.183–5.
43. 'Introducing Glenn's leading man ... herself', *Daily Mail*, 16 December 2010: see http://www.dailymail.co.uk/tvshowbiz/article-1338803/Glenn-Close-plays-cross-dressing-woman-1890s-Ireland-new-film-Albert-Nobbs.html (accessed 04/07/2012).
44. Mark Llewellyn, 'Introduction', Ann Heilmann and Mark Llewellyn (eds), *The Collected Short Stories of George Moore* (London: Pickering and Chatto, 2007), Vol.5, p.xxxix.

CHAPTER TWO

George Henry Moore and Moore Hall During the Famine

FIONA WHITE

Moore Hall is situated on the banks of Lough Carra in County Mayo. Construction on the house started in 1792 and was completed in 1795. The house was occupied continuously from 1795 until 1910. For 13 years it was unoccupied by the Moore family and then eventually destroyed by fire in 1923, during the Civil War. Moore Hall was one of around 7,000 landed estates in nineteenth-century Ireland. The estate witnessed its most stable period during the mid-nineteenth century, under the proprietorship of George Henry Moore (1810–1870). George Henry was an illustrious statesman and respected landlord. The majority of the people living in the locality were associated in some way with the estate, whether as middlemen, agents, cottiers, landless labourers, or big house and demesne servants. Using a number of different historical sources, this article sets out to investigate Moore's management of the estate during the Famine of the 1840s, with particular emphasis on the region around Ballintubber.

George Henry Moore was born 1 March 1810 in Moore Hall, Ballyglass, Co. Mayo, eldest among three sons of George Moore (1770–1840), and Louisa Moore (née Browne), granddaughter of the 1st Earl of Altamont. George Henry was sent to Oscott School near Birmingham to be educated. This was common practice of the Irish gentry at this time. He seemed to show considerable ability at school and was sent to Cambridge. His father hoped that on leaving Cambridge he would become a resident and improving landlord, 'not a prodigal trying to dazzle by a parvenu extravagance either a London society or his toadies and dependants in Mayo'.[1] George Henry's father soon realised that his son's prospects were poor and handed over the decision making for George Henry's future to his wife Louisa. Hone notes that mother and son loved each other deeply and fought as fiercely as they loved.[2] The fact is George Henry learned little at Cambridge except skill at billiards. He emerged as an affable young extrovert who preferred horse racing, hunting, and gambling to more scholarly pursuits.[3]

George Henry was sent to London to study law but fell heavily in debt. He was also involved romantically (much to his mother's dismay) with a well-known married socialite from Cheltenham. As a result of this affair, his mounting debts, and constant pressure from his mother to return to Mayo, George Henry felt the time was right to travel abroad. From 1834 to 1839 he visited Russia, Syria, and Palestine, where he explored the Dead Sea. Following the death of his father in 1840 he returned to Mayo and took charge of the family estate. In the years immediately prior to the Famine it seems that George Henry continued to live the life of a leisured member of the Ascendancy class with his estates providing the funds necessary for the maintenance of his lifestyle. George Henry and his brother Augustus were quickly noted for their skill as horse riders and horse breeders and Moore Hall became a centre of equine activity. Castlebar was the main centre of horse racing in Mayo, which was a highly popular social event among the landed gentry. The races were held at Breaffy outside the town and were second in Connacht only to the Galway races. They were attended by the distinguished families of the county, such as the Knoxes and Gores. The Moores and Moore Hall were the most prominently known, especially for the training of racehorses and hunters.[4] According to Maurice Moore, George Henry and his brother had given up all else and devoted themselves heart and soul to racing and riding by 1841. George Henry was commonly called 'Dog Moore' during the 1840s (after his celebrated race horse *Wolf Dog*). He was noted throughout the country for his hunting bloodstock and the reckless courage with which he rode in the hunt.[5]

A tragic setback and certainly the incident which changed George Henry's life was the death of his brother, Augustus. Augustus died after injuries received whilst riding *Mickey Free* at Liverpool in 1845. George Henry's passion for racing continued, but he sold a lot of his horses and curbed his gambling. Maria Edgeworth who wrote to Louisa after Augustus's death:

> but truth I do pity George; we know how fond [the two brothers] were of each other; but I have no doubt that such a great shock,

instead of being permanently weakening as sorrow sometimes is to the mind, will be serviceable and strengthening and consolidating to his character. He will turn more to quiet literary pursuits, and he will feel in them, along with resource against sorrow, something congenial to his hereditary nature and pleasing and comforting to his mother. His higher nature, his superior tastes and abilities will come out. You will pardon me for this prophecy. I am an old woman.[6]

She was right. His brother's death and the catastrophe that now over-whelmed the country called George Henry Moore to a sense of duty. Documentary sources in the Valuations Office and the Land Commission provide a clear picture of the structure and management of a lot of the Moore's estate under George Henry's proprietorship.[7] The Moores owned over 12,000 acres near Ballintubber, Partry and Ballcally. Agricultural land use included arable, pasture and mountain-commonage. The quality of the land, according to the Field Valuations of 1843, varied from poor mica-slate soil to rather good arable.[8]

Land on the estates was let by Moore either directly to a tenant or to a sub-tenant via a middleman. An agent was employed to oversee the running of the estates. William Mullowney is mentioned as the agent at the time. He combined this duty with those of butler and steward.[9] Tenants included cottiers who paid their rents with their labour, tenant farmers who paid rent either in cash or in kind, and graziers who rented pasture for their cattle. There was also a full staff employed at the hall.

There was always the temptation for middle men to rack rent, and this most certainly happened at Moore Hall. Looking at the holdings of three middle men – Malachy Tuohy, Peter Tuohy and Mr Cheevers – it would seem that they were sub-letting their holdings at between two and three times the rent paid to Moore. The power of the Tuohys stemmed in part from the long leases they had been given; they had secured a lease for lands of Kiltarsaghaun for a period of four lives. A Valuations Officer prior to the Famine judged that rents for portions of the Ballintubber townland were 'greatly too high' and this prompted him to conclude that Mr. Moore was a rackrent landlord.[10] Despite the rent levels in the early 1840s there is no evidence that George Henry evicted any of his tenants for non-payment. Later in the life of George Henry and that of his sons, rent levels on the estate fell generally.

Grazing was a highly emotive national issue in the late nineteenth century, where it became an increasingly attractive financial proposition for large farmers. Extensive grazing reduced employment and forced the eviction of small holders to make way for cattle. Large-scale clearances were common in the east of Ireland. Moore Hall included a livestock farm. At the time George Henry took over the management of the estate cattle and sheep produced an expected turnover of £1,500 per annum.[11] It seems, however, that Moore properties could have yielded much more profit if other parts of the Ballintubber estate had been let out as grassland, yet the Ballintubber estate saw no mass clearance of tenantry for cattle despite the financial benefits that such an action would have brought for George Henry.

During the period 1840–1845 no forceful measures to improve the condition of his estate were taken by George Henry. He did, however, begin to respond to the distress experienced amongst his tenants, particularly around the Ballybanaun and Partry estate, by sending donations as early as July 1842.

When the Famine came to the region around Moore Hall, it hit hard. The population decline overall for the country was about 20 per cent but in Mayo the population fell by 29 per cent from 388,887 to 274,830 due to deaths and emigration.[12]

Father Browne, the parish priest of Ballintubber, observed that of 1,600 houses standing in 1844 at least 800 had been levelled, 3,000 lives had been lost and 500 persons had fled to either America or England. Four thousand souls remained. Some families had been forced to pawn their clothes in order to buy seed in a desperate bid to plant the land and feed themselves.[13]

The areas referred to included parts of George Henry Moore's estates. Local landlords received much criticism from Father Brown and other local priests for their lack of response to the mortal distress of their tenants. George Henry seems to be the exception. He chaired two relief committees at Ballintubber and Partry and was actively involved in the management of relief measures. A famously generous act on behalf of Moore was the provision of funds as a result of a win on one of his horses *Coranna*. *Coranna* was a horse which he had entered in association with Lord Waterford in the Chester Cup in May 1846. Much of Moore's winnings went on settling his debts, but he sent £1,000 pounds to his mother at Moore Hall with instructions for its distribution. Five hundred pounds was to be used to finance relief works, the balance was to be distributed in charity to the very poorest because he believed that the 'horses would gallop all the faster with the blessings of the poor'.[14] Fr. Michael Heaney, parish priest of Mayo Abbey, recalled that every widow on George Henry's property received a milch cow, land was free to tenants under £5 in rent, and relief was given to others paying up to £20 in rent.[15]

As chairman of two relief committees George Henry Moore often wrote to the Lord Lieutenant describing the situation in his committee region. He wrote the following to the Lord Lieutenant on 21 January 1847:

> Able-bodied men can no longer obtain two quarts of meal for a day's work, which has to be divided amongst six individuals ... We have sent from this house several times to Westport within the last fortnight without being able to procure meal. The merchants in this county ... are apprehensive that the enormous profits they have been making will soon be interfered with. ... There is a necessity of having provisions in government depots, sold to the people at a reasonable price. ... If not done, serious and alarming outbreaks are likely to take place. A meeting which will be attended by enormous crowds of people has been convened for Monday next.[16]

Moore also helped finance the voyage of the *Martha Washington*. This vessel shipped a large cargo of foodstuffs from New Orleans to West-port Quay in June 1847 and was financed by a trio of Mayo landlords, Lord Sligo, Sir Robert Blosse, and George Henry Moore. Flour and meal were then sold to the famine stricken at highly subsidised rates, the deficit being met by the three landlords. The venture required £10,000 in capital and incurred an overall loss of £4,800. George Henry's deficit share was approximately £900.[17]

Unfortunately, despite his best intentions, the distribution of relief was not trouble free. George Henry's mother, who had been placed in charge of the fund from the *Coranna* win, found herself in dispute with local priests who prompted tenants to refuse to work except for double wages in the Ballybanaun region. George Henry wrote to his mother to suspend all relief to this region until he returned from England. In this instance both parties were doing what they felt was best for the tenants, but there were other less scrupulous individuals prepared to profit from the crisis. For example, one Tom Lawless was convicted of using false weights when selling flour and meal.[18]

Years of famine relief, low or often non-existent rents, high Poor law Union rates, and gambling debts left Moore in acute difficulty. His estate fell into debt, forcing him during 1854 to sell half his property for £5,900. Some of the lands were purchased by the proselytising Bishop Plunkett, much to the chagrin of Moore who was a Catholic.[19] He owed money to Lord Sligo (who reminded him on more than one occasion of this burden). His later political career added further costs. When he died in 1870, he left the family estate far from healthy. George Augustus found himself saddled with a debt that remained a burden most of his life.

It was in the 1840s that George Henry embarked on his political career. He lost a March 1846 by-election, but succeeded in being elected MP for Mayo during the 1847 general election. At a Dublin convention of liberal MPs, he proposed that all Irish MPs should take a pledge to cooperate closely on matters of particular importance for Ireland; the proposal made little immediate impact. He introduced this idea again in 1851, when he became the spokesman in parliament for Irish Catholics' opposition to the Ecclesiastical Titles Act. Moore took a leading role in establishing the Catholic Defence Association which opposed this Act and helped establish 'The Friends of Religious Freedom and Equality' (which called for the disestablishment of the Church of Ireland).

With Charles Gavan Duffy, Moore played a key role in 1850–1851 in compelling all MPs who supported the Tenant League to take a pledge not to accept government offices until the League's demands were met. He used two platforms – religious inequality and the land question – to unite Irish liberals and Catholic MPs under one movement. One could say that Moore was responsible for formulating 'independent opposition' which became the backbone of this loosely-based independent party in the 1850s. He openly attacked former associates Keogh and Sadlier when they reneged on their pledges and accepted government positions. Moore's support for the Tenant League made him very unpopular among the landed elite in Mayo, especially Lord Sligo, and he lost his seat in the 1852 general election.

In the 1857 general election Moore was re-elected for Mayo but was unseated on the grounds of undue clerical influence being used against his Tory rival. In the 1859 general election Moore and other independents supported the Tory government of Lord Derby to show their irritation with the Palmerstonian liberals. The Tories went on to win a majority of Irish Parliamentary seats.

Moore had been opposed to the Young Irelanders during the 1840s but began to soften and expressed his support for the establishment of a nationalist-orientated party. At the least, he flirted with Fenianism. According to John Devoy, George Henry Moore was asked to join the IRB by Jeremiah O'Donovan Rossa in 1864.[20] He refused to support the National Association of Ireland because it was virtually controlled by Archbishop Paul Cullen. This caused Moore to become politically marginalised.

He served as High Sheriff of County Mayo for a short time during the 1860s. Supported by his great friend Archbishop John McHale, Moore decided to run for Mayo in the 1868 general election on a ticket of tenant rights and an amnesty for Fenian prisoners. He succeeded and began conferring regularly with IRB leaders throughout the following year.[21] Did this demonstrate a desire for some form of political alliance between the Fenians and MPs to form a new movement?

The last few years of his life were clouded with bitter rent disputes on his estate. Fr. Lavelle arbitrated on a number of occasions for Moore while he was absent due to his political career, but on receiving the following letter Moore returned home to settle the rent disputes: 'Important—Caution. Notice is hereby given that any person who pays rent to landlords, agents or bailiffs above the ordnance valuation will at his peril mark the consequences. By order—Signed Rory.'[22]

Moore refused to be blackmailed and warned that he would evict those refusing to pay their rent:

> If it is supposed that because I advocate the rights of the tenants, I am to surrender my own rights as a landlord if it is suspected that I am so enamoured of a seat in Parliament that I am ready to abandon my own self-respect rather than imperil its possession; if it is hoped that because I alone of all the landlords in the parish of Ballintuber have not cleared my estate of the people, the people are to send me to jail—those who count upon taking this base advantage of my political position will find that they have mistaken their man. I did not seek a seat in Parliament for my own personal advantage, and I do not wish to retain it a day longer than I can do so with advantage to the people and honour to myself. I am determined to vindicate my own rights, without fear or flinching, and if it be necessary to evict every tenant who refuses to pay his rent in full—whatever by the consequences—I will take that course.[23]

He arrived on Good Friday 1870 at Moore Hall, demonstrating much fatigue and exhaustion. He died the following Tuesday. The doctor diagnosed apoplexy.

Fr. Lavelle says he died from heartbreak, and his son and biographer Maurice Moore agreed. However, George Augustus, in a preface to Maurice's biography, expressed the belief that his father had committed suicide and died like an old Roman. Although his political friends wanted to bury him as a nationalist hero in Glasnevin, the family wish was fulfilled and he was buried at Kiltoom on the estate. There were a large number of mourners, but some of the Mayo gentry did not attend because of his nationalist politics. Fr. Lavelle (a well-known Mayo man and nationalist priest) said at his funeral: 'the poor deplored him as a lost friend[,] one who was heart and soul in their interests and the stern and uncompromising foe to their enemies and oppressors.'[24]

More than a century later, a monument was erected near the estate at Kiltoom acknowledging the charitable work George Henry had carried out during the Famine. The plaque reads: 'Kiltoom/Burial place of the/Moores of Moore Hall/this Catholic patriot/family is honoured for/their Famine relief/and their refusal to/barter principles for/English gold. Erected by Ballyglass Co/Old I.R.A. 1964.' The irony lies in the fact that the house was burned in 1923 by the anti-Treaty irregular forces during the Irish Civil War. Despite his controversial beliefs, there is no doubt that George Henry Moore by his actions fulfilled the family motto: '*Fortis Cadere Cedere Non Potest*' (He who proceeds with courage shall not fail).

NOTES

1. Joseph Hone, *The Moores of Moore Hall* (London: Jonathan Cape, 1939), p.57.
2. Ibid., p.59.
3. David Barr, 'George Henry Moore and his Tenants, 1840–1870', *Cathair na Mart*, 8, 1 (1988), p.66.
4. Marie Kelly, 'Manners and Customs of the Gentry in Pre-Famine Mayo', *Cathair na Mart*, 8, 1 (1988), p.51.
5. Ibid., p.53.
6. Maurice George Moore, *An Irish Gentleman George Henry Moore* (no existing copyright), p.111.
7. See Barr, *Cathair na Mart*, p.66.
8. Ibid., p.68.
9. Ibid.
10. Ibid., p.69.
11. Ibid., p.71.
12. Statistics derived from www.mayolibrary.ie/en/LocalStudies/TheFamineinMayo/ (accessed 02/07/2012).

13. See Barr, *Cathair na Mart*, p.72.
14. See Hone, *The Moores of Moore Hall*, p.138.
15. See Barr, *Cathair na Mart*, p.72.
16. Liam Swords, *In Their Own Words. The Famine in North Connacht 1845–1849* (Dublin: Columba Press, 1999), p.177.
17. See Barr, *Cathair na Mart*, p.72.
18. Ibid., pp.72–3.
19. Ibid., p.74.
20. Owen McGee, 'George Henry Moore', derived from www.dib.cambridge.org (accessed 02/07/2012).
21. Ibid.
22. J.F. Quinn, 'The Moores of Moore Hall', serialised in the *Western People* (Beginning 28 January 1933).
23. Ibid.
24. Freeman's Journal, 25 April 1870.

REFERENCES

Bence-Jones, M., *A Guide to Irish Country Houses*, Revised ed. (London: Constable, 1988).
Blake, T., *Abandoned Mansions of Ireland* (Cork: The Collins Press, 2009).
Dooley, T., *The Decline of the Big House in Ireland* (Dublin: Wolfhound Press, 2001).
Dooley, T., *Sources for the History of Landed Estates in Ireland* (Dublin: Irish Academic Press, 2000).
Dooley, T., *The Big Houses and Landed Estates of Ireland: A Research Guide* (Dublin: Four Courts Press, 2007).
Frazier, A., *George Moore, 1852–1933* (London and New Haven: Yale University Press, 2000).
Geary, L.M and M. Kelleher (eds), *Nineteenth-Century Ireland: A Guide to Recent Research* (Dublin: University College Dublin Press, 2005).
Genet, J., *The Big House in Ireland: Reality and Representation* (Kerry: Brandon Book Publishers, 1991).
Jordan, D., *Land and Popular Politics in Ireland: County Mayo from the Plantation to the Land War* (Cambridge University Press, 1994).
Knox, H.T., *The History of County Mayo* (Dublin: Hodges, Figgis and Co. Ltd., 1908).
Moore, M., *An Irish Gentleman George Henry Moore: His Travel, His Racing, His Politics* (No existing copyright).
National Library of Ireland: *11 volumes of correspondence of George Henry Moore re; administration of his estates and other family, financial and political matters 1826–1870*.
A Ní Cheanainn, *The Heritage of Mayo* (Dublin: Foilseacháin Náisiúnta Teoranta, 1988).
O'Hara, B., *Mayo: Aspects of Its Heritage* (Mayo: Archaeological, Historical & Folklore Society, 1982).
Ó Tuathaigh, G., *Ireland Before the Famine 1798–1848* (Dublin: Gill & Macmillan, 2007).
Pakenham, T., and V Pakenham, *The Big House in Ireland* (London: Cassel, 2000).
Quinn, J.F., *History of Mayo*, Vol. I. (Ballina: Brendan Quinn, 1993).

CHAPTER THREE

Irish Explorers of the Jordan Rift and the Euphrates Valley in the 1830s: Science, Adventure and Imperialism

HAIM GOREN

'When the Mediterranean first bore me on its bosom with a heart as free and buoyant as its waves, surrounded by countrymen, companions, friends, how little I dream that, two years after, I should be still a solitary and gloomy stranger upon its blue waters, without a friend or companion ...'[1]

George Henry Moore, then twenty-six years old, wrote these words in his diary on 22 May 1837, while trying – in vain – to renew his scientific endeavours at the Dead Sea. Almost six months later, on 13 November, already back in London, he wrote to his mother at Moore Hall:

> My dearest Mother,—You will be astonished at receiving a letter from me at this address, and the surprise will not altogether be an agreeable one, when you learn that I have failed in an enterprise in which I had hoped to gain some little credit, which I pursued through so much toil, danger and mortification, and on which so much money has been expended.[2]

'The reader's attention ought to be called particularly to the fact that it is to this expedition that we owe the direct discovery of the depression of the Dead Sea.'[3] This remark, made by the German geographer Carl Ritter in his highly important *Comparative Geography of Palestine and the Sinaitic Peninsula*, defines the significance that even leading contemporary scholars attributed to the brief notice that was published in the 1837 volume of the *Journal of the Royal Geographical Society*:

> In the month of March 1837, Mr. G.H. Moore and Mr. W.G. Beek,

having made the necessary preparations and produced a good boat, left Beirut in a small coasting vessel for Jaffa, their intention being to make a trigonometrical survey of the Dead Sea, to ascertain its depth, and to procure collections of all that could be of use to science. From Jaffa they conveyed their boat, stores, &c., to the Dead Sea, passing through Jerusalem and descending on Jericho; a work of great labour, considering that they had no assistance from the authorities, but rather the contrary. After surveying a great portion of the shores, these gentlemen were obliged to abandon their work, the guards and guides declaring they would not proceed. The width of the sea has been established beyond a doubt; soundings have also been taken showing great depth, in some parts upwards of 300 fathoms. The length of this sea is much less than is generally supposed. *There appears also to be another remarkable feature in the level of the sea, as from several observations about the temperature of boiling water, it appears to be considerably lower than the ocean* [emphasis added].[4]

Following Carl Ritter, the contemporary study of the history of Dead Sea research repeatedly mentions 'the two Englishmen' as the creators of 'the drama of the scientific community's awareness of the depression of the Dead Sea'.[5] The first 'Englishman' was George Henry Moore of Moore Hall, County Mayo, Ireland.

The mysteries as well as the scientific questions about the Dead Sea had to be solved in a scholarly manner, the rising interest being motivated not only by the sea's religious connotations and scientific motivation, but, probably quite surprisingly, also by Britain's growing need to find a quicker and easier 'route to India' to replace the long sail around Africa. The possibilities included digging canals or forming land-bridges from the Mediterranean to the Gulf of Suez or from the northern coast of Syria to the Euphrates. The British government deliberated the idea intensively from the beginning of the 1830s.[6] Another issue, strongly connected, was the study and development of a means to encourage the use of steamships for transportation to India.[7]

These issues were studied as a result of the continuous work and pressure of Francis Rawdon Chesney (1789–1872). Born in County Antrim, Chesney joined the army and achieved the rank of captain in 1815. He first travelled in the east from the summer of 1829 until September 1831, and then headed the famous Euphrates Expedition from 1834 to 1837.[8] His second in command was Henry Blosse Lynch

(1807–1973), third of the eleven sons of Major Henry Blosse Lynch (1778–1823) of Partry House, Ballinrobe, County Mayo.[9]

The detailed narratives of the scientific study of the Dead Sea and British imperial interests, manoeuvres, moves, projects and processes in the Near East during the fourth and fifth decades of the nineteenth century have been studied and lately published by the current writer.[10] This chapter aims at exploring what might be termed 'the Irish connection', mainly concentrating on the two neighbours, George Henry Moore and Henry Blosse Lynch.

The first step in the study of the Dead Sea was probably the ill-fated exploration of Christopher Costigan (1810–1835), a young Irish student of Clongowes Wood, a Roman-Catholic seminary at Maynooth, who, already in 1835, sailed on the lake in an attempt to explore its shores, measure its depth, explain its buoyancy, and obtain other information. Costigan died in the process and was buried in Jerusalem before he managed to leave even one document relating his story or describing any results of his scientific endeavours.[11] Still, he was known to contemporary travellers, mainly because of the American lawyer, John Lloyd Stephens (1805–1852), the famous 'Maya explorer', who, while visiting Palestine in 1836, traced Costigan's steps, and recounted the story in his popular book, published in 1837.[12]

Moore, together with his English companion William G. Beke, followed Costigan by less than a year and a half. It was striking that both had arrived in Beirut, the Lebanese capital and a central port, with no prior intentions of studying the Dead Sea, and both came up with the idea while in the city. 'It took me five years to find the missing link', said the American missionary John D. Paxton (1784–1868) who had cultivated the idea and most probably had 'planted it in their heads'.[13]

Moore's story was originally told by his son, Colonel Maurice Moore (1854–1939), in a book to which his first son, the novelist George Augustus Moore (1852–1933) contributed the foreword, and of course there is no need to repeat the detailed narrative. Without the important discovery at the Dead Sea, Moore's long voyage, which started as a mere adventure and a way to solve personal problems and 'disagreements' with his mother, could easily have turned into another unimportant routine experience of travel in the East. His route took him to Russia and the Caucasus, where, so typical of him, the first entry in his diary described his visit to the stud farm at Krinavaia, which belonged to the Countess of Orloff and held 1500 horses.[14] Through Georgia he reached Persia, and then there is almost no evidence of his whereabouts during the next twenty months, although we know that he was in Syria in May 1835 (including Palestine, 'the Holy Land') and that he visited Constantinople, Athens, the Greek Isles, and Egypt. Whereas Moore kept drawings he had made in the East, he later destroyed every written document that had passed through his hands, especially those that had revealed his continual agony at his separation from the married woman whom he so loved.[15] It also seems probable – at least this was the accepted rumour and most biographies, following that of his son, Maurice, tend to repeat it as fact – that she had followed him with her husband to the East, and they had travelled together for about a year. She might even be one of the figures mentioned in his Dead Sea diary. This was, as George Moore the novelist wrote in the preface to his father's biography, 'a very wrong thing to do if we consider the question from an ethical point of view, but if we look at it from a literary, how felicitous, how Byronic!'.[16]

Moore's letters and diaries were of great interest, describing his outstanding itinerary, adventures and experiences, but also included considerable scientific data of great value. When visiting Moore Hall, novelist Maria Edgeworth (1768–1849) used to listen to 'the reading aloud by Mrs. Moore of George Henry Moore's latest communications from the East'. The novelist praised Moore's reports, observing that 'it was indeed … uncommon to find both judgment and imagination in one so young…'.[17] She also became aware of the scientific value of his work in the Hauran and around the Dead Sea, and forwarded his reports to the Royal Geographical Society as well as to Sir Francis Beaufort (1774–1857), the Hydrographer of the Navy.[18]

On 3 October 1836 Moore was in Jerusalem, and received a document signed by the Franciscan Purveyor, verifying that he had performed a sacred pilgrimage.[19] One of the diaries that escaped destruction begins on 5 December 1836, and describes Moore's travels from Damascus to the ruins of Bussora (Busra), Djerash (Jarash) and the ruins of other cities in the Hauran area, east of the Jordan. The entries in Moore's biography, where this diary is widely quoted, end in Jarash, on 16 January 1837.[20] On 15 March 1837 Moore was 'busy in preparations all day'. With these words he begins his Dead Sea diary. It ends on 14 July. Between the diaries, there is a gap of two months, during which Moore, together with Beek, reached Beirut, purchased a boat, organised supplies and measuring equipment, and looked for a ship that would take them to Jaffa. The research project on the Dead Sea lasted for four months: the expedition itself took place from 15 March to 28

April (from Beyrout to Jaffa, Jerusalem, the Dead Sea and back to Jerusalem), and between 1 May and 16 July he tried, in vain, to continue (from Jerusalem to Jaffa, Alexandria, and then returned to Jaffa).[21]

The story of the Dead Sea expedition cannot be told here in detail. Generally speaking, the original plan was to encircle the lake, while collecting, measuring, mapping on land, and sailing and measuring at sea. But at the first camp, by the sweet water sources of Ein-Feshkah on the northwestern shore, the Bedouin escorts and helpers refused to continue because of the unstable, even dangerous situation with the different Bedouin tribes living around the lake. Moore made every possible effort to save his mission, but in vain. Consequently, on 17 April the whole group was obliged to turn back to Jerusalem. The boat was left anchored, the heavy equipment remained in Jericho, and Moore and Beek left the Dead Sea. Moore was sure he would return, while Beek decided to 'cut the affair'.[22] Disappointed, Moore wrote:

> He whose heart and sword is mine to-day may desert me tomorrow, if his interest beckon him away; and the love of a woman, that but yesterday seemed passionate and eternal, may to-day have passed, like a shadow on the waters, from her false and reckless heart; but a mother's love lives on alike through storms and sunshine, follows to the grave and the throne alike with unchanged and unchangeable devotion....[23]

This chapter attempts to trace the overlapping points between Moore's narrative and the Euphrates Expedition and to refer to some of its participants. Major-General James Bucknall-Estcourt (1802–1855), Adjutant-General of her Majesty's Forces in the Crimea, 'died of cholera, 23 June 1855, in camp before Sebastopol'. As a captain (later Major) in the 43rd Foot Brigade, from 1835 to 1837 he had served in Chesney's Euphrates expedition, and was placed in charge of the magnetic experiments. He replaced Chesney in command of the ship *Euphrates* in the summer of 1836. The decision to break off the expedition was made in January 1837, and Estcourt took his party across the desert from Baghdad to Damascus on camels. After being repeatedly attacked by Bedouins, they arrived in Damascus on 14 February, then continued to Beirut and sailed for England.[24] This itinerary shows that Moore must have met him in one of the above mentioned cities, or in both. In his diary, Moore writes that he was awaiting a letter from Estcourt which would contain some news, although there is no hint of its nature. There is, though, at least one thing that would have been of common interest: the Lynches and their participation in the Euphrates expedition. Estcourt might have been the first to tell Moore about the loss of the steamer *Tigris*, the smaller of the two boats of the expedition, in a hurricane on the Euphrates on 21 May 1836. Although its commander, Captain Henry Blosse Lynch, survived, his older brother by one year, Lieutenant Robert Blosse Lynch of the Bengal Army, lost his life.[25]

There were many parallels between both families, the Moores and the Lynches. The two families were part of five noble Catholic families living around Lough Carra, County Mayo in the West of Ireland during the eighteenth and nineteenth centuries. They maintained close connections, and Mrs. Elizabeth Lynch was frequently visited by her friend, Louisa Moore. Their estates – Moore's 12,000 acres, and Lynch's 1,500 acres – bordered each other.[26]

Henry Blosse Lynch, the third of the children, volunteered for the Indian Navy at the age of 16.[27] He showed a special gift for Eastern languages, and attained an outstanding knowledge of Arabic, Persian and Hindustani. Being appointed as Lieutenant in 1829, he served until 1832 as the formal interpreter to the Gulf Squadron which measured and mapped the Arabian coasts and the Persian Gulf, and to the Commodore of the Navy. He made a number of journeys in Arabia, and developed the position of an almost formal officer of communications with Arab tribes and their sheiks. In 1832 he took a vacation from the Navy, and made his way home via the Red Sea, Ethiopia, and up the Nile to Egypt. His abilities and experience made him the perfect candidate for Chesney, who took him on as second in command in 1834. He was in charge of the landing of the English delegation at the Gulf of Antioch, and was responsible for the assembly of the two steamers, brought from England in parts, and their launch on the Euphrates. In addition, he crisscrossed the countries, being repeatedly sent by Chesney on data-collecting missions and for negotiations with locals; during one of them his party was also attacked. As mentioned above, he was the Commander of the ill-fated *Tigris* but survived the sinking. Chesney left the delegation in 1837, leaving Lynch in command. By 1839 Lynch had finished surveying the river Tigris, reaching the highest point that had ever been allowed to Europeans.[28]

The Board of Directors of the East Indian Company sent three disassembled steamers around the Cape of Good Hope under the command of Lieutenant William Michael Lynch (1811–1840), the fifth brother. These were assembled and launched at the Harbour of

Bussora, and joined the *Euphrates* in Baghdad: four steamers flying the Union Jack, under the command of Commander H.B. Lynch. The flotilla navigated and surveyed the rivers, but then authority was given to Lynch to retain two steamers, and the others were removed to India.[29] During 1841 they performed a trigonometric survey of Mesopotamia, but were also busy in establishing a postal service between Baghdad and Damascus, almost a family enterprise, along with other commercial ties. From 1842 Lynch was again employed in India, as naval commander as well as in civil duties. He was an active member of the Bombay Geographical Society and founded the Indian Navy Club. He earned the C.B. for his service from 1851 in the battles in Burma. Returning home, he inherited the Mayo estate in 1855 and retired from the Navy the following year. In 1857–8 he headed the Paris negotiations with the Persian Ambassador. The great rebellion in India in 1857 and the difficulties of sending reinforcements there again emphasised the need for a quicker route to India. Great efforts were made to realise a plan for building a railway to the Euphrates; Lynch's view was also asked for.[30]

To put the issue in a wider framework, it must be added that the scientific interest in the Holy Land was usually only marginally connected to global processes. The small, politically undefined country had other reasons for its importance. Consequently, more than geo-political importance or global interest, the personal links of a broad and varied set of individuals who were involved in Holy Land research affected its inclusion in spheres of regional and global discourse. A central supporting argument is the fact that during the short period of only twenty years, the 1830s and 1840s, the scientific discovery of a certain, geographically limited region of this country, also became strongly influenced by geo-political considerations, that is, by interests of the leading powers which were then participating in the 'global game'.[31]

Another aspect is the identification, within this global process, of a so-called 'Irish connection' in Holy Land study as well as its involvement in British imperialism, precisely during the 1830s and the 1840s. In 2004, Jennifer Ridden wrote that: 'Irish perspectives (both Protestant and Catholic) [for supporting the Empire] were shaped by various political ideologies and attitudes, by Irish pragmatic goals, and by various non-English senses of identity. Furthermore, Irish colonisers, both Catholic and Protestant, played important roles in shaping British identity in the colonies'.[32]

She openly wrote of 'the network of connections and movements of Irish people' throughout the Empire, such that people in Ireland 'became increasingly aware of the ways in which the language of imperial Britishness could be turned to their advantage', in particular, for a kind of self-governance.[33]

First to establish this connecting narrative in the case of the Holy Land was the Irish Franciscan Father, well known for his intensive contribution to the study of the country, Eugene Hoade. His 1952 paper, 'Ireland and the Holy Land', was published in the annual of his Alma Mater in Multyfarnham. He named some early and medieval travellers, enumerated the Irish serving in the Franciscan *Costodia terrae sanctae*, and added material concerning other compatriots, such as Costigan.[34] In 1974 he was followed by Con Costello, who had served with the UN forces in the early 1970s and published his most informative book concerning 'Irish links with the Levant from the earliest times'.[35] Undoubtedly, the accounts revealed in these books as well as in my study are the best demonstrations of the special link between the Irish people and the Eastern Mediterranean countries, in which Syria, Palestine and Egypt took a central place. This point has to be considered while exploring the Irish connection with India, and their role in the development of the leading colony.[36]

In my study, I have tried to show the acquaintances and the possible meetings and discussions involving the Irish participants in both areas. The list of Irish mentioned as active participants in both 'routes' – the Dead Sea study and the Euphrates 'road to India', is impressive: Costigan, Moore, Chesney, the Lynches, the learned missionary Josias Leslie Porter (1823–1889),[37] to name only the important ones. One must add dozens of other persons, travellers who visited the East, missionaries and clergy who lived in the East for various periods. The claim that 'affinity with the East had long been part of the Irish temperament', that the Irish were fascinated by the new environment and often submerged in it, some of them ended up converting to Islam, might have some factual basis, although it must be stressed that many of the Irish simply acted in service to the Empire. Other studies have pointed out that 'the number of Irish soldiers, missionaries, and administrators going to India grew tremendously in the nineteenth century', and this must be also true for nearer parts of the East, including Egypt, Syria and Palestine. These far away and exotic countries offered the Irish adventure as well as work opportunities.[38]

From the end of the seventeenth century, the East India Company recruited the Irish as soldiers and low-level civil servants. The numbers and percentage of Irish troops recruited by the company are impressive, approaching 40 per cent. Anglo-Irish aristocrats gained access to the highest positions. The Irish constituted one quarter of the Indian Civil Service. It is also only natural that the mid-1840s saw a tremendous increase of Irish recruits, looking for relief from the Famine. In 1855, the Civil Service and the army of India were thrown open to accepting more Irish into their ranks, and Trinity College started tailoring their curriculum for the civil service exams. These developments hold true for permanent settlers, as well; in addition to soldiers and missionaries, between 1815 and 1910, the Irish constituted about one third of the white settlers in the British Empire. It is also clear that the elite and gentry were particularly significant in this respect.[39] The networks which developed were based on former acquaintance, family connections (as, for example, the Lynch family in the Indian Navy), mutual interest, and a kind of 'compatriotism' (*Landsmannschaft*) based on common origins and culture, and the feeling that one could have more confidence in one's compatriots, mainly in those far away countries.

About two-thirds of the members of Chesney's expedition were Irish. It is difficult to establish the reason, although it might not have been with prior intention as Chesney chose his people according to their proven capabilities and availability. Chesney does not reveal any form of Irish pride in his many writings. On the contrary, he wrote about 'that unhappy country Ireland, about which everyone is greatly alarmed'.[40]

All my efforts to find direct proof of a meeting between George Henry Moore (born 1810) and Henry Blosse Lynch (born 1807) have been fruitless. Lynch volunteered for the Indian Navy at the age of 16, when Moore was only 13 years old. But I did find enough circumstantial evidences for the fact that these neighbours had sufficient possibilities to hear and learn about each other while exploring the East, and probably also to cross paths and to meet. Due to lack of day-to-day diaries, it is impossible to establish their meetings for certain. But I did establish the fact that both Moore and Estcourt stayed in Damascus and Beirut during the second half of February 1837. It is also clear that Moore met Estcourt, and probably many other expedition participants during the years he spent in the East, probably from the spring of 1835 (after returning from Persia) until the end of 1836. Coincidence or not, the fact is that both Mayo people fulfilled a highly significant and important role in the two related and connected processes, the establishing of the Dead Sea level and the British routes to India.

NOTES

1. Maurice Moore, *An Irish Gentleman George Henry Moore: His Travel, His Racing, His Politics*, (London: T.W. Laurie, 1913), p.52.
2. Moore to Mother, London, 13 November 1837, National Library of Ireland, Manuscripts Reading Room [hereafter NLI], Moore 1837, MS 890.
3. C. Ritter, *The Comparative Geography of Palestine and the Sinaitic Peninsula* (trsl. W.L. Gage), III (New York: D. Appleton, 1866, rep. New York: Greenwood, 1968), p.127 n.1.
4. W.G. Beek, 'On the Dead Sea and Some Positions in Syria', JRGS, 7 (1837), p.456. The original letter exists in the RGS Archives, file Beke 1837.
5. B. Kreiger, *Living Waters: Myth, History and Politics of The Dead Sea* (New York: Continuum Publishing, 1988), pp.60–1. The same description is repeated in some Israeli studies, i.e., J. Vardi, 'How was the Height of the Lowest Place in the World Established?', in M. Na'or (ed.), *The Dead Sea and the Judean Desert* (Idan 14, Jerusalem: Yad BenZvi, 1990), pp.23–5 [Heb.].
6. E. Elath, *Britain's Routes to India: British Projects in 1834–1872 for linking the Mediterranean with the Persian Gulf by steam navigation on the Euphrates and by Euphrates Valley Railway* (Jerusalem: Magnes, 1971), pp.25–42 [Heb.]; cf. also W. Allen, *The Dead Sea, a New Route to India, with Other Fragments and Gleanings in the East*, I–II (London: Longman, Brown, Green, and Longman, 1855); H.L. Hoskins, *British Routes to India* (New York: Frank Cass, 1966).
7. J.S. Guest, *The Euphrates Expedition* (London and New York: Kegan Paul, 1992), pp.12–19, 43–4.
8. F.R. Chesney, *The Expedition for the Survey of the Rivers Euphrates and Tigris, Carried On by Order of the British Government, In the Years 1835, 1836, and 1837*, I–II (New York: Greenwood, 1969, 1st ed. London: Longman, Brown, Green, and Longman, 1850); ibid., *Narrative of the Euphrates Expedition, Carried On by Order of the British Government During the Years 1835, 1836, and 1837* (London: Longman, Green, and Co., 1868); Cf.: J. O'Donnell and L. Chesney, *The Life of the Late General F. R. Chesney, Colonel Commandant Royal Artillery* (ed. S. LanePoole, London and Sydney: Eden, Remington & Co., 1893); H.C.G. Chesney, 'General Francis Rawdon Chesney, 1789–1872,' in J.W. Foster and H.C.G. Chesney (eds), *Nature in Ireland: A Scientific and Cultural History* (Dublin: Lilliput, 1997), pp.337–42; See Guest, *The Euphrates Expedition*; H.C.G. Matthew and B. Harrison (eds), *Oxford Dictionary of National Biography*, I–LX (Oxford: OUP, 2004) [hereafter ODNB], 5230.
9. See Chesney, *Narrative of the Euphrates Expedition*, pp.547–8; E.C. Lynch, *Lynch Record, Containing Biographical Sketches of Men of the Name Lynch, sixteenth to twentieth century, together with Information Regarding the Origin of the Name and Topographical Poems Showing the Territories Possessed by Some Branches of the Lynch Family* (New York: William J. Hirten, 1925), 726; ODNB, 17254.
10. H. Goren, *Dead Sea Level: Science, Exploration and Imperial Interests in the Near East* (Tauris Historical Geography Series, 6, London and New York: I.B. Tauris, 2011).
11. E.W.G. Masterman, 'Explorations in the Dead Sea Valley', *The Biblical World*, New Series, 25 (1905), pp.407–421; ibid., 'Three Early Explorers in the Dead Sea Valley: Costigan—Molyneux—Lynch', PEFQS, 43 (1911), pp.13–19; C. Costello, 'Christopher Costigan, Explorer of the Dead Sea', *Irish Geography*, 11 (1978), p.214; ibid., 'Nineteenth Century Irish Explorers in the Levant', Irish Geography, 7 (1984), pp.91–4; ibid., *Ireland and the Holy Land: An account of Irish links with the Levant from the earliest times* (Alcester and Dublin: C. Goodfile Neale, 1974), pp.97–104; E. Eriksen, 'Christopher Costigan (1810–1835): Irish explorer of the Dead Sea', *Holy Land* (Spring 1985), pp.41–9; ibid., 'The Illness of Christopher Costigan—A case of heat stroke', *Dublin Historical Record*, 39 (June 1986), pp.82–5; ibid., *Holy Land Explorers*, Jerusalem 1989, pp.11–51; Kreiger, *Living Waters*, pp.53–60; H. Goren, 'Nicholayson and Finn Describe the Expeditions and Deaths of Costigan and Molyneux', *Cathedra*, 85 (October 1997), pp.65–72 [Heb.], 89–94 [English texts].
12. J.L. Stephens, *Incidents of a Travel in Egypt, Arabia Petraea and the Holy Land, by an American* (New York: Derby & Jackson, 1858, 1st edition, 1837), II, pp.30, 201–2, 213–15; Cf.: V.W. von Hagen, *Maya Explorer: John Lloyd Stephens and the Lost Cities of Central America and Yucatan* (Norman, Oklahoma: University of Oklahoma Press, 1948).
13. See Goren, *Dead Sea Level*, pp.156–7; cf. J.D. Paxton, *Letters from Palestine Written During a*

Residence There in the Years 1836, 7, and 8 (London: Charles Tilt, 1839).

14. See Moore, *An Irish Gentleman*, p.28. Alexej Fedorowitsch Orlów (1787–1861), military commander and diplomat, was engaged in wars against the Ottomans, as well as in agreements and treaties with them.
15. His love affair with 'the lady from Cheltenham', which was the main reason for his travels, is vividly described in his biography.
16. See Moore, *An Irish Gentleman*, p.xvii.
17. J.M. Hone, *The Life of George Moore* (London: Gollancz, 1936), pp.857; M. Edgeworth, *A Memoir of Maria Edgeworth, with selection from her Letters* (ed. by her Children, London: private ed., 1867), III, pp.178–85.
18. To Beaufort's biography, cf. N. Courtney, *Gale Force 10: The Life and Legacy of Admiral Beaufort* (London: Review, 2003); S. Landy, 'Sir Francis Beaufort, 1774–1857', in J.W. Foster and H.C.G. Chesney (eds), *Nature in Ireland*, pp. 327–31. For the central role he played in the processes dealt with in this study, see Goren, *Dead Sea Level*, passim.
19. NLI, MS 890: G. H. Moore II, no. 83.
20. NLI, MS 3510: Syrian Diary; Moore, *An Irish Gentleman*, pp.33–43.
21. NLI, MS 3509: Dead Sea Diary.
22. *Dead Sea Diary*, pp.99–106.
23. *Dead Sea Diary*, p. 133; Moore, *An Irish Gentleman*, p.46.
24. Various documents in Gloucestershire Record Office, Gloucestershire County Council Chesney, D 1571, many cited by U. Naumann, *Euphrat Queen: Eine Expedition ins Paradies* (München: Beck, 2006); See Chesney, *Narrative of the Euphrates Expedition*, pp.251–76, 547–8; E.P. Charlewood, *Passages from the Life of a Naval Officer* (Manchester: Cave & Sever, 1869), pp.43–55; ODNB, 8892.
25. Various letters by John Hobhouse, British Library, Orient/India Reading Room, Mss.; See Chesney, *Narrative of the Euphrates Expedition*, pp.251–76; H. Richardson, *The Loss of the Tigris: A Poem. In Two Cantons. With Notes. Inscribed to the Commander, Officers, and Men of the Euphrates Expedition* (London: J. Hatchard and Son, 1840).
26. H.F. Berry, 'The Partry private cemetery, Townland of Cloonlagheen, and Parish of Ballyovey', *Journal of the Association for the Preservation of Memorials to the Dead in Ireland*, 8/2 (1910), pp.130–4; B. Melvin, 'The Galway tribes as landowners and gentry', in G. Moran and R. Gillespie (eds), *Galway History and Society: Interdisciplinary Essays on the History of an Irish County* (Dublin: Geography Publications, 1996), pp.319–74. Cf. a map of Moorehall, May 1809, NLI, MS 10.
27. For biographies, see above n.9; See Goren, *Dead Sea Level*, pp.73–5. A vast collection of family documents and archive: Henry Blosse Lynch Private Archive, Longcross House, Headley (Berkshire).
28. G.S. Graham, *Great Britain in the Indian Ocean: A Study of Maritime Enterprise 1810–1850* (Oxford: Clarendon, 1967), pp.281–2; See Guest, *The Euphrates Expedition*, p.1407.
29. S.H. Longrigg, *Four Centuries of Modern Iraq* (Oxford: Clarendon Press, 1925), p.293.
30. See Chesney, *Narrative of the Euphrates Expedition*, pp.547–8; See Elath, *Britain's Routes to India*, pp. 120–35; See Longrigg, *Four Centuries of Modern Iraq*, pp.293–6.
31. See Goren, *Dead Sea Level*, passim.
32. J. Ridden, 'Britishness as an imperial and diasporic identity: Irish elite perspectives, c.1820–1870s', in P. Gray (ed.), *Victoria's Ireland? Irishness and Britishness, 1837–1901* (Dublin: Four Courts Press, 2004), p.88. For background, see L.M. Cullen, 'The Irish diaspora of the seventeenth and eighteenth centuries', in N. Canny (ed.), *Europeans on the Move: Studies on European Migration, 1500–1800* (Oxford: Clarendon Press, 1994), pp.113–49.
33. See Ridden, *Victoria's Ireland? Irishness and Britishness, 1837–1901*, pp.88–90.
34. E. Hoade, 'Ireland and the Holy Land', *The Franciscan College Annual*, 20 (1952), pp.69–77.
35. Costello, *Ireland and the Holy Land*, pp.63–160.
36. J. Lennon, *Irish Orientalism: A Literary and Intellectual History* (Syracuse, NY: Syracuse University Press, 2004), pp.169–76.
37. ODNB, 22574; E.J. Aiken, *Scriptural Geography: Portraying the Holy Land* (Tauris Historical Geography Series, 3, London and New York: I.B. Tauris, 2010), pp.89–132.
38. See Lennon, *Irish Orientalism*, pp.169–71.
39. See Lennon, *Irish Orientalism*, pp.171–6; See Ridden, *Victoria's Ireland? Irishness and Britishness, 1837–1901*, pp.88, 91.
40. Chesney to 'My dear Sir', n.d. [1833?], The National Archives, FO 352/26(1).

CHAPTER FOUR

The Metamorphosis of George Moore

MARGARETTA D'ARCY

The impact of the Boer War on Ireland's political development, together with George Moore's contribution to that development, notably through his play *The Bending of the Bough*, has already been examined by scholars; but his own internal metamorphosis (as described in *Hail and Farewell*) prompts a number of questions that – to the best of my knowledge – have not been satisfactorily answered. For example, why did his opposition to British policy in South Africa involve such declarations of visceral revulsion? Was this revulsion the cause of his new recognition of himself as an Irishman, or did the recognition produce the revulsion? And even after the recognition, why did he continue to express contempt toward the Irish? What significance should we attach to his failure to tell his readers the full story of the letters that came to him from the war, exposing Kitchener's atrocities? What are we to understand by his insistence that *Hail and Farewell* is a novel rather than a straightforward memoir? Finally, why did he decide that Ireland needed a book and that Irish women needed to be liberated from the clergy? This chapter will tentatively propose a few solutions to these problems.

When George Moore heard the call to return to Ireland in the unacknowledged role of the nation's Messiah, he was not such a comically ineffectual figure as might appear at first glance. What follows is an examination of the contribution he actually made to the anti-Imperial cause. P.J. Mathews[1] shows how the resistance to the Boer War in Ireland was pivotal in that it not only brought the nationalist separatist movement into a coherent group led by Arthur Griffith, eventually becoming Sinn Féin, but also strengthened the political relevance of the Irish literary movement with the production of *The Bending of the Bough*, a parable of Ireland's deference towards England. The play did not deal directly with the war but was impregnated with the author's turbulent pro-Boer emotions.

Mathews sees this drama as playing 'an important role in critiquing the policies of the Irish Parliamentary Party and articulating the emerging gap between the Home Rulers and the separatists'. Moore believed that the very act of collaborating with Yeats to prepare a workable text from Edward Martyn's unsatisfactory draft, between November 1899 and January 1900, had 'awakened the Irishman that was dormant in me,' while the Boer War was simultaneously turning 'my love of England to hatred of England'.[2]

The resignation of his parliamentary seat by the veteran nationalist MP Michael Davitt, in protest at the government's arbitrary assumption that Ireland must be part and parcel of the war, took place at this very time, an act of separatist vehemence that coincidentally mirrored the thrust of the script. When the play opened in Dublin in February 1900, *Freeman's Journal* described it as 'a biting and political sabre directed against the influences that have destroyed the Irish gentry's sense of patriotism.'[3] Previous productions of the Irish Literary Theatre had opened in London: the deliberately ideological withdrawal from the imperial capital paralleled Davitt's withdrawal from the imperial parliament.

George Moore's letter to the *Irish Times* (its author by then well known in England as well as Ireland), attacking Queen Victoria's visit to Ireland, provoked controversy; Moore wrote that the Queen was visiting in order to recruit Irishmen as cannon fodder for the Boer war, 'to do the work her recruiting sergeants have failed to do. ... With the shilling between her finger and thumb and a bag of shillings at her girdle.'[4] The strength of the attack made Lady Gregory uneasy; she felt that Moore's radicalism was going to be a problem for Yeats. In fact Moore had become weary of collaborative playwriting. *Diarmuid and Grania* had been giving continual trouble and he was 'convinced that any further association with Yeats would be ruin to me. My folly ends on the scene in my pocket, which I'll keep to remind me what a damned fool a clever man like Yeats can be when he is in the mood to be a fool.'[5]

He went back to England to find the whole country eructating in a jingoistic fervour; his younger brother, Colonel Maurice Moore, a soldier on active service, had been posted to the battlefront in South Africa; and his own inner turmoil was increasing by the day. 'I live in a sort of nightmare when I think of the war,' he wrote to Maurice.

> To ponder on it as others do I should go off my head. ... On the subject of the war, I think I am going a little crazy because I

refuse to speak to anyone except those who are against the war.
I met a man the other day whom I had known all my life, he told
me the war was a beautiful thing and this was an exceptional
fine example of war. I said I shall never speak to you again.[6]

His own growing disgust with the England he had once adored led
him to feel personally responsible when his brother wrote to him in
horror about Kitchener's gruesome plans for the Boer community:
totally scorched earth, women and children in concentration camps.
There is no doubt that the anti-war movement was significantly
advanced when George encouraged Maurice to write these anonymous reports. He forwarded them to the campaigning journalist W.T.
Stead, who had detached himself from his previous position as
imperialist advocate and adviser to Cecil Rhodes and was now leader
of the Stop-the-War Committee, a body rapidly growing in strength
and influence. Stead issued the letters in two widely-distributed
pamphlets, *Hell Let Loose: How We Are Waging War In South Africa*, and
The War in South Africa 1899–19?: How Not to Make Peace. They caused
severe embarrassment to government. The atrocities were now in the
public domain: Liberal press and politicians made the most of them;
anti-war, pro-Boer, sentiment was already vocal in British South
Africa, where Olive Schreiner (an old flame of George's) and Albert
Cartwright (editor of the *South African News*) were members of a group
that published a book of subversive poems which although banned
in the Cape Colony was achieving an appreciative circulation in
Britain.[7]

Nonetheless Moore felt that the true evil of the situation had not
yet got through to the British public. His own friends seemed abom-
inably slow to share his anger. He visited the painters, Tonks and
Steer, and was shocked by their apparent complacency.

> I could see [Tonks] sympathised with the Boer women and
> children dying in concentration camps.
> 'The war has put pictures clean out of my head and I don't
> mind telling you that Steer's indifference to everything except
> his values has disgusted me. Can't you see that the war has
> changed me utterly? I can't believe that I present the same
> appearance. Tell me, hasn't the war put a new look on my face?'
> 'No, Moore it isn't as bad as that. They couldn't be left on the
> veldt; we had to do something with the women and children.'
> 'Tonks, I am ashamed of you! After having burnt down their

houses, you had to keep them, as it would be an advantage to you to destroy the Boer race. You keep them in concentration camps where they drop off like flies … children without milk to drink; water, perhaps, from springs fouled with the staling of mules.'[8]

He was wildly obsessive, demented even, hallucinating as he strolled about London.

I walked with a friend and fell out with my friend's appearance, so English did it seem to me. He wore his clothes arrogantly, yet it was not his clothes so much as his sheep-like face that angered me. I saw the same sheep in everyone, in the women as much as the men, a heartless lust for gold was read by me in their faces. For the goldfields of Pretoria which they haven't got and never will. … My thoughts would resolve into a prayer that the means might be put into my hands to humiliate this detestable England, this brutal people![9]

And means were put into his hand: contained in a third letter from Maurice, far more dreadful in its implication than its predecessors because it detailed Kitchener's orders to the army to trap De Wet and his commandos between two rivers, to deceptively accept surrender, and then to shoot them down, every man: 'A murder plot, pure and simple, having nothing in common with any warfare waged by Europeans for many centuries. It must be stopped, and publication will stop it.'[10]

This time he bypassed Stead and his pamphlets, which could not be issued quickly enough; he needed immediate publication in the newspapers; but the first one he tried, the *Daily Chronicle*, presumably his best bet for such an exposé, refused to print the letter if the only indication of its author was 'an Officer in the Field'. Maurice's name could not possibly be given, for Lord Roberts, the Commander-in-Chief, was denying the content of the first two letters and had instituted investigations into the leak. George put his trust in the Irish anti-imperial spirit; he immediately took the mailboat to Dublin, where the editor of *Freeman's Journal*, after some hesitation, published the letter anonymously on 15 January 1901. The next day, it appeared in *The Times*. Albert Cartwright then printed it in the *South African News*, and was instantly arrested and gaoled. But 'the military authorities in South Africa disowned and repudiated the plot … the Boers were safe; it would be impossible to revive the methods of Tamburlane on another occasion.'[11]

On 26 February the treatment of Cartwright was raised as a question in the Commons, with reference to the letter in *Freeman's Journal*; the question was evaded by Joseph Chamberlain, Secretary of State for the Colonies, in the usual po-faced parliamentary manner. Lloyd George denounced the government on the basis of Maurice's first two letters (18 February). In April, Emily Hobhouse was to give Lloyd George a graphic fifteen-page dossier (also published in the *Manchester Guardian*), thereby bringing the atrocities in the concentration camps to the attention of the whole world: 'It is no wonder that in *Ave* he could give "no reasonable account" of his condition at this time, and that he fell back on a story of mysterious voices in the Chelsea Road bidding him to go to Ireland.'[12]

A reader of *Ave* in the twenty-first century (aware of current anti-war agitation, military leaks and Irish neo-paganism) might deduce that the mysterious voices are perhaps there for two reasons. One: security – to conceal the dangerous fact that the anonymous letters were from his own brother. Two: professional practicality – a magical mystical event would be most helpful in fitting him in to the new Irish literary climate. Note that nowhere in *Hail and Farewell* does George reveal Maurice's authorship: when the books of the trilogy were published his brother was still in the army, and could still have been court-martialled. So I suppose that no one in Dublin (save the discreet editor of *Freeman's Journal*) knew about George's role in preventing Kitchener's war crime: otherwise, the caricature reputation of a clownish George Moore that has been handed down to us might well have been very different. The best way for him to hide the truth was to turn the incident into a mock-heroic episode from a comic version of Wagner, where the hero's despair is suddenly lifted by supernatural intervention; his urgent and courageous initiative earns him immediate salvation; Cathleen ní Houlihan calls him out of London in a glorious catharsis that reveals his true self: 'As in a vision I saw Ireland as a god demanding human sacrifices and everybody or nearly everybody, crying, "take me, Ireland, take me; I am unworthy. But accept me as a burnt offering."'[13]

What had made George so passionate in defence of the Boers? He himself seems to have been puzzled by the strength of his own passion.

> One day I stopped in Ebury St. abashed; for it was not a victory for our soldiers that I desired to read in the paper but one for the Boers. It was a long time before I could ask myself the reason

for all this sympathy for illiterate farmers speaking a Dutch dialect in which no book had yet been written; a people without any sentiment of art, without a past, without folklore, and therefore, in some respect, a less reputable people than the Irish.[14]

The obvious reason was one that he shared with other Irish nationalists, a rational dislike of the way the British Empire was forcing itself upon a small agricultural society that wanted nothing to do with it, only because the agricultural society had found gold on its land. But clues throughout the book betray further compulsions. He tells us he was shy and had an inferiority complex; he was unhappily aware that his father didn't think highly of him as an heir to a family with so much to be proud of – the liberalism, the patriotism, the fact that his father had never evicted any one, and had fought hard in parliament for justice toward Ireland. So his brother's third letter from South Africa struck him in a very vulnerable place. Maurice had written, 'Soldiers and regimental officers will be made to bear the blame [of Kitchener's murder plot], and, therefore, I consider the honour of the army is at stake.'[15]

If the blame for a war crime was indeed to be fixed upon Maurice, a senior regimental officer, it would be the end of his reputation in Ireland as a nationally-minded man of integrity, and the end of the reputation of the Moores altogether – the independence movement would make pariahs of Maurice and his children, while George would be included in their disgrace – imagine the reaction from the Transvaal Committee, the likes of Griffith, Maud Gonne, Yeats, Davitt, Martyn – it was not only the honour of the army that was at stake. George could not forget the way Edward Martyn had already told him it would 'take years to obtain forgiveness' for having written *Parnell and his Ireland*: 'Irish memories are long.'[16]

In the election of 1868, when Moore's father ran against the landlord interest and won, breaking the power of the Ascendancy in Mayo, 'he told the electors a story of an old ballad about the dragon of Wantley, which devoured the people and knocked down their houses until—

Moore of Moore Hall
With nothing at all
Slew the dragon of Wantley.'[17]

He had gone out to the fight with neither sword nor shield; the dragon of the old legend was nineteenth-century landlordism; Moore Senior was the people's champion.

Just so did George, 'with nothing at all', humiliate the imperial enemy. His dragon lay dead; he had at last paid his debt to the shade of his father; he could stay true to the memory of his father as a kindly human being. His inferiority complex cast aside, he was able to take his confident and undisputed place in Irish society – not only had he saved the honour of the Moores; he had also saved the Irish-based regiments from unspeakable guilt, and thereby he had saved Ireland. And because his great deed was clutched to his heart as an unbreakable secret, he was able to write in *Ave* 'that no Messiah had been found by me … because the Messiah Ireland was waiting for was in me and not in another.'[18]

> It is difficult for me to believe any good of myself. Within the oftentimes bombastic and truculent appearance that I present to the world, trembles a heart shy as a wren in the hedgerow or a mouse along the wainscoting.[19]
>
> The reader should be able, if he be intelligent, to imagine for himself the hundred other exquisite moments that I owe to my inveterate belief in my own inferiority.[20]
>
> One does not like to speak of a double self. … Yet it seems necessary that I should speak of my self-consciousness. … In my novels I can write only tragedy, and in life play nothing but light comedy. … The reader will kindly look into his mind, and when the point has been considered he will be in a mood to take up my book again and to read my story with profit to himself.[21]
>
> We are moulded, but the influences that mould us are indirect, and are known to nobody but ourselves. We never speak of them, and are almost ashamed even to think of them, so trivial do they seem.[22]

The skill in the writing of *Ave* has often been overlooked: how he so carefully hides his secret and, in a way, turns his book of ostensible fact into a traditional fairy story, something like *The Frog Prince*, or more accurately, *The Mouse Who Became a Lion, or The Wren Who Was Really an Eagle*. As a child his imagination had been deeply stirred by hearing his parents talk about M.E. Braddon's sensational novel, *Lady Audley's Secret*, the tale of a woman who mistakenly hoped she had succeeded in murdering her husband.

He never forgot her desperate and perilous excitement, the more so when he himself became the agent of the honourable secret of his brother's military 'betrayal'. For years, however, he had contained within himself another quite different secret, one he thought he could never be rid of. Another early memory, no less potent:

> … Honor King, an old woman who periodically came begging at the door of Moore Hall; his parents used to joke that he would certainly end up marrying Honor King, then they would all laugh. 'The joke was based on the assumption that I was such an ugly little boy nobody else would marry me.' He traced his self-doubt back to how his parents treated him in childhood.[23]

How many times must little George have wanted to commit, like Lady Audley, his own concealed murder of this terrible (and presumably Catholic) beggar woman? The unfortunate jocularity not only poisoned his early life but conditioned his entire view of Ireland. In 1887 he had published a startling statement in the English magazine *Time*, a long-delayed cry of revenge against his mother.

> Two dominant notes in my character – an original hatred of my native country, and a brutal loathing of the religion I was brought up in, all aspects of my native country are violently disagreeable to me, and I cannot think of the place I was born without a sensation akin to nausea. With Frenchmen I am conscious of a sense of nearness. The English I love, and with a love that is foolish – mad, limitless. England is Protestantism, Protestantism is England. Protestantism is strong, clean, and westernly; Catholicism is eunuch-like, dirty and oriental.[24]
>
> Love of cruelty is inveterate in the human being and remembering this, remorse would sometimes overtake me in the street.[25]

Ulick O'Connor quotes him as saying, fifteen years before the Boer War, that his people were 'degenerate aborigines', and that his hatred for his own race was 'as fierce as that which closes a ferret's teeth on a rat's throat'.[26] Remorse surely overtook him when he came to understand that he had looked at and behaved toward the Irish as the British government toward the Boers.

> We [i.e. the landlords as a class, not in fact the Moores] looked upon our tenants as animals who lived in hovels round the bogs. … If they failed to pay their rents the cabins they had built with their own hands were thrown down.[27]
>
> A cabin in the middle of the Annys bog, a dwelling hardly suited for an animal, yet a man and woman lived there and children

were born in it. ... I remember one day up in the mountains, while grouse-shooting, stabling my horse in a man's cabin.[28]

If we thought that bullocks would pay us better ... we cleaned our lands of tenants. ... I remember how they used to go away by train from Claremorris in great batches bawling like animals.[29]

George had shamefully agreed with such ruthlessness and may have wished his father would serve his tenants in the same way.

There was a dreadful occasion during the Land War, when George as a landlord, taking the place of his dead parent, all but fell into the abyss; the *Connacht Telegraph* called him 'the degenerate son of a worthy father,' as he set about a mass eviction. 'At his request twenty side-cars arrived loaded with police carrying firearms, later joined by a contingent of the RIC from Balla and a process-server. In the village of Coolfox this force met the determined resistance of a dozen women and withdrew after serving four writs of ejectment for non-payment of rent.'[30] Moore's agent persuaded him not to proceed with the business, and he never attempted such a thing again.

At the beginning of Ave he describes how Edward Martyn talked to him in London about the possibility of an Irish literature in the Irish language. He laughed at the idea, but five years later, in 1899, Martyn brought Yeats to see him and to tell him excitedly that a renaissance of literature was about to break out in Ireland and he could be part of it. He tried to put it aside, but Yeats slowly began to seduce him and successfully awoke his interest; he still felt some sort of deep-seated revulsion preventing him from committing himself to the cause. Yeats talked at length to him about various mythological personages, notably Cathleen ní Houlihan, dream-personification of Ireland, who seems to have given serious alarm to Moore's nervous system.

> 'It would be strange if Cathleen ní Houlihan were to get me after all.'[31]
>
> 'I too am sacrificing to Cathleen ní Houlihan; one sacrifice brings many. And to escape from the hag whom I could see wrapped in a faded shawl, her legs in grey worsted stockings, her feet in brogues, I packed my trunk and went away by the mailboat.'[32]
>
> I had caught sight of Cathleen ní Houlihan in the dusk over against the Burren mountains as I returned through the beech woods and the dank bracken. The rewriting of *The Tale of the*

> Town [i.e. *The Bending of the Bough*] had awakened the Irishman that was dormant in me, and the Boer war had turned my love of England to hatred of England and a voice heard on three different occasions had bidden me pack my portmanteau and return to Ireland.[33]

She appeared to be chasing him, alternately out of Ireland and back into Ireland, a grotesque apparition set against the bloody panorama of the Boer War. Is it too much to conclude that this dire figure wore the features, as well as the clothing, of old Honor King – she whom he had feared would forcibly seize him and marry him – she who had made the townlands near Moore Hall into dens of dread for him so many years before? But if Honor King was Cathleen ní Houlihan, she was presumably only waiting for the liberation of Ireland to be returned to her true state as a beautiful, free woman? Moore soon accepted he had no need for either fear or repulsion. He knew now where he was going. Confident and determined, he found himself with two tasks. One: Ireland needed a literary masterpiece in Irish, to complete her culture. Two: remembering the women who had successfully defied his eviction and thus prevented him from the most heinous crime against his people, he would repay them his debt of gratitude by freeing them from the clerical control of Rome, an imperialist hold stronger than that of Britain and inhibiting all joy of life – he himself, after all, had freed himself when he was a boy at boarding school.

> A vile hole, a den of priests. I remember one [whose] arm used to droop about my shoulders with some endearing phrase. When we were alone, his hand nearly slipped into my trouser pocket. I went to confession and mentioned the circumstances. I was curious to test the secrecy of the confessional. I know that Catholics believe that a priest will never reveal a secret revealed in the confessional. The result of my confession was that a few days afterward we heard he was leaving.[34]

As he worked, he came up against one obstacle after another, flaccid native bureaucracy with its never-ending deference to the theocrats. For instance, unable to get anyone in the Gaelic League to share his vision of a great book in Irish, he tried instead to organise a touring company to activate the language with popular plays, only to discover that the rigidity of Gaelic League committee-men contradicted the very purpose of the League. They refused to allow women to take part in such plays, all because a priest had objected to the possibility of un-chaperoned females travelling about with male actors. In his anger at this absurdity, an idea entered Moore's mind – that the new safety-bicycle was already making chaperones irrelevant and was loosing women from the clutches of their mothers, who in turn were in the clutches of the priests. He sallied forth into the street to find Edward Martyn with two priests discussing the wonderful work Lady Aberdeen was doing to get rid of consumption with a campaign against spitting. He interrupted to remark, sensibly enough, that insufficient food is the cause of much consumption; but then audacious fantasy took over, he pronounced his own great cure: 'For the last hundred years no Irish archbishop has died from consumption, not a bishop, nor a parish priest. Therefore I sincerely advocate that all Ireland should take orders.'[35]

He thought he might be pragmatic, and work with the priests rather than against them – 'one can only get the better of the clergy by setting the clergy against the clergy'[36] – so he found an enlightened Jesuit who would publish his short stories for him. Moore did have a true sympathy with, and insight into, the struggle of the man within the priest. He had thought that here was a man who understood. He argued that what Ireland needed was enjoyment – why not let the people dance? Father Tom Finlay said it was already happening – young girls came with their mothers and went home with them after the dance. 'I was much inclined to tell him that to dance under the eye of the priest and be taken home by one's mother must seem a somewhat trite amusement to a healthy country girl, unless indeed the Irish people experience little passion in their courtships or their marriages.[37] I knew full well that my contributions to the *New Ireland Review* were the link that bound me to my friend.'[38] But as a priest his friend would have to place his soul above his intelligence. The contributions were becoming less and less suitable as Moore warmed to his overall theme of everyday life in country parishes. 'Father Tom and I had lain side by side in harbour for a while, but the magnetism of the ocean drew me and I continued to write, feeling all the way that my stories were drawing me away from Catholic Ireland.'[39]

Even the supposedly benevolent land reforms, freeing the people from tenantry, often played into the hands of the church. When his mother's youngest brother gave away his estate to a missionary order to save his soul, George visited the place to call on the new owners.

A plump young priest entertained him with accounts of the difficulty of the order's work in Africa, in particular the unwillingness of polygamous men to give up their wives. George naughtily asks if any provision has been made for the abandoned wives. The missionaries haven't thought of that. 'The children,' says George, 'offer you a fairer field?' 'Yes, we try to get hold of the children.'[40]

The last straw was when a book reviewer referred to him in the press as a Catholic writer. Appalled by this crude pigeon-holing, he decided to throw down the gauntlet with a public statement, a letter to the *Irish Times*, assailing the hierarchy. He had hoped to electrify the country with this indictment; but it was too close to the bone, and the intelligentsia made haste to dismiss it as an absurdity. But how absurd is it?

> When will my unfortunate country turn its eyes from Rome, the cause of all her woe? Rome has betrayed Ireland through the centuries. In the first years of the twentieth century, Maynooth and the Catholic Archbishop deserted the Irish Parliamentary Party, one in the hope of getting a Catholic university, the other in order to get a cardinal's hat. No choice was left to me if I wished to remain an Irishman, but to say goodbye to Rome.[41]

Blocked on all sides but undefeated, George concluded that, 'I have come into the most impersonal country in the world to teach personality – personal love and personal religion, personal art, personality for all.'[42] Slyly, impishly, he decided to overturn his normal pattern of behaviour – tragedy for his novels, light comedy for his life – instead, he would deliberately integrate the comedy with the tragedy and write The Book – not any book, not of course the book in Irish – but a Sacred Book about himself, *Hail and Farewell (Ave, Salve, Vale)*, his own Road to Damascus, wide open to interpretation, just as he himself later on would reinterpret the Bible. This made for difficulties. For the book was to catch on as a piece of mere gossip, mischievous at best, malicious at worst. Moore's protestations were not taken seriously when he called the work as much a novel as any book he had written, so far as the form was concerned. He had *moulded* it from some of his experiences, and readers were inclined to be baffled by its ambiguity.

Near the end of his third volume, he proudly declared he had now become impotent. 'Nature has cast chastity upon me. As soon as my change of life becomes known the women of Ireland will come to me crying, "at the bidding of our magicians we have borne children long enough, may we escape from the burden of child-bearing without sin?"[43] When George described how 'Ireland has lain too long under the spell of the magicians without will, without intellect, useless and shameful, the despised of nations,'[44] who could foresee that a hundred years after the publication of *Ave*, an Irish prime minister in an Irish parliament would have stood up and denounced an 'attempt by the Holy See to frustrate an Inquiry in a sovereign, democratic republic' while 'managing' the 'rape and torture of children'?[45] – a speech swiftly followed by the Vatican's recall of the Papal Nuncio, the senior foreign diplomat in the country.

NOTES

1. P.J. Mathews, 'Stirring up disloyalty: the Boer War, the Irish Literary Theatre and the emergence of a new separatism,' *The Irish University Review* (Spring-Summer 2003).
2. George Moore, *Hail & Farewell*, ed. Richard Allen Cave, (Gerrards Cross: Colin Smythe Ltd, 1985), p.608.
3. See Mathews, *The Irish University Review*.
4. Adrian Frazier, *George Moore, 1852–1933* (Newhaven & London: Yale University Press, 2000), p.290.
5. See Moore, *Hail & Farewell*, p.255.
6. Ulick O'Connor, *Celtic Dawn* (London: Hamish Hamilton, 1984), p.190.
7. Olive Schreiner, Albert Cartwright et al., *Songs of the Veld and other Poems* (London, 1902; Cederberg of Capetown, 2008).
8. See Moore, *Hail and Farewell*, pp.217–19.
9. Ibid., p.221.
10. Ibid., p.256.
11. Ibid.
12. Joseph Hone, *The Life of George Moore* (London: Victor Gollancz, 1936), p.233.
13. See Moore, *Hail and Farewell*, p.213.
14. Ibid., p.215.
15. Ibid., 'Appendix B', p.663.
16. Ibid.. p.235.
17. See Frazier, *George Moore, 1852–1933*, p.9.
18. See Moore, *Hail and Farewell*, p.257.
19. Ibid., p.98.
20. Ibid., p.99.
21. Ibid., p.114.
22. Ibid., p.98.
23. See Frazier, *George Moore, 1852–1933*, p.13.
24. Ibid., p.162.
25. See Moore, *Hail and Farewell*, p.217.
26. See O'Connor, *Celtic Dawn*, p.190.
27. See Moore, *Hail and Farewell*, p.481.
28. Ibid., p.634.
29. Ibid., p.481.
30. See Frazier, *George Moore, 1852–1933*, p.73.
31. See Moore, *Hail and Farewell*, p.208.
32. Ibid., p.214.
33. Ibid., p.608.
34. Ibid., p.419.

35. Ibid., p.323.
36. Ibid., p.337.
37. Ibid., p.340.
38. Ibid., p.346.
39. Ibid., p.347.
40. Ibid., p.639.
41. Ibid., 'Appendix C', p.669.
42. Ibid., p.609.
43. Ibid., p. 608.
44. Ibid., p.609.
45. Dermot Keogh, article in the *Irish Times*, 29 August 2011.

CHAPTER FIVE

Lady Gregory, George Moore, and Gathering Folklore

LUCY McDIARMID

The starting point for this chapter is George Moore's charge, in *Vale*, that Lady Gregory was a proselytiser in her youth. The offending section was published in *The English Review* in January 1914 before the rest of the book, so Lady Gregory had time to threaten a lawsuit if the charge were not removed from the text. Moore objected to the word 'charge' because, as he put it in a letter to Lady Gregory, 'Of course, proselytising to me is a virtue.' But he did, finally, revise the offending passage.[1]

The next point of departure is another time Lady Gregory was accused of proselytising, when she and Yeats were collecting fairy legends, as she describes in one of the prefaces in *Visions and Beliefs in the West of Ireland*.

> Mr. Yeats at that time wore black clothes and a soft black hat, but gave them up later, because he was so often saluted as a priest. But this time another view was taken, and I was told after a while that the curate of the Clare parish had written to the curate of a Connacht parish that Lady Gregory had come over the border with 'a Scripture Reader' to try and buy children for proselytizing purposes. But the Connacht curate had written back to the Clare curate that he had always thought him a fool, and now he was sure of it.[2]

This confusion is by no means outlandish, because – as Sean Ó Domhnaill (b. 1873) of Co. Tipperary remembered – the 'soupers wore black hats and could be easily identified at the local fairs.'[3]

These charges, both untrue and both withdrawn, create suggestive contexts for one another; they offer reason to consider together the two activities, proselytising and folklore-collecting, because to some extent they occupied the same territory and required the same choreography, the entrance of an educated or at least literate Protestant into the space (often the domestic space) of a less-educated Catholic country person. Thus juxtaposed, both proselytising and folklore-collecting can be understood to take place in a 'contact zone', a concept whose theoretical framework provides a way of analysing them. The phrase is taken from Mary Louise Pratt's book *Imperial Eyes*, where she describes it as

> … the space of colonial encounters … the spatial and temporal copresence of subjects previously separated by geographic and historical disjunctures. … It treats the relations … not in terms of separateness … but in terms of copresence, interaction, inter-locking understandings and practices, often within radically asymmetrical relations of power.[4]

Although the 'radically asymmetrical relations of power' Pratt alludes to were operant in both activities, the kinds of 'asymmetry' differ, as do the kinds of power. Taking my inspiration, then, from the external, almost theatrical similarities between gathering folklore and gathering souls – they entail the same clothing, gestures, actions, and space – I want to understand the folkloric encounter, Lady Gregory's in particular, in the light of what it looks like but was not. My aim is to define it precisely by distinguishing it from a practice it was confused with. First I'll look at the Moore–Gregory correspondence; then I'll consider proselytising and folklore-collecting together, the common features and the differences; and then I'll return to Moore and reconsider the passage from *Vale*.

THE MOORE–GREGORY CORRESPONDENCE

In the original text of *Vale* and in his letters to Gregory, Moore's word-ing emphasises proselytising as a cottage-centered activity, a kind of invasion of Catholic domestic space by Protestants. The chapter titled 'Yeats, Lady Gregory, and Synge', as published in the *English Review*, begins by saying that the Persse family was 'a worthy but undistin-guished family in love, in war, or in politics', one that never

> … indulged in anything except a taste for Bible reading in cottages. A staunch Protestant family, if nothing else, the Roxborough Persses certainly are. Mrs Shaw Taylor is Lady Gregory's sister, and both were ardent soul-gatherers in the days

gone by; but Augusta abandoned missionary work when she married, and we like to think of Sir William saying to his bride, as he brought her home in the carriage to Coole, 'Augusta, if you have made no converts, you have at least shaken the faith of thousands. The ground at Roxborough has been cleared for the sowing, but Kiltartan can wait.'[5]

In a 5 January 1914 letter to Sydney Pawling (Moore's editor at Heinemann), Gregory defended her family from the charge that they were 'undistinguished', explained the danger of the proselytising charge to her work at the Abbey Theatre, and also suggested that Moore had gotten this libel from Edward Martyn. At the end she says, 'I do not think you will allow it to be repeated in a book with your name on it, or that I shall be forced to seek legal advice. I shall be very sorry indeed if this becomes necessary.' Denying the proselytism charge directly, she writes,

> My mother an [sic] my two eldest sisters thought it right to point out what they believed to be the different teaching of the Bible to that of the Catholic Church, to any Catholics who would listen. They made no secret of this 'proselytism' which was much mixed up with benevolence and charity in those days. ... But it was not my belief. Although I spent a great part of my girlhood in visiting the sick and poor among my fathers [sic] tenants and supplying their wants, I never 'read Gospels' or taught texts or touched on any controversial matter at all.[6]

When Moore responded to Gregory's letter, he picked up on the 'visiting' and said,

> In your letter to Heinemann you say that though your mother and sisters read the Bible in the cottages you confined yourself to practical help. This will be interpreted by Moran and his like 'that while your mother and sisters read the Bible you distributed tea and sugar.'[7]

In this passage, Moore blends the activities Gregory kept distinct. By distinguishing between what the other women in her family did and what she did, by referring to her mother in one sentence and her father in another, and by the short, definitive sentence 'But it was not my belief', Gregory constructs syntactic boundaries between herself and proselytising. But Moore's response – deliberately, of course – combines the two kinds of cottage-visiting into a single, joint activity: while they read the Bible, she 'distributed tea and sugar'.

Almost any Protestant activity in a 'contact zone' with Catholics seems to have inspired accusations of proselytism. In her letter to Pawling Gregory also mentions that once 'a priest had objected to my gathering some children together to learn needlework', and her friends 'the mother and sisters of so good a Catholic as the Late Rt Hon. C.T. Redington Chief Commissioner of Education in Ireland' wrote to assure the priest 'that the religion of these children would not be meddled with by me, that I had no desire to interfere with the religion of Catholics.'[8] In fact teaching needlework was a common charitable activity of both Catholic and Protestant women, and some- times it was combined with religious teaching. The proselytiser Fanny D'Arcy, collecting money in 1853 for a 'Fund for the Relief of the Converts and Children of Connemara,' listed 'Plain and Fancy Work' and 'Valenciennes Lace' as among the kinds of 'Industrial Instruction' for girls.[9] According to Maria Luddy, the lace-making industry in Ireland was revitalised by women philanthropists beginning in 'the period of the Great Famine'.[10] So both by 'visiting the sick and the poor' among her father's tenants and by teaching needlework, Lady Gregory had engaged in activities that looked like what proselytisers did, though she did not, as she wrote, 'interfere with the religion of Catholics'.

The accusation was of such intense importance to Lady Gregory that she wrote about it to the three most important men in her life. Yeats, of course, was also implicated, in so far as he and Lady Gregory worked closely together, and he wrote her in strong language: 'I saw at once that it was the one damaging statement for it would be separated from the general spitefulness of the essay and so look authoratative' [*sic*].[11] Yeats called Moore's letter to Lady Gregory 'disgraceful – a piece of vulgar bullying'.[12] To John Quinn Lady Gregory wrote,

> I ... feel rather splashed with dirty water ... I was never a pros-
> elytizer, though some of my family were. I was the youngest and
> I suppose in reaction, for I always said it was dangerous to shake
> faith in a religion unless you were quite sure another would be
> put in its place.[13]

And to Wilfrid Scawen Blunt she wrote that she had gone to Heinemann 'to hint at an injunction if he reprinted George Moore['s] assertion that I was a proselytizer. ... This now that it has been printed as a fact might very seriously injure our theatre making parents afraid to entrust their youngsters to me, so it ought to be stopped, and Heinemann seemed ready to stop it, if he can.'[14] Blunt wrote back, 'I am glad you are taking steps against George Moore. It is time he was put a stop to.'[15]

TRANSACTIONS IN THE CONTACT ZONE

Lady Gregory wrote that ' "proselytism" ... was much mixed up with benevolence and charity in those days', and folklore-collecting was also, because it was not merely a series of encounters in contact zones, but transactions, exchanges: something was given and something received on both sides. The Irish Folklore Commission collected stories from people who remembered, or whose parents remembered, proselytising in the mid-and late nineteenth century, and these stories record typical exchanges. The Donegans from Co. Antrim remember, 'It was porridge they would give if you would change your religion.'[16] Seaghan Mac Cártha from Cork had heard of 'Protestant ladies' who 'tried to buy the babies in the district with gifts of food and blankets'.[17] Kathleen Hurley from Co. Galway said that 'those who gave up their religion and attended Protestant worship got contracts for coffins, contracts for roads, contracts for selling manure', and 'were given good farms ... so that the newly turned Protestants ... became rich while the Catholics remained poor.'[18] Sean Ó Duinnshléibhe of Cork said the Protestant church at Glenville offered 'food and clothing'.[19] Not all of the proselytising was accomplished by invasions of domestic space; in many places religious tracts 'were thrown into the cabins by the roadside, handed to children to take home, or thrown about in public spaces'.[20]

The expectation of exchange, as well as the confusion of proselytising with folklore-collecting, is wonderfully illustrated in Carleton's 1845 novel *Valentine McClutchy, the Irish Agent, or, The Chronicles of Castle Cumber*. The corrupt, opportunistic bailiff Darby O'Drive, himself an alleged 'convert', tells the starving tenants that the Reverend Phineas Lucre will give them five guineas a head if they convert, so they line up outside his office ready to become Protestants. They come in one at a time. To give one example of this wild hilarious scene: when Lucre says to one of them, 'Man, what's your business?' the poor man says,

'I come, sirra … to tell your reverence to enter me down at wanst.'

'For what purpose should I enter you down?'

'For the money, sirra; I have seven o'them, and we'll all go. You may christen us if you like, sirra. 'Deed I'm tould we must all be chrishened over agin …'[21]

When the next man comes in, and Lucre questions him, he says,

'Myself, sir, does be thinkin' a great deal about these docthrines and jinnyologies that people is now all runnin' upon. I can tell a story, sir, at a wake, or an my kailee wid a neighbour, as well as e'er a man in the five parishes. The people say I'm very long headed all out, and can see far into a thing. They do, indeed, plaise your reverence.'

'Very good.'

'Did you ever hear about one Fin McCool, who was a great buffer in his day, and how his wife put the trick upon a big bosthoon of a giant that came down from Munster to leather Fin? Did you ever hear that, sir?'

'No; neither do I wish to hear it just now.'

'Nor the song of "Beal Derg O'Donnel," sir; nor the "Fairy River;" nor "the Life and Adventures of Larry Dorneen's Ass," please your reverence?'[22]

The man is ready with legends and folksongs, just in case that's what this Protestant wants. Lucre tells the man that he is 'long-winded', not 'long-headed'. Finally, the (nameless, Irish-speaking) peasant says he has wanted to become a Protestant for a long time and thought it best to come now, rather than later, 'for fraid yez might think it was for the money I am doin' it'. And he adds, 'But is there sich a thing, sir?' To which Lucre replies, 'Not a penny.'[23] Thus each of these practices may be mistaken for or confused with the other, as the identification of Yeats with a Scripture reader, and the peasant's offer to tell the story of 'Fin McCool', make clear.

In folklore-collecting, also, there was the expectation and often the practice of exchange: goods were given as payment for stories or performances. William Motherwell (1797–1835), the Scottish ballad collector, created an almost corporate structure for his collecting: he paid, for example, Andrew Crawfurd who paid 'the poet Thomas

Macqueen' who paid the ballad singers.[24] Jeremiah Curtin, the Irish-American collector who came to Ireland with his wife in the early 1890s, did not initially pay his sources, but on his second trip 'things were on a firm commercial footing', writes Angela Bourke, 'and he paid a Dingle story teller named Sullivan 2/6 for his first story.'[25] Although she doesn't always mention an exchange, Lady Gregory seems generally to have given something to the people who told her stories. She devotes two pages to describing her relationship with one of her regular informants, 'an old, perhaps half-crazed man I will call Michael Barrett'. He lived within walking distance of Coole; she and Yeats 'walked up the long narrow lane' to his 'little cabin'. Once when she was told he was sick, she went to visit him and 'found him better'. But, she writes, 'That was the last time I saw him; I am glad I had been able to help him to more warmth and comfort before the end.'[26] In her journals for 1924, Lady Gregory mentions her tenant Patrick Niland, to whom she gives five shillings because he has overslept and not been able to pick up his pension money. The next week he comes again, and she gives him 'bread and butter and a couple of glasses of port' and half a crown, and – she writes – 'promised him some firing *before* he told me a little story'. The story he tells her is site-specific: a poor woman goes to 'ask charity from our women that were in rich houses', but they won't give her anything. But when she goes home with no food to feed her children, a strange man arrives, asks her what's wrong, and then says 'Go open that chest you have in the room.' She finds it 'full of every sort of thing', and he tells her that it will always be full, but the four women who refused her will come begging to her door. And, says Niland, the man was 'an angel from God'.[27]

The stories are often confirmations that charity is rewarded: the woman Gregory calls Mrs. Sheridan tells her about seeing dead people at a funeral, very well-dressed. 'And look you now', she tells Lady Gregory, 'you should send a coat to some poor person, and your own friends among the dead will be covered, for you could see the skin here.' And Lady Gregory writes, in italics after the story,

> *She made a gesture passing her hand down each arm, exactly the same gesture as old Mary Glynn of Slieve Echtge had made yesterday when she said, 'Have you a coat you could send me, for my arms are bare?' and I had promised her one.*[28]

I mention these examples, and there are others, not to imply that charity compensated for the gross inequities of the Irish social system, but to show that folklore-collecting, like proselytising, created a relationship based on exchange. The encounter existed within an economy, and both parties knew it.

That economy was of course complicated by the fact that in many of these cases, Lady Gregory was listening to stories from her tenants, so the economy in which they both participated pre-dated the folklore conversation. The tenant-informants often made sure to indicate their interest in her family, and she, to give her credit, transcribed their flattery along with their folklore, so what I call 'parafolkloric remarks', the conversational exchanges that occur outside the story, provide a rich sense of social relationships. One of her regular informants tells her to touch a piece of human dung to her finger to avoid getting 'the touch', because, he says of the fairies, 'if they're glad to get one of us, they'd be seven times better pleased to get the like of you'.[29] A blacksmith begins his story saying, 'I know you to be a respectable lady and an honourable one because I know your brothers, meeting them as I do at the fair of Scariff. No fair it would be if they weren't there.'[30] When she asks information about cures, her informants express concern that Robert might be sick. And then there's my favorite bit of flattery: one woman, not given a name, tells Lady Gregory a story about meeting up one time with a 'sheoguey' dog, and then says, 'And what day was that but the very same day that Sir William – the Lord be with his soul! – was returned a Member of Parliament, and a great night it was in Kiltartan.'[31]

The informants' caution as they speak with Lady Gregory, their concern to say things that will please her, also takes the form of a consciousness of levels of diction. When 'an Old Man from Kinvara' tells of a woman who 'let a spit fall on the floor', he says, 'So they gathered that up (with respects to you) ...'[32] Another man uses the same expression: people would 'come out and meet her and – with respects to you – they'd spit in her face.'[33] The second-person singular pronoun apparently required the same kind of apology. After Michael Barrett's death, Gregory talks with his brother, who is skeptical about fairies. He tells her, 'Those things are passed away, and you – I beg your pardon for using that word – a person – hears no more of them.'[34]

All these verbal practices – the flattery, the special language, the almost obsequious reminders of status – exist in the conversations of all the peasants lined up to convert for Rev. Lucre and receive their five guineas. Another common feature is that in folklore-collecting, as in proselytising, a belief system is privileged that, in the nineteenth century, was considered incompatible with Catholicism. As Lawrence Taylor has written, a 'religion' was a specific approved body of doctrine to be sharply separated from 'superstition', and 'superstition' at the time Lady Gregory was collecting, would have included fairy legends as well as keening and wakes.[35] Rural priests would have wanted to educate their parishioners away from fairy legends as well as to protect them from the advances of Protestants. All the converts in *Valentine McClutchy* are ready to condemn the priests and 'malivogue' the Catholics; and the seers and healers, the Biddy Earlys, whom Lady Gregory encouraged people to talk about, are always, in the stories, in professional conflict with the priests. This conflict is common in Irish folklore, and Gregory's stories are typical in this respect.[36] Gregory obviously loved the stories and sought them out, and most of them make the priests look powerless or nasty. Father Andrew used to 'drive away the people from going to' Biddy Early with 'a riding whip in his hand', but after she cured his horse, he let them alone.[37] Biddy Early is always getting back at the priests: when one of them spoke against her, 'she put something on the horse so that he made a bolt into the river and stopped there in the middle and wouldn't go back or forward.'[38]

But these non-Catholic belief systems are only provisionally entertained by the people who are converted and the people who tell fairy stories. In one of the stories collected by the Folklore Commission, from Patrick O'Donnell of Co. Longford,

> The parson gave the grass of a cow to a man if he'd go to church for three Sundays. So the man agreed to the bargain and went to church for three Sundays, but he was going to mass as well and the parson found out about it. So the next time they met the parson says,

> 'I hear you're going to mass.'

> 'Why wouldn't I', says the man, 'I go to you for the grass of me cow, but I go to mass for the good of me sowl.'[39]

Tomás Ó Cearbhall from Co. Cork tells the story of a starving woman who accepted food and agreed to go to the Protestant church, but during the service she went 'up to the foremost portion of the church, knelt down on the floor and said her rosary continuously while the minister officiated'.[40] She was asked not to return. Thomas Kelly from Westport tells of a man who 'turned', i.e. turned Protestant, and ran into the priest of his parish.

'Ah', says the priest, 'you cannot please God and the devil.'

'Ah father', said he, 'It's only till the praties grow.'[41]

A good number of Lady Gregory's folk informants make it clear that they don't 'believe' the stories they're telling her. A woman Gregory calls 'Mrs. Allen' begins her tale this way: 'I don't believe in faeries myself, I really don't. But all the people in Kildare believe in them, and I'll tell you what I saw there one time myself' – and she proceeds to tell a story of a bewitched horse cured by a 'faery doctor'.[42] A chimney-sweep talking to Lady Gregory appears to be trying to reconcile fairy belief and Catholicism, 'I don't believe in all I hear, or I'd believe in ghosts and faeries, with all the old people telling you stories about them and the priests believing in them too. Surely the priests believe in ghosts, and tell you that they are souls that died in trouble.'[43] And a Mrs. Day says, 'My own sons are all for education and read all books and they wouldn't believe now in the stories the old people used to tell. But I know one Finnegan and his wife that went to Esserkelly churchyard ... and all of a sudden there came a pelt of a stone against the wall ... and no one there.'[44] As Angela Bourke has written, 'The essence of fairy-belief is ambivalence.'[45]

To the post-colonial scholar as well as to a nineteenth-century rural priest, both kinds of 'contact zone' encounter might appear to be forms of domination – religious, social, cultural, economic – by educated (or at least literate) Protestants over uneducated or less-educated Catholics. The argument could be made that in the case of Lady Gregory's tenants at least, the story-telling was almost compulsory; wouldn't they want to give the landlord what she asked for? However, I think the provisional nature of the conversions and the denials of belief that precede some of the stories told to Lady Gregory make it clear that the 'ground' was 'not cleared for the sowing' everywhere; or, as the old man said, 'I go to you for the grass of me cow, but I go to mass for the good of me sowl.' Most people knew pretty clearly what they believed and what they didn't believe.

To understand precisely how what Pratt calls 'asymmetrical relations of power' work in the contexts described in this essay, it's important to look carefully at the poor people's part of the exchange:

what did they give for the porridge, the blankets, the old coat, or the half-crown? Here is where proselytising and folklore-collecting look very different. Those who 'turn' or 'jump' give a sometimes temporary, sometimes permanent allegiance to another community; they forsake their own community, or they return to it, but they go through the motions of a new affiliation, whether that entailed going to church, or sending their children to a Protestant school, or working for the missionaries. Their part of the exchange, if indeed it takes place, happens after the encounter in the 'contact zone'. But in the folkloric exchange, the conversation is everything: the talk of the country people who give folklore is their cultural capital; their verbal art is what they're selling. As Lady Gregory writes in *Visions and Beliefs*, '... when I began to gather these stories, I cared less for the evidence given in them than for the beautiful rhythmic sentences in which they were told.'[46] The folkloric conversation is not the means to an end of conversion; it is the end.

And thus the story-teller drives the encounter, determining the length of the conversation, its tone, and its degree of intimacy. The collector – Lady Gregory, or Jeremiah Curtin, or whoever – is there to listen, remember, and record; as audience. The collector's role, especially as Lady Gregory enacted it, was almost a kind of self-efface-ment. We never hear her voice directly talking to the tellers. One of Gregory's informants was a 'very gentle and courteous' old man whose daughters made tea for Lady Gregory, while he sat at the head of the table. He considered her his guest. Another man tells her at least twenty stories, and at the end he tells her how to avoid fairy dis-ruptions within the house. 'Set a little room for them – with spring water in it always – and wine you must leave – no, not flowers – they wouldn't want so much as that – but just what would show your good will.' And then he says to her, 'Now I have told you more than I told my wife.'[47] Sometimes the intimacy is almost confessional; when Mary Glyn tells Lady Gregory about her little boy's death, the emphasis is not on Biddy Early's role but on Mary Glyn's loss:

> My husband went to her the time Johnny, my little boy, was dying. He had a great pain in his temple, and she said, 'He has enough in him to kill a hundred; but if he lives till Monday, come and tell me.' But he was dead before that. ... But Johnny died; and there was a blush over his face when he was going, and after that I couldn't look at him, but those that saw him said that *he* wasn't in it. I never saw him since, but often and often the

father would go out thinking he might see him. But I know well
he wouldn't like to come back and to see me fretting for him.[48]

Although by Mary Louise Pratt's definition this kind of conversation
takes place in 'the space of colonial encounter' between people with
'radically asymmetrical relations of power', I think it also gives the
informants an opportunity – maybe even a therapeutic one – to talk
about traumatic personal experiences.[49] Often the fairy element is
minimal: one man tells Lady Gregory that his wife has been paralysed for 36 years, ever since her last child was born; others tell her
about mental illnesses, broken hearts, children's emigration or deaths,
and terrible accidents.

To the extent that she gives her informants food or clothing or
money, Lady Gregory is treating them professionally. One man
appears pleased to share his expertise: 'I'm sorry I wasn't in to meet you
surely, knowing as much as I do about the faeries.'[50] And one couple
engages in what can only be called a performance. It seems possible
that it was well-rehearsed, but then again it may have been spontaneous. The audience was Lady Gregory, Yeats, and a 'Miss Pollexfen',
presumably a cousin of Yeats's; the location was the Wicklow mountains; and the performers were an elderly couple, Mr. and Mrs. Kelleher.
They are talking about the fairies (I've shortened this considerably):

> *K*: I was not on the right path and couldn't find it and went
> wandering about, but at last one of them said, 'Good-evening,
> Kelleher', and they went away, and then in a moment I saw
> where I was. … They were very small, like little boys and girls,
> and had red caps. … Another time they came about me playing
> music … it is the sweetest music and the best that can be heard,
> like melodeons and fifes and whistles and every sort.
>
> *Mrs. K*: I often hear that music too, I hear them playing drums.
>
> *K*: We had one of them in the house for a while … it was just
> after I married that woman there that was a nice slip of a girl at
> that time. It was in the winter and there was snow on the
> ground, and I saw one of them outside, and I brought him in
> and put him on the dresser, and he stopped in the house for a
> while, for about a week.
>
> *Mrs. K*: It was more than that, it was two or three weeks.
>
> *K*: Ah! Maybe it was – I'm not sure. He was about fifteen inches

high. He was very friendly. It is likely he slept on the dresser at night. When the boys at the public-house were full of porter, they used to come to the house to look at him, and they would laugh to see him but I never let them hurt him. They said I would be made up, that he would bring me some riches, but I never got them. We had a cage here, I wish I had put him in it, I might have kept him till I was made up.

Mrs. K: It was a cage we had for a thrush. We thought of putting him into it, but he would not have been able to stand in it.

K: I'm sorry I didn't keep him – I thought sometimes to bring him into Dublin to sell him.

Mrs. K: You wouldn't have got him there.

*   *   *   *   *   *   *   *

K: I used to feed him with a spoon, I would put the spoon to his mouth.

Mrs. K: He was fresh-looking at the first, but after a while he got an old look, a sort of wrinkled look.

K: He was fresh-looking enough, he had a hardy look.

Mrs. K: He was wearing a red cap and a little red cloth skirt.

K: Just for the world like a Highlander.

Mrs. K: He had a little short coat above that; it was checked and trousers under the skirt and long stockings all in red. And as to his shoes, they were tanned, and you could hardly see the soles of them, the sole of his foot was like a baby's.[51]

It sounds as if the Kellehers have been reading Allingham; they are certainly giving the tourists what they think tourists want:

Up the airy mountain
Down the rushy glen
We daren't go a-hunting
For fear of little men.
Wee folk, good folk,
Trooping all together,
Green jacket, red cap,
White owl's feather.

I cite these quite different stories told to Lady Gregory to indicate the range of conversation possible in folkloric encounters, from traumatic personal stories to practical advice (touch a piece of dung, leave spring water and wine in a room) to performances of an almost Grafton-Street type for the tourists. I assume the Kellehers were well paid. Yeats seems to have paid well; once a wandering poet dropped by Coole and offered to recite his poems to Lady Gregory and Yeats. She didn't think the poems were any good, but Yeats paid the man eight shillings for his recitation.

ETHICAL ISSUES

Of course stories about the fairies and little fifteen-inch fellows in red caps and checked coats are free-floating material. This lore does not form part of any established religious system; there is no institution controlling its dissemination. It exists only in the minds of its tellers; each telling is discrete and distinct; 'Bíonn dhá insint ar gach scéal, agus dhá chasadh dhéag ar gach amhrán' (There are two tellings to each tale, and twelve singings to each song).

And so the ethical question that arises is not about domination but about ownership of this intellectual property: did Lady Gregory pay her informants for the stories that turned into the 350 pages of *Visions and Beliefs in the West of Ireland*? Did the people know she was writing the stories down every evening in the little light green notebooks now in the Berg Collection of the New York Public Library? In the twentieth and twenty-first centuries, debates about this kind of ownership are ubiquitous. An essay on films and novels about Native American culture is titled 'Stop Stealing Native Stories' and complains about 'the theft of voice'.[52] The Chilean miners who were trapped underground in 2010 were more savvy than the country people of Galway and Aran: they made a pact 'to keep the ... details of their ... captivity to themselves' so they could get a book or movie deal; most of them limited what they would tell journalists and asked their families not to speak to the media without permission.[53]

The case can be made that *Visions and Beliefs in the West of Ireland* credits the folk material in an appropriate way; or at any rate, much care has been taken in assigning the various authorships. The content of the volume is framed so as to make clear what is Lady Gregory's own material and what came from her informants. The book is visibly a collaborative effort: everything by Lady Gregory –

introductory material and some connective passages – is in italics, and all the collected stories are not italicised. Each one is preceded by a name, which Gregory explains is invented if the people who told the story are still alive. The book also includes two essays and notes by Yeats, and his name is given in the table of contents. So there are many authors: the title page says,

VISIONS AND BELIEFS IN THE WEST OF IRELAND
COLLECTED AND ARRANGED BY LADY GREGORY:
WITH TWO ESSAYS AND NOTES BY W.B. YEATS

Furthermore, she takes great pains to efface her own voice, putting what are evidently her own questions into the mouths of her informants, as in, 'His wife was taken away in childbirth – and the five children she left … from that day there never was a ha'porth ailed them. Did the mother come back to care them? Sure and certain she did …'[54] And one account begins, 'No, I never went to Biddy Early.'[55] Lady Gregory asked the questions, but we do not hear her ask them.

And then of course, it was she who over a period of almost twenty-five years 'collected and arranged' the stories, writing them in the little notebooks, typing them up, organising them thematically, dealing with the publisher, and so forth. She transformed the raw material into a commercially viable product, and takes appropriate but not excessive credit for her work.

GEORGE MOORE AGAIN

And so having, I hope, clarified both how proselytising and folklore-collecting may be confused with one another, and how they are essentially different, I'd like to return to the original inspiration for this line of thought, George Moore's accusation in *Vale*. Moore apparently couldn't bear to give up what he'd written about Sir William, so he kept it in, in revised form:

We are glad that Sir William chose Augusta rather than one of her elder sisters, either of whom would certainly have fired up in the carriage when Sir William, on his way to Coole, suggested to his bride that she should refrain from pointing out to his tenants what she believed to be a different teaching of the Bible from that which they received from the parish priest. He would probably say: You have made no converts – (we have forgotten

Mrs Shaw Taylor's Christian name, but Agnes will serve our purpose as well as another) – you have made no converts, Agnes, but you have shaken the faith of thousands. The ground at Roxborough has been cleared for the sowing, but Kiltartan can wait.[56]

Why, you might wonder, did he keep this passage, substituting a sister (an invented sister) for Lady Gregory? No doubt he wanted to retain his original witticisms, but in addition, I believe he wanted to get into his text an anecdote in which Lady Gregory – even by proxy – is controlled and almost punished by a strong man. Moore presents the Persses as weak men, men who did nothing ('undistinguished … in love, in war, or in politics'); the only people who did anything in the family were the women, Mrs. P 'and her two elder daughters', who 'indulged … a taste for Bible reading in the cottages.' Originally, as you know, Lady Gregory was in that category, and although Moore had to state that she did not 'join them in their missionary work', it's obvious that she is the one Sir William married, and the vignette still seems to apply to her, because she was the one who accompanied Sir William in the carriage to Coole.

A strong man – not like the Persse men – is needed to control this strong woman. This is Moore's punishment to Lady Gregory for being too powerful, and for not using that power to favour Moore. In fact, as he says immediately after, she didn't even ask him to sign her fan at a London dinner party, despite inviting other men at the party to sign it.[57]

Moreover, Moore appears to like Sir William, and identifies him with his (Moore's) own father, though he finds Sir William deficient in masculinity: 'Sir William's travels were not so original as my father's, and the racehorses that he kept were not so fast.'[58] Sir William is only two steps away from being Moore himself, and he functions here as a surrogate. The carriage is in that passage because it belongs to Sir William; it is the small space in which the woman who has been wandering free in the cottages is now confined by her husband. The carriage, in short, is a space of domination, the space where not two social classes but two genders meet, and it's clear which one is the more powerful – in Moore's imagination, at least. Like all of *Vale*, like all of *Hail and Farewell*, the passage is a tiny corrective to the world outside the book.

NOTES

For reading this chapter and offering comments I am grateful to Angela Bourke, whose own scholarship in the field of folklore has been of immense help to me. I would also like to thank Adrian Frazier for discussing aspects of this topic with me, and Maureen O'Rourke Murphy for generous help with books.

1. George Moore to Lady Gregory, typed letter, 9 January 1914. Henry W. and Albert A. Berg Collection. Astor, Lenox, and Tilden Foundations, New York Public Library.
2. Lady Gregory, *Visions & Beliefs in the West of Ireland* (Gerrards Cross: Colin Smythe Ltd, 1970), p.63.
3. Cathal Póirtéir, *Famine Echoes* (Dublin: Gill & MacMillan, 1995), p.170.
4. Mary Louise Pratt, *Imperial Eyes: Travel Writing and Transculturation* (Abingdon: Routledge, 1992), pp.6–7.
5. George Moore, 'Yeats, Lady Gregory, and Synge', *English Review* (January 1914), p.175.
6. Lady Gregory to Sydney Pawling, typed letter, carbon, dated 5 January 1914. See Berg Collection.
7. George Moore to Lady Gregory, typed signed letter, 15 January 1914. See Berg Collection.
8. See Gregory to Pawling, 5 January 1914. Berg Collection.
9. Miriam Moffitt, *Soupers & Jumpers: The Protestant Missions in Connemara 1848–1937* (Dublin: Nonsuch Publishing, 2008), p.31.
10. Maria Luddy (ed.), 'Philanthropy in Nineteenth-Century Ireland', *The Field Day Anthology of Irish Writing. Volume V: Irish Women's Writing and Traditions* (Cork: Cork University Press in association with Field Day, 2002), p.693.
11. W.B. Yeats to Lady Gregory, typed signed letter, 4 January 1914. Berg Collection.
12. W.B. Yeats to Lady Gregory, signed holograph letter, 10 January 1914. Berg Collection.
13. Lady Gregory to John Quinn, typed signed letter, 1 January 1914. Berg Collection.
14. Lady Gregory to Wilfrid Scawen Blunt, typed signed letter, undated (probably January 1914). Berg Collection.
15. Wilfrid Scawen Blunt to Lady Gregory, holograph signed letter, 9 January 1914. Berg Collection.
16. See Póirtéir, *Famine Echoes*, p.167.
17. Ibid., p.171.
18. Ibid., p.174.
19. Ibid., p.176.
20. Ibid., p.178.
21. William Carleton, *Valentine McClutchy, the Irish Agent, or, The Chronicles of Castle Cumber* (Dublin: James Duffy, 1845), p.200.
22. See Carleton, *Valentine McClutchy*, p.201.
23. Ibid., p.202.
24. William B McCarthy, 'William Motherwell as Field Collector', *Folk Music Journal* 5, 3 (1987), p.310, and Mary Ellen Brown, *William Motherwell's Cultural Politics* (Lexington, KY: University of Kentucky Press, 2001).
25. Angela Bourke, 'The Myth Business: Jeremiah and Alma Curtin in Ireland, 1887–1893', *Éire-Ireland* (44:3&4, Earrach/Samhradh, Fall/Winter 2009), p.160.
26. See Gregory, *Visions and Beliefs*, p.203.
27. Lady Gregory, *Journals* (New York: Oxford University Press, 1988), Vol. 1, pp.577–8.
28. See Gregory, *Visions and Beliefs*, p.61.
29. Ibid., p.64.
30. Ibid., p.37.
31. Ibid., p.285.
32. Ibid., p.48.
33. Ibid., p.221.
34. Ibid., p.203.
35. Lawrence Taylor, *Occasions of Faith: An Anthropology of Irish Catholics* (Philadelphia: University of Pennsylvania Press, 1995), p.53.

36. See, for instance, Pádraig Ó Héalaí, 'Priest versus Healer', *Béaloideas* Iml. 62/63, 1994/1995.
37. See Gregory, *Visions and Beliefs*, p.34.
38. Ibid., p.39.
39. See Póirtéir, *Famine Echoes*, p.167.
40. Ibid., p.171.
41. Ibid., p.180.
42. See Gregory, *Visions and Beliefs*, pp.153–4.
43. Ibid., p.192.
44. Ibid., p.224.
45. Angela Bourke, 'The Virtual Reality of Irish Fairy Legend', *Eire-Ireland* (31:1&2, Earrach/Samhradh, Spring/Summer 1996), p.12.
46. See Gregory, *Visions and Beliefs*, p.16.
47. Ibid., p.68.
48. Ibid., p.49.
49. See Bourke, 'Virtual Reality', for a discussion of the way fairy legends express 'emotions which might be unacceptable if more directly expressed', p.13.
50. See Gregory, *Visions and Beliefs*, p.279.
51. Ibid., pp.219–21.
52. Lenore Keeshig-Tobias, 'Stop Stealing Native Stories', in Bruce Ziff and Pratima V. Rao (eds), *Borrowed Power: Essays on Cultural Appropriation* (New Brunswick, NJ: Rutgers University Press, 1997).
53. Alexei Barrionuevo and Simon Romero, 'Rescued Miners' Secrecy Pact Erodes in Spotlight', *The New York Times* (18 October 2010).
54. See Gregory, *Visions and Beliefs*, p.111.
55. Ibid., p.126.
56. George Moore, *Hail and Farewell* (1911; Gerrards Cross: Colin Smythe, 1976), pp.546–7.
57. Ibid., p.548.
58. Ibid., p.547.

REFERENCES

Bourke, A., 'The Virtual Reality of Irish Fairy Legend', *Eire-Ireland*, (31:1&2, Earrach/Samhradh, Spring/Summer 1996), pp.7–25.
Bourke, A., 'The Myth Business: Jeremiah and Alma Curtin in Ireland, 1887–1893', *Éire-Ireland* (44:3&4, Earrach/Samhradh, Fall/Winter 2009), pp.140–70.
Brown, M.E., *William Motherwell's Cultural Politics* (Lexington, KY: University of Kentucky Press, 2001).
Carleton, W., *Valentine McClutchy, The Irish Agent, or, The Chronicles of Castle Cumber* (Dublin: James Duffy, 1845).
Lady Gregory, *Journals. Volume 1* (New York: Oxford University Press, 1988).
Lady Gregory, *Visions & Beliefs in the West of Ireland* (Gerrards Cross: Colin Smythe Ltd, 1970).
Luddy, M., 'Philanthropy in Nineteenth-Century Ireland', *The Field Day Anthology of Irish Writing. Volume V: Irish Women's Writing and Traditions* (Cork: Cork University Press in association with Field Day, 2002), pp.691–3.
McCarthy, W.. 'William Motherwell as Field Collector', *Folk Music Journal* 5, 3 (1987), pp.295–316.
Moffitt, M., *Soupers & Jumpers: The Protestant Missions in Connemara 1848–1937* (Dublin: Nonsuch Publishing, 2008).
Moore, G., *Hail and Farewell* (1911; Gerrards Cross: Colin Smythe, 1976).
Póirtéir, C., *Famine Echoes* (Dublin: Gill & MacMillan, 1995).
Pratt, M.L., *Imperial Eyes: Travel Writing and Transculturation* (Abingdon: Routledge, 1992).
Taylor, L., *Occasions of Faith: An Anthropology of Irish Catholics* (Philadelphia: University of Pennsylvania Press, 1995).

CHAPTER SIX

George Moore's Dana Controversy Revisited:
A Plea for an Irish Théâtre Libre?

MICHEL BRUNET

In the September 1904 issue of *Dana*, there appeared a polemical article entitled 'Stage Management in the Irish National Theatre'.[1] The author was a certain Paul Ruttledge, obviously a pseudonym, forcibly bringing to mind the name of the rebellious hero himself of William Butler Yeats's play *Where There is Nothing*, published in 1902.[2] It was not too difficult to attribute the essay to George Moore inasmuch as both men of letters had had a quarrel about the paternity of the play two years before and were still at loggerheads.[3] George Moore's return to the attack might be ascribed to the fact that he was also probably resentful at having been eased out of the Irish dramatic movement when the Irish Literary Theatre was dissolved, soon to be reorganised as the Irish National Dramatic Society with Yeats as president and William G. Fay as stage-manager. George Moore first launched his scathing attack on Fay to question his 'method or lack of method' in staging Yeats's play *The Shadowy Waters*, which was performed on 14 January 1904, but the attack was more generally, albeit covertly, directed at Yeats and his idea of a poetic national theatre.

The interest of this highly vindictive text is twofold. It can be read as a diatribe against the newly self-appointed directors of the Abbey Theatre and the style of theatre then promoted by the dramatic movement of the Irish Revival, but it can also be regarded as a sort of manifesto propounding acting principles directly derived from André Antoine's Théâtre Libre. This article will seek to analyse both aspects of George Moore's essay. It will be informed by discourse analysis and conducted more particularly in the light of the metaphoric concept of scenography. First, a distinction must be made between scenography, properly speaking, and generic scene. Scenography is generated by the text and basically depends on a particular discourse whereas 'generic scene' refers to the literary type of writing which conventionally assigns parts to the actors, that is, speakers, and prescribes the medium used. In the case in point, Moore's article can be regarded as belonging to the polemic genre in that it consistently makes derogatory remarks intended to detract from the achievement of the Irish National Theatre, and at the very least arouse a controversy over its staging practices, as if the management of the theatre were a national cause open to debate among the literati.

It is not altogether surprising that George Moore should have chosen to publish his article in the magazine *Dana*, edited by John Eglinton in conjunction with Frederick Ryan. Moore was a close friend of Eglinton's and had already contributed a number of essays or translations to the short-lived periodical.[4] The little review, rightly subtitled *An Irish Magazine of Independent Thought*, was accustomed to publishing texts touching on the theatre but above all evincing a readiness to open its pages to dissenting voices and intellectual debates. Moore availed himself of the forum of discussion it provided to inveigh against William Fay's style of production and direction and by so doing, to voice the grudge he had been bearing against Yeats for years.

The essay openly attacks William Fay and, as such, falls under the umbrella of *argumentum ad hominem*, that is 'argument against the person', and not about the subject-matter (*ad rem*), though the types may overlap at times. What Fay is criticised for is his ignorance of or lack of expertise in basic stagecraft. The crux of the matter is that Moore makes his point by illustrating his demonstration with the production of Yeats's play, *The Shadowy Waters*. The play is inherently poetic which makes it admittedly difficult to stage. The words taking precedence over action and physical movement, the work ran the risk of being static and unspectacular. Although it had been revised several times, it had never attained any convincing dramatic intensity, partly on account of Yeats's penchant for cryptic symbolism and poetic speeches which had to be chanted rather than naturally delivered. The irony is that Moore took part in the collective doctoring process, pruning down much of the mythological material but proving unable in the end to redeem the play, as some critics have suggested: 'It was in part the theatre and Moore's technical and conventional competence that bedevilled the work.'[5] Moore's taking Fay to task might have been motivated by the actual performance of the play and his method which consisted, as Moore puts it, in having his actors recite their texts rather than play their parts: 'the actors stood in different corners of the stage, and fired off their lines.'[6] But his disapproval might also stem from the mere fact that Moore did not appreciate, more generally, poetic drama, which he deemed 'as dead as the civilisation that produced it',[7] and objected, in the circumstances, to a play which Yeats claimed to be 'more a ritual than a human story'.[8] Not surprisingly, Moore's jibes chime with the widespread impression that the play was not really successful, in fact 'the least successful of Yeats's verse plays', to quote Lennox Robinson.[9] For his part, such an aficionado as Joseph Holloway 'felt quite sad that such a beautiful work of art should have failed owing to the dense obscurity of the text'.[10] Thus, Moore's conclusion that Fay did not know how to have his actors move around on the stage does not seem to be equitable. It rather shows that Yeats's revised version of the play was inherently weak in actability and stage worthiness. Bringing the failure of the play to bear on his assessment of the stage-director's achievement and making Fay the object of his attack comes down to charging him with 'guilt by association', which is ethically suspect, not to say fallacious in terms of rhetoric. Pragmatically speaking though, it probably fulfilled George Moore's desire to attack the Abbey directors who had discarded him.

While any given piece of polemical writing as a macro-speech act responds to generic expectations imposed by a pragmatic frame in terms of circumstances, rhetoric, actors, however ambivalent they might be in this case, Moore's article produces its own idiosyncratic scenography. Scenography is not to be viewed as a social context. It is to be apprehended as a discursive process putting its communicative devices into place so as to construct a self-image or ethos of the writer. By ethos, we refer, following Aristotle's tenet, to the representation of the voice enacted through the reading process. George Moore, under the name of Paul Ruttledge, constructs a certain self-image which can be spelled out as one of a knowledgeable person well acquainted with theatrical practices, in particular with the continental dramatic experiments that had been carried out by André Antoine in Paris. References to acting methods used in the staging of Ibsen's *Ghosts* are also instrumental in substantiating the representation. Peremptory assertions contribute to reinforcing the credibility of the author and defining him as an expert in theatrical matters though he does not or cannot proffer any credentials, apart from numerous references to Antoine. The scenography elaborates on a discourse implementing the argument of authority or expertise, in other words what is called the *ad verecundiam* argument. Nevertheless, by dropping Antoine's name no less than seven times in the essay, George Moore does not only appeal to and rely on his acknowledged expertise to make his point, he also intimates that his own familiarity with staging practices somehow partakes of the French director's production methods. The demonstration is all the more forcibly made as the discursive process is achieved to the detriment of the victim of the polemic, that is, William Fay. Indeed, conversely, Fay emerges and is dismissed as a complete beginner, one who starts from scratch, as it were, and should be enticed to learn the basics of his trade: 'Our contention is that Mr. Fay does not know his A. B. C. of stage management, and we are anxious that he should set about learning it.'[11] This condescending piece of advice is part and parcel of a whole discriminating and discrediting enterprise, starting with a sustained unfavourable comparison with Antoine. Pointing to a similarity between their first professional employments, the discourse sets out to show the discrepancy in their respective careers. Antoine was a gas-company employee and Fay an electrician but the former 'has become one of the most successful actors in Paris, more even than a successful actor he has become an actor of genius', whereas the latter 'is an actor not without talent'. Objectively speaking, Fay had gained some valuable experience in acting and stage managing, however amateurish most of his commitments might have been by the turn of the century. As befits the genre of polemic, Moore is led to make some allowances for Fay's talent as an actor at some stage of his demonstration but his concessions are granted in an ambiguous way. He recognises only his 'real sense of humour and power of infecting his audience with his enjoyment of the drolleries of life'.[12] As regards his achievement as a stage-director, Moore admits that Fay has managed 'to struggle on'. Even though he has been praised in London by Mr. William Archer and Mr. A.B. Walkley, the flattering remarks he was honoured with are, however, flatly dismissed by Moore/Ruttledge as insignificant and worthless compliments only due to exotic personalities. The final blow or coup de grâce is dealt when Moore suggests that Fay should take on a professional stage manager. The argument builds up to a climax but seems to go awry when, carried away by his initial impetus, Moore makes the allegation that Miss Annie Horniman, the

English patron, had bought Fay a theatre. At that point the *ad hominem* argument lapses into what is sometimes called an *ad personam* argument, verging on libel, as the innuendo refers to her private life.[13]

The self-image of an author is not solely associated with what he explicitly says about himself, it is also filtered, as it were, by his manner of speaking and behaving. In this case, nothing is disclosed about the identity of Moore/Ruttledge which remains strategically disguised under the mask of an authoritative 'We'. The reader is progressively induced to adjust the ethotic representation as it is produced by the text in various directions, but not necessarily in accordance with the author's primary intention. Besides casting himself in the role of a knowledgeable stage-manager or a fervent disciple of Antoine, George Moore shows himself to be a humorous polemicist through such ironic sentences as 'We do not speak derisively' or even 'This article is not written in any carping spirit.' But irony can also turn out to be double-edged, all the more so as the reader can possess pre – or extralinguistic – knowledge of the actual writer and, as far as we are concerned, with the benefit of hindsight, even a post-discursive representation interacting with the intended necessarily positive discursive ethos.

That Moore should choose, as a second example, his own play, *The Strike At Arlingford*, without naming it explicitly, naturally enough lest he should be identified, after mentioning Ibsen's *Ghosts*, in order to illustrate his lesson on staging methods à la Antoine, does not necessarily carry his point home. Moore's own play does not compare favourably with Ibsen's pioneering work, especially in view of its denouement, which bears some resemblance to that of Ibsen's play. While Ibsen's drama achieves some tragic and pathetic grandeur, Moore's 'Ibsenish' but not so 'unconventional'[14] play seems to sink into melodrama and dilute the social purport, the convoluted analytical dialogues together with the stage directions being unable to make up for the spurious quality of the dramatic action that builds up to the climactic suicide scene. It is not altogether certain either that the performance in London on 21 February 1893, for those who attended it, was as effective as he had expected. The acting was deemed poor and the staging hardly natural and convincing. Too much movement was probably involved in the staging, Moore running 'too much into duets', according to Bernard Shaw.[15] One critic working for *The New York Times* even wrote: 'The mere question of getting the people on and off the stage was handled with so little skill that one could almost see the wires by which they were jerked from the wings'.[16] Admittedly, Moore was critical of his own plays and conscious of their shortcomings. In his preface to *The Coming of Gabrielle* published in 1921, talking of his early plays, including *The Strike at Arlingford*, he admits to his lack of investment: 'I have never put my back, as the phrase goes, into a play.'[17]

Whatever Moore's achievement as a playwright and as a stage-director, it is evident that his indictment of Fay and of the National Theatre is largely informed by his knowledge of Antoine's ground-breaking theatrical enterprise and fuelled by his personal involvement and first-hand experience with the Independent Theatre in London in collaboration with Jacob Grein in the early 1890s. His derogatory remarks and instructions to Fay show that he endorsed some dramatic principles that Antoine advocated for a number of practical points. Moore pays particular attention to the interaction between speech and physical movements and points to the dramatic benefit one can derive from their association or their dissociation. For instance, speaking 'on the rise' can be fatal to the interpretation of the very words being pronounced: 'the author's meaning may be spoiled by a change of position'.[18] In that respect, George Moore seems to reflect and comply with Antoine's belief in the necessity to coordinate speech and non-verbal expression in order to achieve a synthetic dramatic effect. Admittedly, the question of the symbiosis between speech and movement relates to the problematic discrepancy between writing a play and staging it, and therefore to a stage-director's responsibility in a theatrical production. George Moore's opinion, according to which, 'A piece well-staged amounts to a re-writing',[19] certainly owes much to, or at any rate, is inspired with Antoine's clear-cut views on the respective roles in the production of a play: 'His [The writer's] business is to write the play: mine is to have it acted.'[20] Stage-directing no longer consists in organising a perform-ance but in imagining and interpreting a literary text. George Moore's artful, if not trumped-up, use of his own play, *The Strike at Arlingford*, to illustrate his point reveals how much he was subjugated by Antoine's theories and practice and possibly how highly he rated his own competence as far as stagecraft is concerned.[21] Moore first posits the academic hypothesis that, in the final scene of the (his) play, the one and only stage-direction is: 'He drinks the poison', only to extrapolate that Antoine's responsive *mise en scène* of this given situation would not consist in representing the action proper in its physicality and sensational practicality but in suggesting it by relying on the audience's readiness to anticipate the act: 'As you lift the glass the curtain falls.' Moore briefly concludes that Antoine's stage instruction is nothing short of 'miraculous'. It is bound to be all the more so as it comes extremely close to the very words one can read in Moore's actual script of the play: 'He raises the glass to drink; as he does so, the curtain falls.'[22]

The scenography which defines Moore as a knowledgeable theatrical mentor not only gives his discourse authority and legitimacy, it also aims to have persuasive effects on the alleged mentee and whom it may concern. It should not, however, be regarded as a purely rhetorical strategy; it is consubstantial with an aesthetic stance that is basically associated with a belief in stage realism, whether it be in style or in content. When Moore defines himself as an upholder of the philosophy of Antoine's Théâtre Libre, he develops a self-constituting discourse that implicitly outlines what should be a contradictory and illegitimate discourse for him. In other words, the article can be construed as an act of positioning in relation to the acting practices that were being developed and implemented by the National Theatre Society.

Moore's essay responds to the lecture 'The Reform of the Theatre' that Yeats delivered on 14 March 1903. Sharing Moore's desire for a literary theatre that would break new ground in opposition to the commercial theatre, Yeats nevertheless departed from him by laying the emphasis on the necessity 'to restore to the stage beautiful speech' and, as a *sine qua non* condition 'to simplify acting', in particular as regards movements on the stage:

> Modern actors slurred over the solemnest passages, and strove constantly to attract attention to their bodily movements. According to English ideas of what was known as 'business' an actor when not speaking must always be moving his hands or feet or jigging about somewhere in a corner, and so attention was constantly drawn away from the central character. Gestures should be treated rather as a part of decorative art, and the more remote a play was from daily life, the more grave and solemn should the gesture be.[23]

Moore and Yeats could not have more divergent views on the art of acting, though neither of them was really proficient in stage direction. Yeats had neither practical experience nor much theoretical knowledge and largely relied on the technique taught by the Fay brothers, who incidentally tried to convert Yeats to the fundamentals of Antoine to no avail, as he profoundly disliked the art of Antoine and wanted to put it out of the picture.[24] He described it as 'the art of a theatre which knows nothing of style, which knows nothing of magnificent words, nothing of the music of speech'.[25] By that time, he was also elaborating on his own theories of acting. Moore was certainly much further ahead of him, as he had gained some hands-on experience in London as a playwright and a stage director[26] but had not fully explored the resources of the dramatic form and had certainly distanced himself from Antoine's staging principles. Moore did not feel, for example, as bound as Antoine was to such basic naturalistic stage techniques as the use of true-to-life decor and real props as prerequisites for any *mise en scène*.[27]

As a matter of fact, the point of contention had not so much to do with staging methods strictly speaking as with the moot question of the direction a national theatre should take. In that respect, Moore's polemical article seems to be an epilogue to a nexus of essays which had been published in various reviews and newspapers, in particular in the Saturday issues of the Dublin *Daily Express* at the end of 1898.[28] John Eglinton had aroused a controversy over the irrelevance of the plays that were being or were to be staged by the Irish Literary Theatre under the aegis of Yeats. He had taken issue with works depicting the legendary deeds of past heroes when, for him, a national theatre should address the realities of contemporary life, a position which was not a far cry from Moore's earlier wish to see plays dealing with 'the moral and ethical problems of the day'.[29]

We may wonder, however, about the significance of Moore's *Dana* article which reads like a somewhat vain vindication of an Irish Théâtre Libre. Indeed, we may ask ourselves whether he was not fighting a rearguard action, by claiming an outdated brand of stage realism as was suggested by Yeats,[30] against a newly-established poetic trend on the Irish stage, especially at a time when Moore had turned to other literary interests and forms of expression and had obviously outgrown naturalistic principles in fiction. Edward Martyn probably did more or, at any rate, he did his utmost, to promote realistic and social drama by producing plays in the wake of Ibsen and setting up amateur theatre groups to perform them.[31] So we might come to the conclusion that Moore was not so intent on acting as a conduit of the Théâtre Libre in Ireland in its philosophy and its practice as he had been in London, along with J. T. Grein, though he had never really urged a French Théâtre Libre in England either. If such is the case, Moore's offensive article then essentially boils down to a personal squabble, a locus where there might be next to nothing. However, when abstracted from its immediate context, his essay can be still regarded, interestingly, as a piece of counter-discourse challenging the master narrative that was being spun around the Irish National Theatre.

NOTES

1. Paul Ruttledge (aka George Moore), 'Stage Management in the Irish National Theatre', *Dana*, 5 (September 1904), (Dublin: Hodges and Figgis), pp.150–2.
2. In the *United Irishman* on 1 November 1902 and in an American edition published by John Quinn in New York a few days later.
3. Jack Wayne Weaver provided internal and external evidences pointing to such a conclusion in 'Stage Management in the Irish National Theatre: An Unknown Article by George Moore?', *English Literature in Transition, 1880–1920*, 9, 1 (1966), pp.12–17.
4. Ironically, George Moore had Chapter 6 of *Moods and Memories, a section of Memories of My Dead Life*, published under his own name in the same Dana issue.
5. Michael J. Sidnell, George P. Mayhew, and David R. Clark, (eds), *Druid Craft: The Writing of 'The Shadowy Waters'* (Dublin: Dolmen Press, 1972), p.317.
6. See Ruttledge, *Dana*, p.150.
7. George Moore, *The Times* (London), 15 October 1891.
8. W.B. Yeats, 'Letter to Frank Fay, 20 January' [1904], in John Kelly and Ronald Schuchard (eds), *The Collected Letters of W. B. Yeats, Volume III*: 1901–1904 (Oxford: OUP, 1994), p.527.
9. Lennox Robinson, *Ireland's Abbey Theatre: A History 1899–1951* (London: Sidgwick & Jackson, 1951), p.40.
10. Robert Hogan and Michael J. O'Neill (eds), *Joseph Holloway's Abbey Theatre* (Carbondale and Edwardsville: Southern Illinois University Press, 1967), p.33.
11. See Ruttledge, *Dana*, p.151.
12. Ibid., p.150.
13. The editors published a correction in the December 1904 issue of *Dana*, 8, p.256.
14. George Moore, 'On the Necessity of an English Théâtre Libre', in *Impressions and Opinions* (London: David Nutt, 1891), p.240.
15. Bernard Shaw, *Collected Letters, 1874–1897*, Vol. 1, edited by Dan H. Laurence (London: Max Reinhardt, 1965), p.383.
16. H.F., 'Dared to write a play', *The New York Times*, 5 March 1893.
17. George Moore, 'Preface', *The Coming of Gabrielle* (New York: Boni and Liveright, 1921), p.8.
18. See Ruttledge, *Dana*, p.151.
19. Ibid.
20. Moore's interview of Antoine, 'The Patron of the Great Enacted', *St James's Gazette*, 5 February 1889, p.3–4.
21. George Moore claims that Antoine called him his 'confrère', when he first met him in Paris, in 'Note on *Ghosts*'. See Moore, *Impressions and Opinions*, p.215.
22. David B. Eakin and Michael Case (eds), *Selected Plays of George Moore and Edward Martyn* (Gerrards Cross: Colin Smythe, 1995), p.52.
23. W.B. Yeats, 'The Reform of the Theatre', see Robinson, *Ireland's Abbey Theatre: A History 1899–1951*, p.32. A revised version of the lecture was published in Samhain 4 (September 1903), pp.9–12, reprinted in W.B. Yeats, *The Collected Works of W.B. Yeats, Volume VIII: The Irish Dramatic Movement*, edited by Mary FitzGerald and Richard J. Finneran (Houndmills: Palgrave Macmillan, 2003), pp.26–8.
24. Gabriel Fallon, 'The Abbey Theatre Acting Tradition', in Sean McCann (ed.), *The Story of the Abbey Theatre* (London: Four Square, 1967), pp.105–6.

25. W.B. Yeats, 'Letter to F. J. Fay, 28 August' [1904], see Yeats, *The Collected Letters of W. B. Yeats, Volume III: 1901–1904*, pp.642–3.
26. Before *The Strike at Arlingford* (1893), originally a five-act play reduced to three with the help of Arthur Kennedy, George Moore had written or co-written several plays, namely *Worldliness* (c.1874), *Martin Luther* (1879), *The Honeymoon in Eclipse* (1888), and taken part in the direction of several dramatic productions.
27. Emphasising the role of the stage director, Moore incidentally claims that: 'A theatre can dispense with everything else, with scenery, costumes, wigs and paint', See Ruttledge, *Dana*, p.152.
28. The articles were collected and published in book form under the title *Literary Ideals in Ireland*, T. Fisher Unwin (London, 1899), reprinted by Lemma Publishing Corporation (New York, 1973).
29. See Moore, *Impressions and Opinions*, p.246.
30. '[…]Because he is an amateur in plays and stage management, he does not understand that his kind of play and his kind of management is equally obsolete', 'Letter to F.J. Fay, 28 August' [1904], see Yeats, *The Collected Letters of W. B. Yeats, Volume III, 1901–1904*, p.642.
31. See Jerry Nolan, 'Edward Martyn's Struggle for an Irish National Theater, 1899–1920', *New Hibernia Review*, 7, 2 (Summer, 2003), p.96.

REFERENCES

Antoine, A., 'L'Invention de la Mise en Scène', in Jean-Pierre Sarrazac and Philippe Marcerou (eds), *Anthologie des Textes d'André Antoine* (Arles: Actes Sud, 1999).

Eglinton, J. et al., *Literary Ideals in Ireland* (London: T. Fisher Unwin 1899), reprinted by Lemma Publishing Corporation, (New York, 1973).

FitzGerald, M. and Finneran, R.J. (eds), *The Collected Works of W.B. Yeats, Volume VIII: The Irish Dramatic Movement*, (Houndmills: Palgrave Macmillan, 2003).

Hogan, R. and O'Neill, M.J. (eds), *Joseph Holloway's Abbey Theatre*, (Carbondale and Edwardsville: Southern Illinois University Press, 1967).

Kelly, J. and Schuchard, R. (eds), *The Collected Letters of W. B. Yeats, Volume III: 1901–1904* (Oxford: OUP, 1994).

Maingueneau, D., *Le Discours Littéraire* (Paris: Armand Colin, 2004).

McCann, S. (ed.), *The Story of the Abbey Theatre* (London: Four Square, 1967).

Moore, G., 'The Patron of the Great Enacted', St James Gazette, 5 February 1889.

Moore, G., *Impressions and Opinions* (London: David Nutt, 1891).

Moore, G., *The Times* (London), 15 October 1891.

Moore, G., *The Strike at Arlingford* (1893), in Eakin, D.B. and Cases, M. (eds), *Selected Plays of George Moore and Edward Martyn* (1893; Gerrards Cross: Colin Smythe, 1995).

Moore, G. [Paul Ruttledge], 'Stage Management in the Irish National Theatre', *Dana*, 5 (September 1904), (Dublin: Hodges and Figgis), pp.150–2.

Moore, G., 'Preface', *The Coming of Gabrielle* (New York: Boni and Liveright, 1921).

Nolan, J., 'Edward Martyn's Struggle for an Irish National Theatre, 1899–1920', *New Hibernia Review*, 7, 2 (Summer, 2003).

Robinson, L., *Ireland's Abbey Theatre: A History 1899–1951* (London: Sidgwick & Jackson, 1951).

Bernard Shaw, *Collected Letters, 1874–1897*, Vol. 1, edited by Dan H. Laurence (London: Max Reinhardt, 1965).

Sidnell, M.J., Mayhew, G.P. and Clark, D.R. (eds), *Druid Craft: The Writing of 'The Shadowy Waters'* (Dublin: Dolmen Press, 1972).

Tindale, C.W., *Fallacies and Argument Appraisal* (Cambridge: CUP, 2007).

Weaver, J.W., 'Stage Management in the Irish National Theatre: An Unknown Article by George Moore?', *English Literature in Transition, 1880–1920*, 9, 1 (1966), pp.12–17.

CHAPTER SEVEN

George Moore and his Dublin Contemporaries: Reputations and Reality

MARY S. PIERSE

When George Moore moved from London to take up residence in Dublin in 1901, he came with a certain reputation that, for some, promised enlivenment and enlightenment to the Irish literary and social scenes. Shades of that reputation lingered for decades in disparate locations. However, any reported aura of daring and excess in the period between 1900 and 1911 deserves particularly critical scrutiny since Moore's published works in those years are not immediately suggestive of revolutionary spirit. While Æ hoped for Ireland's Voltaire and Susan Mitchell would refer to Moore as 'a high-explosive shell', there was a marked diminution of the sort of activities in which Moore formerly engaged for publicity purposes. One might ask what was his impact in a capital city that was well supplied with opinionated littérateurs, one that was apparently alive with nationalist and dramatic activity, and yet was deeply conservative? Did the fruits from Moore's Dublin sojourn furnish much that differs from the work of other writers of that time and place? How would Moore's presentation of potentially controversial subject matter measure up to any produced by those around him at the time of the Irish Revival? Some writings by Padraic Colum, Pádraic Ó Conaire, Edward Martyn, James Stephens, and Susan Mitchell provide grounds for revising and rebalancing their respective images, as well as repositioning them in relation to George Moore in the Revival years.

The portrayal of writers and artists is invariably achieved against a backdrop, whether of their times or of a later period. At the turn of the twentieth century, concerns of the Irish Revivalists, and of Irish nationalists, were centred on promulgation of a differentiating culture, on projection of a Golden Age in ancient Ireland, and thus of the Irish as inheritors of an ancient and wonderful civilisation that had been side-tracked and demeaned by foreign domination, but which if restored through recourse to myth and legend – and through independence, or at least Home Rule – would blossom. The Gaelic heritage would once more make the country a pleasant and prosperous place in which to live. With the eagerness to win respect, and to justify a move from subaltern status to self-determination, came hyper-anxiety concerning the reception of the revivalists' art, conduct and pronouncements. That nervousness could frequently result in romantic and conservative pictures of the country and its inhabitants, not realistic pictures. The marked diversity of class, church and state allegiances produced variations on what was acceptable on the grounds of 'decency' and of 'national ambition', and very centrally, of gender roles. Nowhere is this diversity more clearly illustrated than in varying reactions to Synge's *The Playboy of the Western World*. The differences are instructive: *Freeman's Journal* said the play's violence and patricide constituted a libel on Irish peasants; Arthur Griffith viewed it as a slight on Irish women; Lady Gregory did not like the 'bad language' and, in her private communications, discerned class differences based on toothbrush usage. More generally, it was clear that the play's concern was not with fostering nationalist feeling, it did not connect with any ideas on Home Rule, and it certainly did not depict a community adhering to the tenets of Christian or Catholic religion. Those reactions furnish some idea of the prevailing sensitivities confronting any artist; it was remarkably easy in 1907 to fall foul of the numerous standards of political correctness.

SOME DUBLIN CONTEMPORARIES

With the clear-eyed fearlessness of youth, Padraic Colum (1881–1972) would wound several susceptibilities. In 1902, his one-act play *The Saxon Shillin'*[1] won the Cumann na nGael prize, but, alarmed at its potential to cause controversy, the Irish National Theatre Society immediately reneged upon a promise to stage it. Colum thought he heard 'whispers of Castle influence'; unease in some revivalist circles is the probable explanation.[2] While a play that sought to discourage enlistment by Irish men in the British Army might have been welcomed by many, the play exposed a degree of economic and social interdependence between the colonisers and the colonised which was more widespread than just Irish acceptance of army pay. The story concerns the imminent eviction, by British soldiers backed up by local police, of the Kearney family, and then of all their neigh-bours because they cannot pay the increased rent demanded by the landlord. One of the soldiers is Hugh Kearney, who offers money to pay the rent, but the sum he can pay (presumably his pay and savings) is too small. What is needed immediately is £10. Hugh's two brothers are migrant labourers in England, but their remittances are also insufficient. Hugh refuses the order of his sergeant to rejoin the evicting group. Instead, he takes his father's old gun to defend the family home, and he is shot dead. The troubling ingredients in this drama included the financial relationship between an Irish local agent and his landlord, the ambiguous position of local people in the police force, the hopelessly inadequate return from emigrant agricultural labourers, the cynical view taken of those who pay lip service to revolt while actually doing nothing, the doubt cast over any possi-bility of overturning the well-entrenched status quo, and the clear intimation that the landlord class is not a benevolent one presiding over a folkloric peasantry. All of this is conveyed in just a few lines, spoken with the directness and clarity of people on the edge.

Through Hugh Kearney's unambiguous ripostes to the accusations hurled at him, Colum throws down the gauntlet to dreamers who would ignore painful reality. He asks two questions, the second of which the Gaelic League might have preferred to remain unasked: 'How many young people in the village can speak Irish? How many old people want them to speak it?' When his sister accuses him of having 'the drop o' Cromwell' in him because he joined the British Army, Kearney is more than realistic: 'I couldn't stay here any longer doin' nothin', a burthen to you all, an' the hard times that was in it. If I had to get the passage-money I'd ha' gone to America gladly.' He underscores local acceptance of Irishmen in the Constabulary: 'But because he has aisy times an' big pay he's a good Irishman.' He draws attention to Irish MPs, and land agents, and all who work for the Crown: 'An' above the polisman an' the soldier, there's many an Irishman that takes the Saxon shillin', ay, and the Saxon £500 a year, who isn't called traitor.' Kearney's bitter conclusion is that he and Mike Hanlon, the landlord's agent, have 'both taken the wan price – the Saxon shillin''.

Maud Gonne and Arthur Griffith left the National Theatre Soci-ety in protest against the refusal to produce *The Saxon Shillin'*. The play was eventually staged in Dublin in 1903 by Gonne, women from Inghinidhe na hEireann, and the students in their drama classes.[3] That group was not afraid to depict the limited survival choices for the poor, and the chasm between reality and the favoured fairy and folk tales themes of some revivalists. Padraic Colum would be equally powerful and searching in his 1906 play *The Land*. That play illustrates the incompatible outlooks of an older generation who fought in the land war, and those of the younger generation who seek material comfort and do not believe in the idealised picture of rural Ireland.[4] Most strikingly, the last act shows the defiant independence of Ellen Douras who says: 'The house and the land you offer would be a drag on me.' It's my freedom I want'.[5] A new generation of more educated women (and men) appears in Colum's play, who reject the dated, self-important notions of the land war veterans. Indirectly, but very strongly, Colum contests any visions of an easy path to successful independence and financial success for individual or nation.

Pádraic Ó Conaire (1883–1928) has been called a trailblazer and a revolutionary in Irish literature,[6] and those descriptions are justified by at least one of his short stories. His Irish-language story 'An Bhean a Ciapadh' (The Woman who was Tortured) was published in 1909; it was translated into English as 'Put to the Rack' in 1913.[7] In an almost dispassionate tone, the tale foregrounds the chattel status of Mary Finnerty, a young woman of about 18 years, and the horror of a marriage arranged, against her will, to one of her father's former work comrades, a man of almost 50. As James Burke says to her father: 'Don't you remember the Christmas night long ago when we gave our word that one of us wouldn't want for a wife so long as the other had a daughter?' Her father is willing, but Mary swears she will not marry Burke. 'All the same they were married.'[8] Mary is to be the provider of an heir for Burke. The first child is stillborn, and Mary is told that a second pregnancy would kill her. She runs away from her rich but violent and drunken husband who is obsessed with acquiring more and more land, and on keeping it from anyone else. Her flight is too late; pregnant as the result of marital rape, she dies in giving birth to a son. It is intimated that Mary's father is being sued for calling Burke a murderer. Burke's prayer over her grave gives thanks to God because Mary 'has left me an heir'. The stark brevity of the narrative emphasises the horror, but still allows space for a critique of the pursuit of land and money, the made marriage, the ills of the dowry system, the insistence on male inheritance, and the murderous effects of marital rape; moreover, it posed a challenge to those who advocated female submission and who condemned birth control. Ó Conaire's story is a very weighty confrontation in just nineteen short pages.

James Stephens (1880–1950) is yet another important contemporary literary figure not instantly associated with controversy. A versatile author, Stephens composed fiction and poetry and perhaps on account of his wonderfully beguiling speaking voice, he is often thought of as a gentle soul who produced fresh versions of fairy tales and legends. That is, of course, only part of the story. In 1909, one of his poems was published in *Bean na hEireann*, the journal of Inghinidhe na hEireann, whose most prominent members included Maud Gonne and Constance Markievicz. The stanzas of 'The Red-haired Man's Wife' show that Stephens had a very unusual and modern approach to the nature of marriage and the status of women. He engages with the apparent illogicalities of the customary transition from single to married state, 'you were my friend / But yesterday, now / All that's at an end / And you are my husband and claim me / and I must depend'; he notes the enforced effacement, 'My old name is lost, / My distinction of race'; but the internal determination is phrased as:

> I am separate still,
> I am I and not you,
> And my mind and my will
> As in secret they grew
> Still are secret, unreached, and untouched,
> And not subject to you.[9]

That particular *non serviam* did not feature in the marriage vows of any church, nor was it envisaged in common understanding and practice. It was one from which George Moore would not dissent.

Edward Martyn (1859–1923), cousin of George Moore, has not been well served by his remembrance as 'Dear Edward' of *Hail and Farewell*; the name and the anecdotes suggest ineffectual bumbling, idiosyncratic and compulsive pursuit of esoteric interests, and some degree of social inadequacy. Apart from the multiple portrayals in *Hail and Farewell*, and the rather disparaging ones provided by Yeats, other descriptions of Martyn provide a fuller picture. They give Martyn competence, acuity and sophistication. He was a co-founder of the Irish Literary Theatre with Yeats and Lady Gregory, although they would later part over differences related somewhat to Martyn's leaning towards Ibsenism and his lack of enthusiasm for what he saw as 'peasant' plays and folk drama at the Abbey. Martyn was a good musician, an enthusiastic Wagnerite, a prime mover in establishing and funding the Feis Ceoil, in setting up and subsidising the stained-glass workshop An Túr Gloine, in founding and endowing the Palestrina choir that still sings in Dublin, and in starting the Irish Theatre in 1914. He was also the first president of Sinn Féin. On the more literary side, his laboured satire *Morgante the Lesser: His Notorious Life and Wonderful Deeds* (1890) is a complex and detailed work. *Maeve* and *The Heather Field* are two of his better-known plays.[10] The sum of those attributes and achievements contrasts not just with the picture of 'Dear Edward' but also differs markedly from the tone and the message of his 1907 play *Romulus and Remus*.[11] On the surface, *Romulus and Remus*, or *The Makers of Delights* is not a parlour drama, or a peasant one; surprisingly, it is a hairdressing salon piece, and a rather camp one that Martyn subtitled 'a symbolist extravaganza'. The cast consists of the salon owner, Denis d'Oran, described as a master hairdresser, his two journeyman hairdressers Romulus Malone and Remus Delaney, his shop assistant Daisy Hoolihan, and a customer, the widow Mrs. Cornucopia. There is an amount of running in and out through doors, a screaming hairpulling fight between Daisy and Mrs. Cornucopia, farcical petulance between Romulus and Remus over ingredients for the perfume that Denis d'Oran intends to make – and a conclusion that sees Remus exiting, possibly to marry Daisy, and Romulus hiding from Mrs. Cornucopia but staying to work for Denis. This farce is a barely concealed assault by Martyn on Yeats and Moore for their carving up of *The Tale of a Town* into *The Bending of the Bough*. For Romulus, read George Moore; for Remus, read Yeats; for Denis, read Martyn; and, in the characters of Daisy and Mrs. Cornucopia, there are strong hints in the direction of Lady Gregory and Annie Horniman. The stage directions are interesting and give some indication of how Martyn viewed their relationship:

> Remus Delaney, wearing a short coat and white apron, stands by table at left, and combs a female wax figure maker. He is a cadaverous and altogether fantastic looking personage, with long hair falling, divided like window-curtains, and bespangled with various-sized combs ready for use. Denis d'Oran, in ordinary clothes, stands doggedly behind the counter at right. Romulus Malone, in the same costume as that of Remus, walks very excitedly up and down the shop.[12]

The initial exchanges are ostensibly about perfume making: Remus/Yeats wishes to add an ingredient that he obtains from the carcasses of dead flies, and at this point, Romulus/Moore backs Remus. d'Oran/Martyn complains: 'I don't see why I should consent to have my invention destroyed.' Remus/Yeats takes a superior tone: 'Neither you, d'Oran, nor Romulus are really able to invest your inventions with the distinction of bouquet.'[13] Martyn's identification of the Yeats/Gregory focus on folk and peasantry as extract of dead flies is blatant; he views Moore's realist approach as common peppermint; his attack on them is to depict their attitudes of super-iority in matters dramatic and cultural as baseless and unsuitable posturing. The play is trivial and would not merit a re-staging but, as an intra-cultural exchange of the early twentieth century, it is a quite overt needling of a Celtic mystic and revivalist, and of one who thought of himself as the Irish Messiah.

From the desk of the *Irish Homestead*, and in her socialising, and with her Pollexfen/Yeats connections, Susan Langstaff Mitchell (1866–1926) occupied a strategic place in Dublin's literary life. She defies simple classification in terms of her writings. They range from soulful and religious poetry, to a vengeful and barbed biography of George Moore which was both unauthorised and unappreciated by him. She also produced witty doggerel that made biting social and personal comment.[14] Mitchell's verse can be clever, humorous and wounding. In 'The Voice of One', when writing of Bates, Barton and M'Clure – or Yeats, Martyn and Moore – Mitchell zones in on their quirks and weaknesses. Yeats/Bates is made to intone: 'The Drama of to-morrow draweth nigh, I its inventor, its creator I. / No theatre, no scenery, no stage, / No clothes the roving fancy to engage, / No actors either, for their gestures rude / Break in upon the spirit's solitude.'[15] Mitchell also made poetic comment on the *Playboy* riots of 1907. The tone is mock-comical, but the darts are poisoned. They are targeted particularly at those strait-laced pedants who would demand the substitution of 'chemise' for 'shift' but could easily opt for kilts instead of trousers, apparently in the belief that this was nationalist dress. Over and above her support for Yeats and Synge on this occasion, she is publicly querying the notions of some Gaelic Leaguers, sticking a pin in the balloon of a nationalist narrative, removing herself from any Irish–Ireland consensus – and doing so with the easily remembered rhyming of 'Oh no, we never mention it.' The pamphlet *The Abbey Row: not edited by William Butler Yeats* begins:

Oh, no, we never mention it, its name is never heard—
New Ireland sets its face against the once familiar word.

They take me to the Gaelic League where men wear kilts, and yet
The simple word of childhood's days I'm bidden to forget!

The attitude in that response is mirrored in all editions of Mitchell's
Aids to the Immortality of Certain Persons, Charitably Administered. In a
1913 edition of that work, she too offered an anti-recruiting composition but its mocking, ironic lines appear to play more to the gallery
than to voice the painful difficulties of a Hugh Kearney: 'He'd
bullets in his right arm, he'd bullets in his leg, / He had no grá for
working, and he had no leave to beg.'[16]

MOORE IN DUBLIN

George Moore's attacks on John Pentland Mahaffy in 1901 and his
proclaimed conversion to the Church of Ireland in 1903 are the most
high-profile of his public jousts in Dublin. On the other side of the
scale is his remarkable and serious literary production during his
Dublin residence. *Sister Teresa, The Untilled Field, The Lake, Reminis-
cences of the Impressionist Painters* and *Memoirs of my Dead Life* were the
main prose works published by him between 1900 and 1910. To those
titles, one might add *The Bending of the Bough* (1901), that much-
contested and re-written version of Martyn's play *The Tale of a Town*. It
is a considerable output. Amongst the titles, *The Untilled Field* and *The
Lake* are the books that relate closely to contemporary Ireland.[17]
Neither volume bears any relationship to Mitchell's prose or poetry,
nor are they pitched at the purposely farcical level of Martyn's play.
However, as do Colum and Ó Conaire, both books engage with
contemporary Ireland, with its rural realities, its varieties of nationalism, its gender prescriptions, clericalism and squinting windows; yet,
nothing is sensationalised. Although Moore deals with the same
economic difficulties and social issues and ills as did his contemporaries,
the results are achieved somewhat differently.

Centrality of land problems, and attitudes to land, and the nature of
rural community particularly at the turn of the century, are as
obviously present in Moore's *Untilled Field* stories as they are in Padraic
Colum's play *The Land*, but Colum's obvious respect for Moore does not
produce imitations, he ploughs his own furrow.[18] The plain dialogue of
Colum's *The Saxon Shillin'* outdoes Moore by a long distance when it
comes to unmistakable voicing of the economic realities and the weaknesses of the idealistic nationalist agenda. Where the speech in Colum's
dramas is direct, Moore's prose is atmospheric. Even in 'The Wild

Goose' where Moore provides more dialogue than is his wont, the disparate attitudes of Ned and Ellen to the nature of a new Ireland, and how it might be achieved, are always vague, never clarified, never grounded in practicalities. Ellen's reported views are that 'the ancient language of the Gael' could bring back glory days, and that 'the new political movement' would achieve regeneration.[19] Moore's scepticism regarding those suppositions emerges only tangentially in the later story 'Fugitives' when Harding reports that Edward Martyn told him 'as soon as the old language is revived all differences will disappear'.[20] If Hugh Kearney asks the direct question, Moore weaves a richer tapestry but one that does not seek to shirk or hide decay. In 'The Exile', as the story moves on to Catherine's abandonment of the convent, the rural backdrop is sketched in: 'The fences were gone, cattle strayed through the woods, the drains were choked with weeds, the stagnant water was spreading out.' The town scene is no better, with 'broken pavements and dirty cottages'.[21] The scenery is not spotlighted but its misery is nonetheless put on record.

In *The Untilled Field*, Moore provides differing pictures and outcomes for attempts at made marriages: that of Catherine and Peter in 'The Exile' will prove stable if unexciting and its success will be at the expense of the dreams of Catherine and James; that of Kate Kavanagh and Peter M'Shane ('The Wedding Feast') fails because Kate decides to escape its forced nature; Julia Cahill hears the dowry price that Michael Moran asks of her father and utterly refuses marriage to him ('Julia Cahill's Curse'). A demanded dowry of one pig jeopardises the planned marriage between Catherine Mulhare and James Murdoch although the day is saved for them when Father MacTurnan can provide the money not just for one pig but for two ('A Letter to Rome'). In several of *The Untilled Field* stories, the standard of living is barely above subsistence but snobbery perceives the degrees of poverty: Mrs. Connex has risen in the world and can now look down on Mrs. M'Shane ('The Wedding Feast'). The attitude is very akin to Ó Conaire's depiction of community reaction to Mary's marriage to James Burke: 'a fine match for Miss Finnerty. What had the Finnertys ever had even at their best?'[22] The destitution, isolation, jealousies and envies of rural Ireland are recognised by Moore, Colum and Ó Conaire and each decides to present the difficulties and human tragedy rather than resort to picturesque folklore or idyllic imagery. Their messages might not have been the ones preferred by some contemporaries, yet the pictures they painted provided a degree of realism and balance for Revival aims, debates and development.

In painting relationships and marriage in *The Lake*, Moore confronts contemporary societal attitudes to single mothers, and he smoothly normalises the non-marital relationship between Nora and Mr. Poole. In each of those cases, the persuasion of readers is accomplished almost surreptitiously, and by degrees. Where women are concerned, Moore would appear to be utterly in support of the message in the Stephens poem albeit his agreement is not openly stated. His challenge to the standard treatment and fate of the unmarried, pregnant woman comes in the clear opinion contained in a letter from Father O'Grady in London: 'The ordinary course is to find out the man and force him to marry the girl; if this fails, to drive the woman out of the parish ... I believe the practice to which I have alluded is inhuman and unchristian.'[23] In this way, Moore totally distances himself from the viewpoint and invests the charitable stance with significant sacerdotal authority. With a similar dissembling stratagem, the petty squabbling and baby-snatching disputes over baptisms are seen to bring those sectarian arguments into disrepute, and to do so without any open condemnations by Moore.[24] Both issues were 'live' in rural communities and Moore had previously engaged with them in the story of 'Some Parishioners' in *The Untilled Field*. In that instance, the more extreme views are those of Father Maguire, the considered ones are held by his uncle, Father Stafford: 'Only two or three days ago, he had come running down from Kilmore with the news that a baby had been born out of wedlock, and what do you think? Father Stafford had shown no desire that his curate should denounce the girl from the altar. ... And a few days later, when he told his uncle that the Salvationists had come to Kilmore, and that he had walked up the village street and slit their drum with a carving-knife, his uncle had not approved of his conduct.'[25] In a period when religious difference was so marked and contentious, and where overt 'respectability' was narrowly defined and deemed a vital badge of worth and status, Moore chips away at the certainty and hypocrisy but he does not launch open warfare. In terms of his literary compositions, this is not a new approach; his method of lauding the single mother in *Esther Waters* (1894) had been equally indirect, as was his mode of querying several stereotypes in *Celibates* (1895). The difference in Dublin was his relatively low-key self-promotion, both for author and work.

PARES COMPARIBUS?

The parlous condition of Ireland in the early years of the twentieth century emerges, albeit to differing degrees and with varied angles, from the writings of Moore, Colum and Ó Conaire. It is a place from which many are forced to leave, but to which there is ongoing attachment: that bond brings Burke back from America to Galway in Ó Conaire's story ('The old enchantment! the old call of the blood!'),[26] and it has Bryden oscillate physically and mentally between New York and Duncannon in Moore's 'Home Sickness' in *The Untilled Field*.[27] For Bryden, the grind of the new world is balanced against the paralysing poverty of the old one where 'the potatoes failed … all agreed that they could make nothing out of their farms. Their regret was that they had not gone to America when they were young'.[28] Looking at the returned Burke, he is described as 'a bit rough', and Mary wonders if this is due to his life in the States, but it is clear that he is 'so coarse that he doesn't even know when he is insulting!'[29] The pull and tug are present for Matt and Ellen in *The Land*: Ellen asks 'Do you ever think of America? The streets, the shops, the throngs?' and Matt's response is 'The land is better than that when you come to know it.'[30] Ellen knows that America is no Utopia; it is the intransigence of the older generation (Matt's father) which finally drives both to America.

Neither Edward Martyn nor Susan Mitchell provides any pictures of rural hardship even though Martyn deals with land fixations in *The Heather Field*. However, both engage vigorously with the cultural climate of the period and with its main protagonists from W.B.Yeats and Lady Gregory to Moore, Æ and Synge. Their tones are those of the sophisticated theatregoers rather than those of the socially concerned, and the clash of personal artistic rivalries sparks off the pages. The fractures between Martyn and Yeats reflect some of the issues that led Gonne and Griffith to leave the National Theatre Society, the gap is between those determined to put Irish nationalist interests first and those who, in the words of Yeats, 'stand above their subject and play with it'. Those latter, in Yeats's mind, were Synge, Lady Gregory and himself; he defined others, 'Colum and Edward Martyn for instance, are dominated by their subject'.[31] On his part, Colum understood the installation of a Yeats 'directorate' as the 'deposition of the politically minded members and of a very sincere element who wanted a really democratic organization'.[32] Martyn's potshots at Moore and Yeats in *Romulus and Remus* result from his experience of dictatorial direction, even if it might conceivably have been intended to save him from public failure with a less-than dramatic play.

Mitchell's biography of George Moore is but another illustration of sharp personality clashes in the Dublin circle. It was probably for intensely personal reasons, concerning Moore's exposure of her relationship with Æ, that she chose to interpret the Manet portrait of Moore in terms of volatile ordinance: 'That portrait which is like nothing so much as the human symbol of a high-explosive shell'.[33] Yet, as has been seen, Moore was comparatively quiet in Dublin. His literary contemporaries at least equal, and often exceed any indulgence on his part in stinging or aggravating the reading and theatre-going public of the day. Without any fruitless attempt to establish an authorial scale of the controversial and disturbing at that time, it could be confidently asserted that Mitchell's description was exaggerated, and that it is Moore's literary artistry in those years which escapes her notice. Perhaps Mitchell herself said as much later in that biography when she softened the portrait by such phrases as 'his natural kindness' and 'his interior sincerity'.[34] Truly in Dublin of that period, it was not just any 'birds of a feather' but *pares comparibus facile congregantur* (Equals with Equals most easily flock together).

NOTES

1. P. Colum, *The Saxon Shillin'*, in Robert Hogan & James Kilroy (eds), *Lost Plays of the Irish Renaissance* (Newark, Delaware: Proscenium Press, 1970), pp.65–71.
2. P. Colum, 'Preface', in *Three Plays* (Dublin: Allen Figgis, 1963), p.4.
3. While Colum wrote that the departure of Gonne and Griffith was in response to the non-staging of *The Saxon Shillin'*, it has also been claimed that the reason was the actual staging of Synge's *The Shadow of the Glen*. Griffith stated that the play was 'no more Irish than the *Decameron*' (*United Irishman*, 17 October 1903).
4. P. Colum, 'The Land', in *Three Plays* (Dublin: Allen Figgis, 1963), pp.9–47.
5. Ibid., p.44.
6. Called 'Ceannródaí liteartha' ['Literary Pioneer'] by Pádraigín Riggs, and 'Réamhlóidí i litríocht na Gaeilge' ['A Revolutionary in Irish literature'] by Alan Titley. P. Riggs, 'Réamhrá' i *Pádraic Ó Conaire, Scothscéalta* ['Preface' in *Pádraic Ó Conaire, Best stories*] (Indreabhán, Conamara: Cló Iar–Chonnacht, 2009), p.11 & clúdach [book cover].
7. P. Ó Conaire, 'Put to the Rack', in *The Woman at the Window and Other Stories*, trans. by Éamonn O'Neill, (Dublin: Talbot Press, 1931), pp.43–61.
8. Ibid., pp.46–7. The Irish version is even more grimly terse: 'Ach phós' ['But they married'].
9. J. Stephens, 'The Red-Haired Man's Wife', *Bean na hÉireann*, (February 1909), p.9.
10. E. Martyn, *Morgante the Lesser: His Notorious Life and Wonderful Deeds* (London: S.Sonnenschein & Co., 1890).
11. First printed in *Irish People*, December 1907. Edward Martyn, *Romulus and Remus*, or The *Makers of Delights*, in William J Feeney (ed.), *Edward Martyn's Irish Theatre* (Newark, Delaware: Proscenium Press, 1980), pp.87–106.
12. Ibid., p.88.

13. Ibid., pp.88–9.
14. Examples of more soulful poetry are found in S. Mitchell, *The Living Chalice and other poems* (Dublin: Maunsel, 1908).
15. S. Mitchell, *Aids to the Immortality of Certain Persons in Ireland, Charitably Administered* (1908), (Dublin: Maunsel, 1913), pp.12–13.
16. Ibid., pp.42–3.
17. G. Moore, *The Untilled Field* (Gloucester: Alan Sutton Publishing, 1990). *The Lake*, (Gerrards Cross: Colin Smythe, 1980).
18. His description of Moore at the Oireachtas in 1902 records 'George Moore with his pallid face and blonde hair, an alert look in his china blue eyes as he takes mental notes of the characters around him'. P. Colum, *Ourselves Alone: the story of Arthur Griffith and the origin of the Irish Free State* (New York: Crown Publishing, 1959), p.63.
19. G. Moore, 'The Wild Goose', in *The Untilled Field*, p.169.
20. G. Moore, 'Fugitives', in *The Untilled Field*, p.206.
21. G. Moore, 'The Exile', in *The Untilled Field*, p.14.
22. See Ó Conaire, 'Put to the Rack', in *The Woman at the Window and Other Stories*, p.47.
23. See Moore, *The Lake*, p.31.
24. Ibid., pp.163–6.
25. See Moore, 'Some Parishioners', in *The Untilled Field*, p.35.
26. See Ó Conaire, 'Put to the Rack', in *The Woman at the Window and Other Stories*, p.46.
27. See Moore, 'Home Sickness', in *The Untilled Field*, pp.23–34.
28. Ibid., p.26.
29. See Ó Conaire, 'Put to the Rack', in *The Woman at the Window and Other Stories*, pp.48, 49, 58.
30. See Colum, 'The Land', in *Three Plays*, p.17.
31. W.B. Yeats, Letter to Florence Farr in October 1905, in Allan Wade (ed.), *The Letters of W.B.Yeats* (London: Rupert Hart-Davis, 1954), p.462.
32. See Colum, 'Preface', in *Three Plays*, p.5.
33. S. Mitchell, *George Moore* (Dublin: Maunsel, 1916), p.15.
34. Ibid., pp.35, 71.

CHAPTER EIGHT

Female Vocation and Convent Life in Moore's Narrative

Mª ELENA JAIME DE PABLOS

The number of nuns in Ireland rose enormously throughout the nineteenth century.[1] In 1800 there were six religious orders with 120 nuns inhabiting eleven houses; by 1851 that number had increased to 1,500 nuns residing in ninety-five convents and to over 8,000 by 1901 in a total of thirty-five religious orders or congregations.[2]

Insufficient opportunities for marriage,[3] the fact that wives, mothers and daughters occupied a subordinate position within the family unit,[4] the prospect of a communal life of shared values, purpose and commitment,[5] and obviously, the revitalisation of Catholicism which took place in Ireland during the nineteenth century, all led a significant number of Irish women to take the veil. The convent provided celibate women with an alternative to marriage. There postulants, mostly in their twenties, offered a dowry and vowed chastity, poverty, and obedience. They became the symbolic wives of Christ. Most wore a ring reminding them of this mystic wedding.

'Nuns' sense of self had been shaped by the prevailing philosophy regarding the attributes of the ideal woman. They themselves personified this ideal state through self-abnegation, committed work, and religious vocation.[6] 'Obedient and submissive, her vows of chastity endowing her with "purity, innocence and grace", the nun embodied all that was perceived to be ideal in Irish womanhood.'[7] Indeed, being respected by both laity and clergy, they enjoyed a higher social status than single women in the secular world.

Mary Francis Cusack, popularly known as the Nun of Kenmare, in 'Woman's Work in the Cloister' explains that being holy both in body and spirit has a special reward:[8] 'Thus while the Catholic Church honours marriage as one of her seven sacraments, giving it true dignity and all respect, she does not forget that Christ was the Virgin

Son of the Virgin Mother, and that He has called some chosen souls to follow Him in a more excellent way.'[9] May Shiel added: 'Christ and Mary are both virginal, as in Paradise before the Fall. The Christian who is vowed to virginity shares that perfection and that paradise. So virginity is the essential nucleus of Christian virtue. Sanctity is purity.'[10]

The religious commitment of nuns to charity[11] work also contributed to the enhancement of their position and their removal from the ordinary sphere of lay women.[12] They, for instance, responded to urgent needs of education and welfare in Ireland after the Great Famine by working at schools, hospitals, and charity institutions.[13] They did so to such an extent that, according to Mary Luddy, the 'devotional revolution' that took place in post-Famine Ireland 'where a more entrenched Catholicism came to be practised by an apparently more devout population, probably owed more to the nuns than has ever been acknowledged'.[14]

In *The Transforming Power of the Nuns* (1988), Mary Peckham Magray argues that the nineteenth-century Irish Catholic cultural revolution was achieved not only by the efforts of male elites, but also by the hard work of nuns. They employed their wealth and their authority to effect changes in both the religious practices and the daily activity of the Irish Catholic population.

But while fostering the 'devotional' or 'Catholic cultural' revolutions, Irish nuns were nevertheless socially conservative, and they contributed to the status quo. As a matter of fact, their social structures reflected the social divisions regarded as natural outside the convent. There were two main types of sisters: choir sisters and lay sisters. Choir sisters, who granted the institution bigger dowries than lay sisters, came from wealthy families, took higher vows, and devoted themselves to worship and prayer. The lay sisters, from more humble families, were less educated than the choir sisters, took simple vows, had no vote and their ordinary occupation was 'the discharge of the domestic duties, as cooking, laundry-work and the like'.[15]

Caitriona Clear affirms that only choir sisters were trusted to rule religious congregations. Their authority had to be accepted and respected by lay sisters, who were told to play the role of servants for their salvation.[16] The 'Guide for the Religious Called Sisters of Mercy'[17] states that with the Choir Sisters, 'she [the lay sister] is always to consider herself under subjection to them … and she should obey and act towards them with respectful deference.'[18] Thus, social asymmetry outside the convent was kept within it. Lay sisters' inferior position was similar to that held by women within the secular Irish society.[19]

C.L. Innes points out that though there were twice as many nuns as priests and seven times that of men in religious brotherhoods at the beginning of the twentieth century, historical or literary accounts of the period seem to offer little evidence of their existence.[20] George Moore, however, once more an exception to the rule, devotes hundreds of pages to their portrayal. He interested himself in what he called 'the pale innocent life of nuns, some few of whom have renounced the world, others who have never known it'.[21]

This chapter analyses passages from *The Untilled Field, A Drama in Muslin, The Lake, Celibate Lives,* and *Hail and Farewell* that represent female vocation and convent life in late nineteenth-century and early twentieth-century Ireland. Virginia Crawford's information was of great help to Moore.[22] According to him, she was a thoughtful and deeply religious minded woman who, unlike many other Roman Catholics, thought and felt and dreamt with her own brain and her own heart.[23] Her information was of great help to Moore. An expert on saints' lives and convent life, Mrs. Crawford became Moore's paid researcher and sometimes near collaborator for almost forty years. The author drew on her for *Evelyn Innes, Sister Teresa, The Lake,* and *Héloïse and Abélard.* 'She did not merely check factual information for GM but also wrote some of the letters of Evelyn and of Rose (in *The Lake*) and she often wrote out some descriptive passages that GM then revised to suit his style.'[24] From Mrs. Crawford's point of view, Moore's style had 'a tendency to individualize very sharply but to miss portraying the type of convent nun'.[25]

While living in Ely Place, Dublin, Moore could gather objective information about nuns by looking over a wall into the neighbouring convent. He witnessed how convents occupied a significant part of the urban landscape of Ireland's capital and how nuns played a major role in binding citizens to a revitalised Catholic Church. In *Hail and Farewell,* Moore presents what he sees as a reality, that is, the proliferation of nuns and female religious congregations in Dublin as a sort of plague citation. Nuns are 'birds' that compete with each other to invade and control more and more neighbourhoods in the city. They teach the young, nurse the sick, take care for the mentally handicapped, rescue sinners, and cater for the needs of the destitute:

> Nothing thrives in Ireland like a convent, a public-house, and a race-meeting. Any small house will do for a beginning; a

poor-box is put in the wall, a couple of blind girls are taken in, and so salubrious is our climate that the nuns find themselves in five years in a Georgian house situated in the middle of a beautiful park. The convent whose music distracts your meditations is occupied by Loreto nuns[26] – a teaching order, where the daughters of Dublin shopkeepers are sure of acquiring a nice accent in French and English. St Vincent's Hospital, at the corner, is run by nuns who employ trained nurses to tend the sick. The eyes of the modern nun may not look under the bedclothes; the medieval nun had no such scruples. Our neighbourhood is a little overdone in convents; the north side is still richer. But let's count what we have around us: two in Leeson Street, one in Baggot Street and a training college, one in Ballsbridge, two in Donnybrook, one in Ranelagh; there is a convent at Sandy mount, and then there is John Eglinton's convent at Merrion; there is another in Booterstown. Stillorgan Road is still free from them; but I hear that a foreign order is watching the beautiful residences on the right and left, and soon as one comes into the market – You have been out hawing, my dear Moore, and I appeal to you that the hen bird is much stronger, fiercer, swifter than the tiercel.

The tiercel, of course, for while he was pursuing some quarry at a Blackrock, the larger and the stronger birds, the Sister of Mercy and the Sister of the Sacred Heart, struck down Mount Annville, Milltown, and Linden. All the same, the little tiercel has managed to secure Stillorgan Castle on the adjacent hillside, a home for lunatic gentlemen, most of them Dublin publicans.[27]

Convents, in George Moore's Catholic Ireland, were supposed to be places to enjoy placid and contemplative lives.[28] Far from a corrupted secular world, vocations could be developed. However, the writer undermines this idealised vision of the institution by putting forward the true reasons women had to take the veil. He depicts the inequities inside the convent. He regarded a convent as a sort of prison. He warned of the power of convents to alienate the women who entered them. He tries to prove that the mystery in convent life, in the life of every nun, was not the mystery of Divine grace.[29]

According to Moore, women entered convents for reasons outside of religion. He thought that most women joining religious orders in the nineteenth century and early twentieth century did not do so because they had experienced a spiritual call or had a philanthropic vocation, but because they wanted to avoid paternal or marital pressure, to elude the risks of maternity, to empower themselves (by ascending up within the convent hierarchy), to overcome a failed sentimental relationship, to develop themselves by performing a social task, to hide from society when physically or mentally handicapped, or simply, as stated before, to enjoy an apparently calm and peaceful existence. He was to be of those men Mary Francis Cusack accused of going 'out of the way to find out some other motive' than 'the love of God' for nuns to enter convents.[30]

Some cases will illustrate those assertions.

THE CONVENT AS A PLACE FOR EMPOWERMENT

Maria Luddy points out that convents were institutions of power, where women could create their own systems of labour and have the opportunity of rising to positions of power and authority unmatched by lay Catholic women.[31]

In *The Lake*, Eliza Gogarty decides, at the age of fifteen, to take the veil. When she reveals her intention to her family, every single member is astonished. No one had ever observed any spiritual inclination in her before. Ambitious, she is convinced that 'one day she would be Reverend Mother of the Tinnick Convent'.[32] What she envisages is the chance to develop her intellect and to empower herself. We are told that she could have married, but Eliza shares the belief, widespread in nineteenth-century Ireland, that 'becoming a wife and mother' is the 'second best option' for young Catholic women.[33]

Taking the vows implies a life marked by deep spirituality and harsh deprivation, but Eliza does not celebrate this side of religious life. When her young brother Oliver tells her he is to build and live in a hermitage on Castle Island emulating old Irish Saints, she disapproves of the project. Oliver cannot fully assimilate 'her inability to understand an idea so inherent in Christianity as the hermitage, for at that time Eliza's mind was made up to enter the religious life'.[34]

Oliver's amazement increases when he asks Eliza if she intends to found a new Order or to go to far away places to teach indigenous people. He discovers that she is much more interested in a laundry than in the Indians. Her plea that the Tinnick Convent was always in straits for money did not appeal to him then any more than it did today.

'The officers in Tinnick have to send their washing to Dublin.'

'A fine reason for entering a convent,' he answered.

But quite unmoved by the sarcasm, she replied that a woman can do nothing unless she be a member of a congregation. He shrank from Eliza's mind as from the touch of something coarse, and his suggestion that the object of the religious life is meditation did not embarrass her in the very least.[35]

In a convent, she can perform a socially relevant task; she has freedom of choice; she can get ahead. She has decided she will be 'directing the affairs of the convent'[36] because she considers that an attractive occupation, one that will let her fulfil her desire to do something worthwhile and to attain a certain level of power. It has nothing to do with vocation. Indeed, she exhorts Oliver, 'don't let us waste our time talking about vocations';[37] or religious ideals. In fact, her brother has 'never met anybody less interested in opinions or in ideas than Eliza'.[38]

When he announces to Eliza that he wants to take holy orders, she backs his decision thinking 'of the advantage this arrangement would be to her when she was directing the affairs of the convent'.[39] Eliza is moved by pragmatism and not by religious vocation, but as Moore would state in a letter sent to Emily Lorenz Meyer on 9 January 1907, 'the truth is that women are natural pagans and have never been Christianized. Man has never succeeded in Christianizing woman. Women say they are Christians to please men, that is all and the proof of this is that women have never (God bless them) invented a religion.'[40]

THE CONVENT AS AN ASYLUM FOR HELPLESS WOMEN

Mary Gogarty, persuaded by her siblings Oliver and Eliza, also takes the veil. Both Oliver and Eliza think that Mary will not be able to cope with the real world on her own, since she has proved to be unable to fulfil with success the tasks that she has so far undertaken:

Her life up to the time she entered the convent was little else than a series of failures. She was a shop-assistant, but standing behind the counter gave her varicose veins; and she went to Dublin as nursery-governess. Father Oliver had heard of musical studies: she used to play the guitar. But the instrument was not popular in Dublin, so she gave it up, and returned to Tinnick with the intention of starting a rabbit and poultry farm. Who put this idea into her head was her secret, and when he received Eliza's letter telling him of this last experiment, he remembered throwing up his hands. Of course, it could only end in failure, in a loss of money.[41]

In order to prevent more 'foolish experiments',[42] that is more failures, Mary is accepted at Tinnick Convent, where Eliza exercises a powerful control over the nuns. Mary soon becomes another victim of Eliza's unquestionable authority and strong censorship. She is deeply upset. Nobody seems to care about that fact though, not even Oliver, who ignores the real problems of nuns at convents:

> 'You don't know, Oliver, what it is to live in a convent, and your own sister the head of it?'

> 'I should have thought; Mary, that it was especially pleasant, and that you were especially fortunate. And as for thinking that Eliza is not wishing you to see me alone I am sure—'

> 'You are sure I'm mistaken.'

> 'What reason could she have?'

> 'Eliza doesn't wish the affairs of the convent discussed. You know, I suppose, that the building of the new wing has put a burden of debt on the convent.'

> 'I know that; so why should Eliza—'

> 'Eliza tries to prevent my seeing any of the visitors. Now, do you think that quite right and fair towards one's sister?'

> ...

> 'Eliza loves ruling everybody, and just because I am her sister she is harder on me than anyone else.'[43]

For her part, Eliza refers to Mary as stupid, lazy, gossipy and absent-minded. When Mary's lack of attention provokes an accident at the laundry which harms irreparably another nun's arm, Eliza says that Mary 'can't keep her attention fixed on anything, not even on her prayers, and what she calls piety I should call idleness'.[44]

But Mary is not the only one who does not carry out her tasks properly. According to Eliza, the convent is an asylum for lazy women with little intelligence: 'It's terrible to have to do with stupid women, and the convent is so full of them',[45] she affirms. The nuns' efficiency ratio is so low that Eliza wonders 'what is the good of having a convent at all'.[46] Obviously, she measures the usefulness of the institution she runs in purely economic terms, much in the way real nuns did. As Maria Luddy states, nuns 'were above all pragmatic and their institutions had to be run as businesses'.[47]

THE CONVENT AS A RETIREMENT PLACE FOR PEOPLE
'CROSSED IN LOVE'[48]

In 'The Exile', a short story included in *The Untilled Field*, Catherine enters the religious life because the man she loves, Peter Phelan, 'hoped to be admitted into the minor orders'.[49] That is 'she didn't go into the convent because she had a calling, but because she was crossed in love'.[50] When Peter abandons Maynooth before becoming a priest because his essays are censored, his brother, James, and his father, Pat, determine that 'A good wife is the only thing for Pether.'[51] Pat goes to Catherine's convent to arrange the match, but once in the convent, 'He began to think how much easier was this pious life than the life of the world – the rearing of children, the failure of crops, and the loneliness. Here life slips away without one perceiving it, and it seemed a pity to bring her back to trouble.'[52] The Superior Mother won't let him talk to Catherine, not even after being informed that Catherine did not enter religious life for the expected reason:

> 'But, my lady, you see Catherine wanted to marry my son Pether, and 'tis because he went to Maynooth that she came here. I don't think she'd want to be a nun if she knew that he didn't want to be a priest.'
>
> 'I can't agree with you, Mr Phelan, in that. I have seen a great deal of Sister Catherine – she has been with us now for nearly a year – and if she ever entertained the wishes you speak of, I feel sure she has forgotten them. Her mind is now set on higher things. … I know her very well. I can answer for Sister Catherine.'[53]

Like Eliza Gogarty, this Superior Mother is a totalitarian ruler. She is not afraid of losing a vocation; what she does fear is losing the lay sister who knows how to manage the convent farm. Paradoxically, Catherine, who is to be clothed within days, goes to see her and confesses both her real reason for entering the convent and her lack of a solid religious vocation. Without knowing about Pat's visit to the convent, she announces she is to leave it in order to assist him, who is – in a vision she has had – sad and lonely. She shows a tender, but dynamic, personality who is eager to help others following the Christian principles of kindness, sympathy, and charity; however, she is sure that she will be able to carry out this duty much better outside rather than inside the convent walls:

> 'It was the second day of my retreat, mother. ... I remembered those at home. I remembered Mr. Phelan, and James, who wanted to marry me, but whom I would not marry; and it seemed to me that I saw him leaving his father – it seemed to me that I saw him going away to America. I don't know how it was – you won't believe me, dear mother – but I saw the ship that is to take him away lying in the harbour. And then I thought of the old man sitting at home with no one to look after him, and it came over me suddenly that my duty was not here, but there. Of course you won't agree with me, but I can't resist it, it was a call.' ... 'I only know that I must go home. ...' But after all, mother, there are many duties besides religious duties.'[54]

THE CONVENT AS A LABOUR CAMP

Sarah Gwynn, the protagonist of the eponymous short story in *Celibate Lives*,[55] flees from her home in Co. Down when a series of disasters take place in her county and she is accused of provoking them for being 'the only Catholic there',[56] since 'if anything goes wrong in County Down it's the fault of the Catholics'.[57] Boys in the village keep on saying: 'To hell with the Pope and his witches.'[58] She feels the need to move to Dublin, where she meets by chance Phyllis Hoey, who provides her with a post at the biscuit factory where she herself is employed. As their salary is so meagre, they are forced to get some extra money to cover food and accommodation expenses. Phyllis resorts to prostitution, so that Sarah can devote herself to a less profitable second employment, sewing. From the tiny room they share, they can observe the nuns in the adjacent convent. Once more, it is perceived from the outside as an idyllic place that provides a happy life of meditation and prayer.

Pushed by Phyllis, Sarah visits the priest to hear 'a little more of the Catholic religion than was spoken about in the County Down'[59] and she enters religious life without knowing what it really involves. As she would admit years later it was 'No more than an accident.'[60]

> If I had time, I'd like to know more of the nuns, they seem so quiet and happy. But we were, as I've said, at work all day, and it wasn't till there was a strike in the factory that the days were our own, with no bell ringing and nobody to take our names as we went in. ... The strike lasted a fortnight, and I heard a little more of the Catholic religion than was spoken about in the County Down. Phyllis said: If you have a feeling that way, tell the priest who hears your confession that you'd like instruction in the Catholic religion; he'll give it to you and jumping. So I did, and entered the Church just about when the strike was to end.[61]

She wants to take the vows to escape a life of hard work and alienation both at the biscuit factory and at home, and to enjoy a life of retirement and prayer in a convent in Wales. The priest's intervention makes it possible, but money is needed to pay for the price of the passage and the clothes she is to wear during the probationship. One of Phyllis's night clients is ready to provide the money on condition that Sarah prays for his salvation, and she accepts. Within the convent walls, Sarah develops a sense of guilt. She thinks of Phyllis and her precarious situation. She wants to go back to Dublin to help her survive, but Mother Prioress prevents it by encouraging her to stay and pray to God for Phyllis's welfare: 'all things are in the hands of God; he alone can help'.[62] Remorse does not disappear but Sarah stays in Wales and becomes a lay sister. She is glad that Mother Prioress is good to her by letting her hear mass, a right not always granted to lay sisters: 'Mother Prioress, ... was very good to me and understood that the lay sisters had as much right to hear Mass as the choir sisters.'[63]

However, this Mother Prioress is replaced by another one who is not so kind to lay sisters, one who exploits them to the extreme. Endless, unbearable duties undermine their health, and when the oldest die, nobody comes to take their place, therefore the burden on the remaining ones leads to their complete exhaustion. Sarah becomes deeply troubled by the fact that she has no spare time to pray for Phyllis and her Dublin benefactor.

One day, overtired, a tray falls from Sarah's hands and she is harshly rebuked by the Sub-Prioress and the Mother Prioress.

Stressed by fatigue and offended by false charges, Sarah stands up in front of them and openly denounces the discrimination and exploitation lay sisters like her suffer:

> I spoke without knowing what I was saying, telling them that while they were walking idly in the garden we were working our lives away. Yes, I think I said that two nuns had died already of hard work and bad food, and that we had not time for prayer; that the nunnery was no house of prayer but just a sweaters' den, and that I'd sooner go back to a biscuit factory, where at all events I had the evenings to myself for prayer.[64]

She is dismissed from the convent and handed one miserable sovereign in return for ten years of hard labour, approximately the amount of money Phyllis could get in one night in either Sackville or Grafton Street. With that money, she returns to Dublin to find her friend. To make a living, she works as a parlour-maid for Doctor O'Reardon, who, on hearing Sarah's story, criticises the Sub-Prioress and Prioress for promoting a hierarchical system, for ruling the convent in a merciless way, for suppressing any dissident voices, and especially for treating Sarah unfairly: 'You were in a convent for nearly ten years, and because you answered the Sub-Prioress, or maybe the Prioress herself, sharply, they bundled you out, clapping a straw hat on your head and an alpaca jacket on our shoulders, giving you but your bare fare to Dublin, nor caring—'. However, Sarah, so accustomed to playing a subservient silent role, sees herself the only one responsible for what had happened: 'Oh, but you mustn't talk like that, sir! It was all my fault. I spoke to our Sub-Prioress in a way that I shouldn't have. I lost my temper, and all the blame is with me.'[65]

Some time later, she can admit she entered religious life not because she experienced a calling, but because she, young, ignorant, without relatives or friends to support her, and without a satisfactory job, considered the convent a comfortable refuge: 'I was only eighteen and knew nobody except Phyllis and the girls at the factory. If I had known then what I know now, I could have gone to an agent and do some charring, maybe a situation.'[66] With the passing of time, according to Doctor O'Reardon, Sarah 'is no longer religious',[67] but she seems unable to find her place in the secular world. She rejects a marriage proposal not because she does not like the man who makes it, but because she cannot forget about her duty towards Phyllis: 'My duty is towards Phyllis, sir; I have promised her my prayer, and there's the man that paid for me, too, to be considered. If I married I would be having children and I'd have to look after them, and Phyllis would be forgotten; I couldn't be remembering her always except in a convent.'[68] As Elizabeth Grubgeld affirms, 'because she believes in the morality preached by the church, she must spend her life attempting to redeem Phyllis from eternal punishment'.[69] Moore, who thought that 'religious orders absorb[ed] the country, and ... what is more unfortunate the will [of its citizens]',[70] presents Sarah Gwynn as an 'an underdeveloped and childlike mentality' forged in 'a world where sexuality is denied through church law'.[71] She is an example of someone who is alienated by religious narrow-mindedness.

THE CONVENT AS A PLACE FOR HIDING WHEN PHYSICALLY AND/OR MENTALLY HANDICAPPED

Cecilia, in *A Drama in Muslin*, illustrates another reason to take the veil; that is to conceal a misshapen body. In a patriarchal society where women's value depends greatly on their capacity to be appealing to men, beauty becomes one of their most appreciated assets. Cecilia, with a deformed body, is clearly set on the margins of a secular world which discriminates against her, both for being a woman and being 'ugly'. Her need to escape a society which despises her, together with sweet remembrances of childhood at St. Leonard's Convent are some of the reasons moving her to become a nun. She refuses rather than renounces the world.

Born into a Protestant family, she meets her sisters' opposition to her conversion to Catholicism by placing rosaries and holy-water fonts everywhere at home, thus provoking her sisters' wrath and removing any possibility of a peaceful existence. Their religious discussions prove to be unfruitful since they are based on arrogance, intolerance and radicalism:

> Cecilia, as I told you yesterday, has been filling the house with rosaries and holy-waterfonts; Jane and Sarah have been breaking these, and the result has been tears and upbraidings ... Last night at dinner I don't really know what they didn't say to each other; ... Jane asked Cecilia how many Gods there were in the roll of bread she was eating if the priest were to bless it ... Jane had no sooner spoken than Cecilia overthrew the teacups and said she was not going to stay in the house to hear her religion insulted, and without another word she walked down to the

parish priest and was baptised a Catholic; nor is that all, she
returned with a scapular round her neck, a rosary about her
waist, and a Pope's medal in her hand. ... She was going to pack
up her things and return at once to St. Leonard's and become a
nun.[72]

Religious beliefs separate the sisters. Once more 'spiritual love' is set
above any other type of love, including, as in this case, family love.
But Cecilia's 'weird love of the spiritual'[73] is also connected to 'her
hatred of all that concerned sexual passion'.[74] The narrator deems
Cecilia's hatred of sex unnatural and proceeds to explain its genesis:

Her hatred of all that concerned sexual passion was consequent
on her father's age and her mother's loathing for him during
conception and pregnancy; and then, if it be considered that this
transmitted hatred was planted and left to germinate in a
misshapen body, it will be understood how a weird love of the
spiritual, of the mystical, was the almost inevitable psychical
characteristic that a human being born under such circumstances would possess.[75]

As Mark Llewellyn affirms: Celibacy 'becomes not only a subject
placed in relation to religion, but also an issue which is intimately
related to a pessimistic philosophy about the value and purpose of
life itself. ... celibacy is a family issue.'[76] The narrator of *A Drama in
Muslin* implies that Cecilia's mother's hatred of her father, and her
own body deformity, determine her psyche. Her 'dark and illogical
mind'[77] is unfit for loving but prone to hating people – men, 'obscene
animals',[78] above all, the culprits of women's both subjection and
degradation.[79] She has deeply assimilated the Catholic principle that
'virginity ... alone is ideal Christianity'.[80] In a conversation with Alice
Barton, she warns:

...man's love. It is a vile and degrading thing. How women can
endure it I don't know; the thought fills me with horror. Women
are pure, men are obscene animals. Their love is our degradation. Love! A nice name they give it. How can a sentiment that
is merely a gratification of the lowest passions be love? And that
is all they seek; I know it; in their heart of hearts they despise
us.[81]

Indeed, Cecilia represents 'The hostility of the Catholic Church to
love, sexual love between men and women, [that] brought about in

Moore a mounting irritation.'[82] For Moore, sex is life. In *Confessions of a Young Man*, he declares that 'the bold fearless gaze of Venus is lovelier than the lowered glance of the Virgin'[83] and that he is in favour of 'a new creed proclaiming the divinity of the body';[84] in *Hail and Farewell*, he even talks about the 'healthy love of sex'.[85] On the contrary, celibacy, understood as sexual abstinence, is death: 'celibates cannot continue a country',[86] he says in a letter to Virginia Crawford (16 December 1902).

Cecilia opts for the convent, where her misshapen body, concealed by a habit, will not be an object of derision, where she can enjoy the only company she tolerates, that of women, and where she will devote herself to a mystic destiny without being mocked at.

Cecilia could exemplify one of those 'rare' cases mentioned by Mary Francis Cusack:

> ...some persons will be admitted into the cloister who would have been a trial everywhere. There are persons of almost constitutionally bad tempers, selfish dispositions, and rough manners, who will neither be quiet themselves, or suffer others to be quiet. They are always imagining offence, and forgetting they are always giving offence.[87]

In *Hail and Farewell*, Moore also mentions another nun whose mind is disturbed. The description of her death as accidental preserves the idealised image of Irish nuns. According to the author, her cause of distress might be 'some thought', 'some fear', 'some suffering', or else some 'scruples of conscience' experienced within the convent, which represents a sort of prison to her, one she can only escape by suicide:

> A nun had been found drowned ... the verdict returned was of accidental death. The verdict of suicide in a moment of temporary insanity would not have been agreeable to the nuns, but to me, a teller of tales, it is more interesting to think that she had gone down in the night to escape from some thought, some fear, some suffering that could be endured no longer. She was free to leave the convent; the bars that restrained her were no iron bars, but they were not less secure for that. She may have suffered, ... from scruples of conscience, and gone down in despair to the pond.[88]

Though briefly referred to, she is one clear example of what Gerber calls

George Moore's 'religion-haunted personalities',[89] that is, self-tormented figures.

Although Moore very often undermines the stereotyped conception of nuns as spiritual and altruistic beings by depicting nuns as totalitarian rulers, as women who lack real vocations, sound knowledge, or helpful talents; as sisters who may be either physically or mentally handicapped; he nevertheless cannot but feel compassion for those who live in convents, apparently places of beatitude, but in reality prisons or labour camps. Moore's nuns are victims of dogmatism, prejudice, and abuse. In a conversation with John Eglinton included in *Hail and Farewell*, Moore asks:[90] 'Do you think the flood of intelligence will penetrate into the convents and release the poor women wasting their lives?'.[91]

NOTES

1. According to Maria Luddy: 'The most important of the new congregations were the Sisters of Charity, founded in 1815 by Mary Aikenhead; the Loreto Sisters formed in 1820 by Frances Ball; the Sisters of Mercy established by Catherine McAuley in 1831; the Sisters of the Holy Faith created by Margaret Aylward in 1867; and the Sisters of St John of God, founded in 1871 by the Bishop of Ferns. The other foundation made by a bishop occurred in 1807, with the establishment of the Brigidine community in the diocese of Kildare and Leighlin. A large number of European communities also made foundations in Ireland in the nineteenth century.' See Luddy, M., *Women and Philanthropy in Nineteenth-Century Ireland* (Cambridge: Cambridge University Press, 1995), p.26.
2. Fahey, T., 'Nuns and the Catholic Church in Ireland in the Nineteenth Century', in M. Cullen (ed.), *Girls Don't Do Honours: Irish Women in Education in the 19th and 20th centuries* (Dublin: Women's Education Bureau, 1987), pp.7–30.
3. 'Recent studies have shown that a large proportion of Irishwomen could not expect to marry in post-famine Ireland. Their options were then emigration or spinsterhood. The convent provided another alternative.' See Luddy, *Women and Philanthropy in Nineteenth-Century Ireland*, p.34.
4. To illustrate this point, let's add that in Fraser for June, 1874, readers are told that the reason why so many girls become nuns is that 'They find home unbearable.' See Cusack, M.F., *Women's Work in Modern Society* (Co. Kerry: Kenmare Publications, 1874), p.347.
5. Hill, M. and Pollock, V., *Image and Experience. Photographs of Irishwomen c.1880-1920* (Belfast: The Blackstaff Press, 1993), pp.129–30.
6. Luddy, M., *Women and Philanthropy in Nineteenth-Century Ireland*, p.53.
7. See Hill and Pollock, *Image and Experience*, pp.129–30.
8. Cusack, M. F., *Women's Work in Modern Society*, p.335.
9. No doubt, the Nun of Kenmare remembers Saint Ambrose's words uttered in 377 A.D.: 'A virgin is concerned with the Lord's claim, intent on holiness of body and spirit; whereas the married woman is concerned with the world's claim, asking how she is to please her husband.' See Saint Ambrose, *The Nun's Ideals*, translated by J. Shiel, (Dublin: Cepter, 1963, p.26. Ambrose posits that by abstaining from all pleasures of sex, nuns may be holy in body and spirit (Ibid., p.27).
10. Shiel, M., 'Introduction', in Saint Ambrose, *The Nun's Ideals*, p.14.
11. 'Catholic nuns organised, and managed, the most extensive network of charitable organisations and societies' . See Luddy, *Women and Philanthropy in Nineteenth-Century Ireland*, p.8.
12. Ibid., p.53.
13. See Hill and Pollock, *Image and Experience*, p.130.

14. See Luddy, *Women and Philanthropy in Nineteenth-Century Ireland*, p.4.
15. Luddy, M., *Women in Ireland, 1800–1918. A Documentary History* (Cork: Cork University Press, 1995), p.81.
16. Clear, C., 'Walls within walls: Nuns in Nineteenth-century Ireland', in C. Curtis et al. (eds), *Gender in Irish Society* (Galway: Galway University Press, 1987), p.149.
17. Maria Luddy provides her readers an extract of the 'Guide for the Religious Called Sisters of Mercy' (London, 1866).
18. See Luddy, *Women in Ireland, 1800–1918. A Documentary History*, p.81.
19. See Clear, *Gender in Irish Society*, p.149.
20. Innes, C.L., *Woman and Nation in Irish Literature and Society: 1880–1935* (London: Harvester Wheatsheaf, 1993), p.120.
21. Gerber, H. (ed.), *George Moore in transition: Letters to T. Fisher Unwin and Lena Milman, 1894–1910* (Detroit, Illinois: Wayne State University Press, 1968), p.98.
22. As a researcher, Virginia Crawford produced abundant work 'on labour problems, Christian democracy, education, feminism, cooperative banks, workhouses, saints and convents, and a wide range of literary figures. Her work appeared in Cosmopolis, one of Unwin's periodicals, *The Review of Reviews, Fortnightly Review, Month, Dublin Review, Contemporary Review, and other reputable journals'*. See Gerber, *George Moore on Parnassus. Letters (1900–1933) to Secretaries, Publishers, Printers, Agents, Literati, Friends, and Acquaintances* (Delaware: University of Delaware Press, 1988), p.27.
23. Ibid., p.90.
24. Ibid., p.28.
25. Ibid.
26. 'The music of harp and violin practice penetrated his house at Ely Place [Dublin] from the convent behind it.' See Frazier, A., *George Moore 1852–1933.* (London and New Haven: Yale University Press, 2000), p.309.
27. Moore, G., *Hail and Farewell* (Buckinghamshire: Colin Smythe, 1987 [1914]), p.441.
28. It was generally understood that girls went into convents 'to be comfortable'. See Cusack, *Women's Work in Modern Society*, p.341.
29. Mary Francis Cusack affirmed: 'There is indeed a mystery in convent life, in the life of every nun; it is the mystery of Divine grace; it is the mystery which leads her to prefer the kingdom of heaven to the kingdoms of earth.' See Cusack, *Women's Work in Modern Society*, p.357.
30. Ibid.
31. Luddy, M., 'Women and Philanthropy in Nineteenth-Century Ireland', in K.D. McCarthy (ed.), *Women, Philanthropy, and Civil Society* (Bloomington, Indiana: Indiana University Press, 2001), p.13.
32. Moore, G., *The Lake* (Buckinghamshire: Colin Smythe, 1980 [1905]), pp.7–8.
33. See Luddy, *Women, Philanthropy, and Civil Society*, p.13.
34. See Moore, *The Lake*, p.10.
35. Ibid.
36. Ibid., p.11.
37. Ibid., p.58.
38. Ibid., p.11.
39. Ibid.
40. See Gerber, *George Moore on Parnassus. Letters (1900–1933) to Secretaries, Publishers, Printers, Agents, Literati, Friends, and Acquaintances*, p.130.
41. See Moore, *The Lake*, pp.49–50.
42. Ibid., p.50.
43. Ibid., pp.55–6.
44. Ibid., p.58.
45. Ibid.
46. Ibid.
47. See Luddy, *Women, Philanthropy, and Civil Society*, p.34.
48. Moore, G. *The Untilled Field* (Dublin: Gill & Macmillan, 1990 [1903]), p.12.
49. Ibid., p.8.
50. Ibid., p.12.
51. Ibid.
52. Ibid., p.15.

53. Ibid., p.16.
54. Ibid., p.18–19.
55. Published for the first time in *Single Strictness* (1922).
56. Moore, G., *Celibate Lives* (Leipzig: Bernhard Tauchnitz, 1927), p.263.
57. Ibid.
58. Ibid.
59. Ibid., p.269.
60. Ibid.
61. Ibid.
62. Ibid., p.273.
63. Ibid., p.274.
64. Ibid., p.275.
65. Ibid., p.251.
66. Ibid., p.270.
67. Ibid., p.260.
68. Ibid., p.276.
69. Grubgeld, E., *George Moore and the Autogenous Self: The Autobiography and Fiction* (Syracuse, New York: Syracuse University Press, 1994), p.94.
70. See Gerber, *George Moore on Parnassus. Letters (1900–1933) to Secretaries, Publishers, Printers, Agents, Literati, Friends, and Acquaintances*, p.107.
71. Llewellyn, M., 'Celibacy and its Artistic Discontents', in M. Pierse (ed.), *George Moore: Artistic Visions and Literary Worlds* (Newcastle: Cambridge Scholars Press, 2006), p.228.
72. Moore, G., *A Drama in Muslin* (Belfast: Appletree Press, 1992 [1886]), pp.240–1.
73. Ibid., p.146.
74. Ibid.
75. Ibid.
76. See Llewellyn, *George Moore: Artistic Visions and Literary Worlds*, p.224.
77. See Moore, *A Drama in Muslin*, p.146.
78. Ibid., p.144.
79. For Moore, states Frazier, the passion of love is 'Not degrading at all, was Moore's subversive claim, but inspiring, indeed ennobling, even when the love in question did not lead to the altar and the home.' See Frazier, *George Moore 1852–1933*, p.346. Moore stated that Christians feel 'every attempt to make love a beautiful and pleasurable thing is a return to paganism'.
80. See Shiel, *The Nun's Ideals*, p.16.
81. See Moore, *A Drama in Muslin*, p.144.
82. See Frazier, *George Moore 1852–1933*, pp.308–9.
83. Moore, G., *Confessions of a Young Man* (London: Penguin, 1939 [1888]), p.61.
84. Ibid., p.62.
85. See Moore, *Hail and Farewell*, p.187.
86. See Gerber, *George Moore on Parnassus. Letters (1900–1933) to Secretaries, Publishers, Printers, Agents, Literati, Friends, and Acquaintances*, p.107.
87. See Cusack, *Women's Work in Modern Society*, p.346.
88. See Moore, *Hail and Farewell*, p.444.
89. See Gerber, *George Moore on Parnassus. Letters (1900–1933) to Secretaries, Publishers, Printers, Agents, Literati, Friends, and Acquaintances*, p.83.
90. This may be connected with an idea widely spread within intellectual circles and mass media, such as the *Fraser's Magazine* (May 1869), that 'because nuns believe in God's revelation, and practise the Christianity which the Bible teaches, it is at once set down that their "lives are petty", that they spend their time in miserable squabbling, and that the whole concern is unutterably weary and stupid'. See Cusack, *Women's Work in Modern Society*, p.345.
91. See Moore, *Hail and Farewell*, p.446.

CHAPTER NINE

More Moore in Joyce than Joyce in Moore

MARK CORCORAN-KELLY

According to his biographer, Richard Ellmann, James Joyce found George Moore a good man to improve upon.[1] He outlined Joyce's use of the ending in *The Lake* in *A Portrait of the Artist as a Young Man*. Adrian Frazier stresses the importance of *The Untilled Field* to *Dubliners*, making reference to the ending of *Vain Fortune* in relation to 'The Dead'.[2] This chapter will examine direct links between *Dubliners* and *The Untilled Field*, pinpointing where the Moore influence lies at this juncture in Joyce's career, in particular how one story from *The Untilled Field*, 'The Clerk's Quest', was used by Joyce as the backbone for a number of stories, both in terms of character conception and theme. Central themes of these stories are celibacy and love within and outside marriage.

'The Clerk's Quest' seems to have resonated with James Joyce from 1904 to 1906, when he was writing 'Clay', 'The Boarding House', 'A Painful Case', and 'A Little Cloud'. These stories include either a clerk or a celibate. Marriage is either a dominant theme, or the elephant in the room.

The earliest version of Moore's 'The Clerk's Quest' appeared in *St. James Gazette* in September 1890, entitled 'Mr Dumpty's Ideal'. Initially conceived for an English audience, Moore reworked and renamed the story. It resurfaced as 'The Clerk's Quest' in the 1903 edition of *The Untilled Field*.

The main character is Dempsey. His position as bank clerk mirrors Joyce's own short-lived position as a bank clerk in Rome in 1906, here described by Robert Spoo: 'The months Joyce spent in Rome were some of the unhappiest of his life. Having given up his post at the Berlitz School in Trieste, he had come to Rome, accompanied by Nora Barnacle and their son, Giorgio, to accept a more lucrative job as a correspondence clerk in a bank.'[3]

The clerk characters that Joyce creates after the publication of *The Untilled Field* bear Moore's influence. Robert Spoo, however, accepts Joyce's claim that no treatment of such subject matter had ever been attempted by an Irish writer:

> ...in *Dubliners* Joyce depicted a society in which the ascetic ideal had come to dominate, rendering its practitioners morally abject and spiritually docile. Insisting that an honest, probing diagnosis had yet to be attempted by an Irish writer, Joyce felt obliged to supply the missing chapter of moral history. He chose 'Dublin for the scene because that city seemed to me the centre of paralysis'.[4]

Yet Joyce was very much aware of Moore's own very recent depiction of paralysis in Irish society. The Italian clerks with whom Joyce worked in 1906 may have served as Joyce's experiential models – they annoyed him and 'were forever having something wrong with their testicles ... or their anuses', which they described at length to the Irish writer – but Moore's stories were his pre-existing literary models.[5] Unlike Moore, Joyce had lived the life of his characters as a clerk and had inhabited their class as a Dubliner.

Joyce's 1905 letters to his brother Stanislaus show irritation with inaccuracies in the detail of Moore's portrayals in *The Untilled Field*, such as a local looking up a regular train route that a realistic character would surely already know.[6] Joyce's own stories would be careful to be correct on such matters, but they repeat Moore's fixation on clerkship, celibacy, the loss of celibacy, and marriage. Celibacy in this context refers to a state of being unmarried, not abstention from sex. Complete sexual abstinence, as Havelock Ellis put it in *Sex in Relation to Society*, is 'unreal and ... in the strict sense perhaps impossible'.[7]

In 'Celibacy and its Artistic Discontents' Mark Llewellyn notes that 'Moore's attitude to the positive elements of both celibacy and marriage is highly ambiguous; indeed, in at least two of his celibacy narratives, it is marriage itself, or the horrors children perceive within their parents' marriages, that prompts a desire for the celibate life.'[8] For Moore and Joyce celibacy involves the choice not to marry. In Irish society the scandal of sex and children out of wedlock was taboo.

Joyce's clerk stories build upon Moore's narrative style, characterisation, and aesthetic. 'The Clerk's Quest' is the tale of a man who has spent his life immersed in work; he has rejected all other aspects of life. He has taken one holiday in thirty years, and during that holiday, he still calls into the office. He develops a delusional crush on a Scottish woman based on the pink perfumed cheques she sends to the office. The clerk's fixation on Henrietta Brown builds up into a psychotic delusion. He neglects his work. He neglects everything. Ultimately, it is the death of him. Joyce takes this celibate, friendless character-type and reinvents it. The clerk is not a solitary celibate character but a celibate in a family setting in 'A Little Cloud', and 'Counterparts'. In 'A Painful Case' Joyce gives us a cynical clerk on the margins of society and family á la Dostoevsky's *Notes from the Underground*.

In 'A Little Cloud', a newlywed clerk has a deluded ambition to become a poet. To be a celibate poet bachelor with Jewish princesses available to him becomes the fantasy. One of the passages in 'A Clerk's Quest' most influential upon 'A Little Cloud' is the following:

> …the cheque was written in a thin, feminine handwriting, and was signed 'Henrietta Brown,' and the name and handwriting were pregnant with occult significances in Dempsey's disturbed mind. …and he grew suddenly aware of some dim, shadowy form, gracile and sweet-smelling as the spring – moist shadow of wandering cloud, emanation or earth, or woman herself? Dempsey pondered, and his absent mindedness was noticed, and occasioned comment among the clerks.[9]

Joyce also uses the name Henrietta, the object of Dempsey's delusion, in three ways in 'A Little Cloud'. There is a direct reference to Henrietta Street, and Bolton Street involves an indirect reference to another Henrietta. Henrietta Street is named after Lady Henrietta Somerset, the wife of Charles FitzRoy, 2nd Duke of Grafton. Bolton Street is named after Charles Paulet, 2nd Duke of Bolton. Paulet's third wife was called Henrietta Crofts. It was often thought by Dubliners that Henrietta Street was named after the Duke of Bolton's Henrietta rather than the 2nd Duke of Grafton's Henrietta.[10] The woman in Moore's story in Joyce's version becomes the streets outside the clerk's window in King's Inns.

Another alteration or substitution by Joyce of a detail from Moore's story concerns the image of a flower that first excites Dempsey's interest in the distant female correspondent. Moore states that Dempsey had not seen a flower in thirty years: '"He was interested only in his desk." It seemed that Dempsey had no other ambition than to be allowed to stagnate at a desk to the end of his life, and this modest ambition would have been realised had it not been for a slight accident.'[11]

Such symbolism was of a sort to irritate Joyce, in the same way he was irritated by Moore's character checking a train timetable when he would not have needed to do so. It was a blatant narrative mechanism. If Moore wanted to stress Dempsey's virginity, he could have come up with a better indication than Dempsey not having seen a flower in thirty years despite living in Ireland's capital. That a man living in a city would not have seen a flower in thirty years beggars belief. It is also incredible that Dempsey would never have looked out of his office window. One of the first things Joyce has Little Chandler do is look out of his window: 'As he sat at his desk in the King's Inns he thought what changes those eight years had brought. The friend whom he had known under a shabby and necessitous guise had become a brilliant figure on the London Press. He turned often from his tiresome writing to gaze out of the office window.'[12]

At the end of the story, Chandler, as he cradles his child and poetry ambitions, reads Bryon:

> '...Whilst I return to view my Margaret's tomb
> And scatter flowers on the dust I love.'

> He paused. He felt the rhythm of the verse about him in the room. ... There were so many things he wanted to describe: his sensation of a few hours before on Grattan Bridge, for example. If he could get back again into that mood.[13]

Joyce's character reads about a lover laying flowers on the grave of a dead love. The gesture, and the emotion, are trite, literary, false, and therefore like what Little Chandler really is. He is not a true writer.

A third historical figure in Joyce's story is Henry Grattan, the Irish leader, after whom a Dublin bridge was named. Grattan's wife was also called Henrietta. There is no mention of this in the story itself; Joyce leaves this to be noticed by a discerning reader. He rejects the heavy symbolism of Moore, in favour of super-subtle hints. In place of a delusion are the very real streets where Chandler walks daily, named after the men and the wives of the men, who had shaped the country. Both of the Dukes, after whom streets are named, are former Lord Lieutenants of Ireland. As Donald T. Torchiana points out, the other street mentioned in the story, Capel Street, was named after another Lord Lieutenant.[14] Moore's Henrietta was merely an English sort of female forename for an undeveloped character from Edinburgh. Joyce's proper names are carefully selected for their historical connotations. The men alluded to by Joyce are key Irish and

English figures whose actions had very real consequences for Ireland. Joyce layers his story with the past through politics and history. Henry Grattan studied at King's Inns to become a barrister, Little Chandler's place of work. Both of the Dukes for whom the streets are named also held positions as clerks, albeit the ultimate highest such position, Privy Counsellor. Joyce's remapping of Moore's story allows him to multi-layer the narrative.

Moore's text is Joyce's foundation. It allowed him to believe that he was becoming a better writer than Moore, because his stories corrected Moore's, and elaborated upon them. Joyce's story undermines the reclaiming and repackaging of Irish dialect and Irish history through the Revival by revealing how Ireland's history was formed in tandem with Britain's history and the English language. There is nothing the Revival can do to rewrite or reframe this language of description. It is there on the everyday streets and names that *Dubliners* use. All else is illusion and myth.

Joyce adds complex layers to location, character, and narrative. There are copious notebooks and manuscripts to reveal his method. His composition has, to use Joyce's own phrase, 'a copy and paste' quality. In one of Joyce's notebooks (entitled VI.B.10) used in the construction of Ulysses there are notes for the corrections of the 'Cyclops' episode.[15] In the middle of the notes there is a section where Joyce seems to be leaving *Ulysses* behind and shifting into his next work. The notes are taken from the *Irish Times* on 20 October 1922. Joyce collected words from various sections of the paper. Presumably, these are words that Joyce liked and wished to use.

The notebook also contains words from journals. The vast majority of *Finnegans Wake*'s language is utilised from notes taken from newspapers, journals, and overheard conversations. Joyce, it seems, was from the beginning collecting random words, phrases, and what not. Joyce returned again and again to his notebooks to write and rewrite *Finnegans Wake*, crossing off the words and phrases from articles and conversations which he had used. It is possible that Joyce used Moore in a similar vein to construct his own collection of stories. He uses Moore's work as a skeleton to build upon, akin to his use of Homer's epic as a framework for *Ulysses*. It is not the only work Joyce utilised in his construction of *Dubliners*; however, it is the key work in terms of structure and storyline.

In 'A Little Cloud' Joyce's married clerk, Chandler, meets his successful celibate journalist 'friend' who has briefly returned to

Ireland. The men compare the benefits of their respective lives. Each wants to be seen as the more successful and happy. This is a device used by Moore in *The Untilled Field*. Married and unmarried characters operate on opposite philosophies. Throughout the stories, the narrative is animated by this contrast. In 'Two Parishioners' two men of different personalities and means vie for the one woman. In 'The Wild Goose' two characters of different political and religious persuasions are brought together in matrimony.

In some ways the authors differ in approaches to authorship, despite having similar influences in terms of French literature. Moore, a self-educated author, possessed a faster and looser approach to fiction: '[Moore] had so little formal education that he was very impressionable. It took little to dissuade him from what ideas of tradition he had. He was also extremely lucky in the influences to which he was exposed as a result of his migration to Paris.'[16]

Joyce was heavily and traditionally educated by the Jesuits and then in University College Dublin. He has a slower and more de-tailed approach to writing. As Adrian Frazier has suggested, Moore at the time of writing *The Untilled Field*, knows who he is, he desires to be the centre of social attention, and he will adopt whatever position is required for his art. He shifts from Catholicism to Protestantism, and from literary school to literary school. He had found his principle of authorship – unflinching truth. In *The Untilled Field*, Moore's dedication to truth makes him rebel against the Literary Revival even as he is trying to be part of it; he cannot help himself from exposing patriotic illusions. The original manifesto, signed by Yeats states:

> We will show that Ireland is not the <the locus> home of buffoonery and of easy sentiment, as it has been represented, but the home of an ancient idealism, and we are confident of the support of all Irish people, who are weary of misrepresentation, in carrying out a work <which> that is <above> outside all the political questions that divide us.[17]

The hope is to define the country away from its history through a definition against England in a revisionist history. However, this is futile and goes against the internationalist ambitions of Joyce.

Joyce is equally dedicated to truth, of course. In fact, he has a more exacting demand for accuracy in details, as mentioned earlier. Another detail from Moore's story that Joyce seizes upon is the pink perfumed cheque from Henrietta Brown which begins Dempsey's illusion. Joyce uses perfume in three different stories about clerks.

Moore's pink cheque suggests dowries. Preceding stories in *The Untilled Field* often concern arranged marriages and the bargaining that takes place regarding the dowry the female will bring to the husband. In *Dubliners* the clerks Bob Doran, Mr. Alleyne, and Farrington are excited by the perfume of females in 'The Boarding House' and 'Counterparts'. Chandler of 'A Little Cloud' does not seek nor is he enamoured by the perfume of a female, but he perfumes his own handkerchief:

> He was called Little Chandler because, though he was but slightly under the average stature, he gave one the idea of being a little man. His hands were white and small, his frame was fragile, his voice was quiet and his manners were refined. He took the greatest care of his fair silken hair and moustache, and used perfume discreetly on his handkerchief. The half-moons of his nails were perfect, and when he smiled you caught a glimpse of a row of childish white teeth.[18]

He grooms himself to perfection; he is prim and pretty. Perfume is a symbol of the self-applied illusion that Chandler is a poet.

Gallaher in 'A Little Cloud' shares Moore's distaste for marriage. Joyce knew Moore was anti-marriage; everyone did; it was his hallmark. Joyce's hero Ibsen was no supporter of marriage either. The response to marriage as an experience and concept is a dominant feature of 'A Little Cloud'. At the time of its composition, Joyce was not married but he had eloped with Nora. They had an infant when he wrote this story in 1906, hence, the job as a clerk which he hated. He lives a married life but is not married by law. This elopement, Nora's pregnancy, and their cohabitation are an experience which has Joyce scrambling for self-understanding. The arrival of a child at first brings enchantment: 'The event staggered and delighted him; a few years later he said to his sister Eva. "The most important thing that can happen to a man is the birth of a child."'[19]

Years later, as a settled family man in terms of acceptance and gratefulness in family life, Joyce could not understand those without children: 'The most natural act for living beings which are complete is to produce other beings like themselves and thereby to participate as far as they may in the eternal and divine.' Joyce said to Louis Gillet, 'I can't understand households without children. I see some with dogs, gimcracks. Why are they alive? To leave nothing behind, not to survive yourself – how sad!'[20]

In bad health and ageing the perception of progeny is one of surviving yourself, a form of continuation to be rejoiced in. During Nora's first pregnancy, however, he was not happy:

> I think it is best for people to be happy and honestly I can see no prospect of her being happy if she continues to live this life here. You know, of course, what a high esteem I have for her and you know how quietly she gave our friends the lie on the night when she came with us to the North Wall … I think that her health and happiness would be much improved if she were to live more suited to her temperament. … The child is an unforgettable part of the problem. … After all, it is only Skeffington, and fellows like him, who think woman is man's equal…[21]

In 1905 the potential child is a problem and women are not equal. The pressures of new and great responsibility have Joyce floundering. Earlier in the year he rejects plainly the ceremonial and conceptual traditions of marriage and the religious decrees imposed upon infants: 'But why should I have brought Nora to a priest or a lawyer to make her swear away her life to me? And why should I superimpose on my child the very troublesome burden of belief which my father and mother superimposed on me?'[22]

In December of 1905 he writes to his aunt:

> I have hesitated before telling you that I imagine the present relations between Nora and myself are about to suffer some alteration. … I daresay I am a difficult person for any woman to put up with but on the other hand I have no intention of changing. Nora does not seem to make much difference between me and the rest of the men she has known and I can hardly believe that she is justified in this. I am not a very domestic animal – after all, I suppose I am an artist – and sometimes when I think of the free and happy life which I have (or had) every talent to live I am in a fit of despair. At the same time I do not wish to rival the atrocities of the average husband and I shall wait until I see my way more clearly. … I am not sure that the thousands of households which are with difficulty held together by memories of dead sentiments have much right to reproach me with inhumanity.[23]

The responsibilities of cohabitation and his own drinking are causing him to believe that a separation is in the offing. The hampering of
his artist self is cause for despondency. His perception of the average
household is not positive. He is contemplating escape. As Ellmann
records his attitude will change with time:

> Instead of being man's faithful, passionate slave, woman, as he
> now began to see and, in a different mood, would later write to
> Frank Budgen, was 'perfectly sane full amoral fertilisable
> untrustworthy engaging shrewd limited prudent indifferent
> *Weib'*. ... Stanislaus was able to help his brother and Nora over
> this crisis, not so much, as he supposed, by the force of his
> admonitions, as by supplying them with a common target of
> complaint – himself.[24]

The more he came to terms with his role as a father and husband the
more dimensions were built into his characters, making them more
rounded, however far from feminist ideals. The abuses witnessed and
experienced at the hands of Joyce's father would be repeated under
the stressful circumstances of Joyce's life at this time. His drinking
became chaotic, to the detriment of his family life, and Stanislaus was
left to pick up the pieces: 'Sometimes Stanislaus, in a fury over his
brother's resolute efforts to cause his own ruin, would pummel James
when he got him home.'[25]

These are the changing attitudes and beliefs of James Joyce as he
makes the transition from a young artist with aspirations to become
a great artist, to a father, lover, and head of a family with those
same aspirations. This fluctuating state of mind is reflected in the
clerkship stories in *Dubliners*. The man of fresh family responsibility,
Chandler, and the celibate Gallaher, contest the benefits of their lives.
Chandler begins to look upon his successful friend Gallaher with
jealousy:

> He felt acutely the contrast between his own life and his friend's,
> and it seemed unjust. Gallaher was his inferior in birth and
> education. He was sure that he could do something better than
> his friend had ever done, or could ever do, something higher
> than mere tawdry journalism if he only got the chance. ... He
> saw behind Gallaher's refusal of his invitation. Gallaher was
> only patronising him by his friendliness just as he was patron-
> ising Ireland by his visit.[26]

Gallaher is snobbish because he is a journalist on the London scene who frequents Paris, a single man who has the run of Jewish princesses and a successful career, but Chandler has his own little conceit. The accusation thrown at Gallaher by Chandler of patronising Ireland may be a veiled swipe at Moore, a writer who returned from London via Paris as a famous and revered author to join the Revival. Joyce could also be suggesting Moore's symbolic return to England through his conversion to Protestantism in 1903 highlighted by the letter to the *Irish Times*. The ego of the author in both cases is continually seeking assertion and success. The crossover in terms of the men's egos, similar ambitions, allegiance to a past, and a family history is apparent in Moore and Joyce.

Gallaher dangles the Paris life in front of Chandler: "'Every place is immoral,' he said. "Of course you do find spicy bits in Paris. Go to one of the students' balls, for instance. That's lively, if you like, when the cocottes begin to let themselves loose. You know what they are, I suppose?" "Ah" he said, "you may say what you like, there's no woman like the Parisienne – for style, for go.'"[27]

Notions of freedom, success, and happiness would seem to lie away from the responsibility of new family as Chandler begins to daydream of being a poet and 'spicy bits'. This is similar to Joyce's position as an artist with family responsibilities. The celibate life was not a problem for Moore, however. He could pick and choose his moments for women:

> Henry Grattan and Wolfe Tone, Charles Dickens and Edmund Burke. The Temple was still infested with writers who neither practised nor studied the law. Arthur Symons, W.B. Yeats, and Havelock Ellis would all come like Moore and Martyn to live in the Temple. ... Moore himself found an escape in the Temple 'from the omniscient domesticity which is so natural in England.' For both Moore and Martyn, one of the Temple's charms was 'young male life ... and the absence of women.'[28]

Moore believes that his literary work is more important than the pursuit of women for marriage or anything else. However, he needs the admiration and belief of a woman to produce his best work. George Moore's relationship with his brother Augustus was tested when Augustus filed for divorce against his showgirl wife for adultery.[29] George felt it brought shame upon the family. Could this be another ingredient in the character of Gallaher? Both Moores,

Augustus and George, had journalistic careers in London. Both were associated with the scandal of adultery. Chandler ponders adultery over, hand in hand, with his fantasies of being a poet. The London antics of the brothers Moore may have informed Joyce's portrayal of Gallaher.

The exploitation of aspects of Moore's characters and storylines from *The Untilled Field* for use in Joyce's short stories may well have been subconscious. What is certain is that Joyce engaged with Moore's text to a meaningful extent, perhaps in the hope of building upon and bettering Moore's effort. This enables him to derive a complexity and realism which is not apparent in the work of Moore. He melded these literary pieces with his own life experiences to produce his first great work.

NOTES

1. Richard Ellman, *James Joyce* (Oxford: Oxford University Press, 1982), p.234.
2. Adrian Frazier, *George Moore 1852–1933* (New Haven: Yale University Press, 2000), p.307.
3. Robert Spoo, *James Joyce and the Language of History* (New York: Oxford University Press, 1994), p.15.
4. Ibid., p.24.
5. See Ellman, *James Joyce*, p.226.
6. Ibid., p.193.
7. Havelock Ellis, *Sex in Relation to Society, Studies in the Psychology of Sex* (London: Heinemann, 1948), p.215.
8. Mark Llewellyn, *Celibacy and its Artistic Discontents, George Moore: Artistic Visions and Literary Worlds*, edited by Mary Pierse (Newcastle: Cambridge Scholars Press, 2006), p.223.
9. George Moore, *The Untilled Field* (London: Heinemann, 1931), p.122.
10. Maurice Craig, *Dublin 1660–1860* (Dublin: The Royal Society of Antiquaries of Ireland, 2006), p.129.
11. See Moore, *The Untilled Field*, p.121.
12. James Joyce, *Dubliners* (London: Penguin, 1996), p.76.
13. Ibid., p.92.
14. Donald Torchiana, *Backgrounds for Joyce's Dubliners* (Boston: Allen & Unwin, 1986).
15. Luca Crispi and Sam Slote, *How Joyce Wrote Finnegans Wake* (Wisconsin: Wisconsin University Press, 2007), p.5.
16. Linda Bennett, 'George Moore and James Joyce: Story-teller versus Stylist Author(s)', *Studies: An Irish Quarterly Review*, Vol. 66, No. 264 (Winter, 1977), pp.275–291.
17. R.F. Foster, *W.B. Yeats A Life* (Oxford: Oxford University Press, 1998), p.184.
18. See Joyce, *Dubliners*, p.76.
19. See Ellman, *James Joyce*, p.204.
20. Ibid.
21. Ibid., pp.202–3.
22. Ibid., p.198.
23. Ibid., p.214.
24. Ibid., p.215.
25. Ibid.
26. See Joyce, *Dubliners*, p.88.

27. Ibid., p.84.
28. See Frazier, *George Moore 1852–1933*, p.185.
29. Ibid., p.195.

A Class Apart:
The Baptism of Stephen Dedalus

CONOR MONTAGUE

In 1922, George Moore allegedly referred to James Joyce as a nobody from the Dublin docks: 'no family, no breeding'. *Portrait of an Artist as a Young Man* was a 'book entirely without distinction; why, I did the same thing, but much better, in the *Confessions of a Young Man*. Why attempt the same thing unless you can turn out a better book?'[1]

There are two issues that warrant scrutiny here, both of which relate to Moore's 1905 novel, *The Lake*. Firstly, there is Moore's jibe at Joyce's class, a jibe that typifies their public jostles and an accusation that Moore knew would rile his compatriot. Secondly, Moore refers to *A Portrait of the Artist as a Young Man* as an inferior version of *Confessions of a Young Man*. He made this statement shortly after completing an extensive revision of *The Lake*, a novel that has more in common with *Portrait* than *Confessions*.

In the distinction between classes both writers repeatedly sought the higher literary and moral ground, and it was during those years when Moore was working on *The Lake* that those battle-lines were first drawn up. In late autumn 1901, Stanislaus Joyce knocked on the door of 4 Ely Place and handed *Day of the Rabblement* to the servant,[2] a pamphlet in which James Joyce delivered a stinging criticism of the Irish Literary Theatre and those involved in producing plays in Ireland. Of George Moore he said:

> Mr Moore, however, has wonderful mimetic ability, and some years ago his books might have entitled him to the place of honour among English novelists. But though *Vain Fortune* (perhaps one should add some of *Esther Waters*) is fine original work, Mr Moore is really struggling in the backwash of that tide which has advanced from Flaubert through Jakobsen to

D'Aununzio [sic]: for two entire eras lie between *Madame Bovary* and *Il Fuoco*. It is plain from *Celebates* [sic] and the latter novels that Mr Moore is beginning to draw on his literary account, and the quest for a new impulse may explain his recent startling conversion. Converts are in the movement now, and Mr Moore and his Ireland have been fitfully admired. But however frankly Mr Moore may misquote Pater and Turgeuieff [sic] to defend himself, his new impulse has no kind of relation to the future of art.

Published while Moore was working on *The Untilled Field*, this was stinging criticism. Like the satirical 1891 portrait of George Moore by Walter Sickert, or the caricatures of Max Beerbohm, it might have been enjoyed by Moore. George Russell (Æ), mentions Joyce, and Moore's reaction to *Day of the Rabblement*, in a letter to W.B. Yeats dated August 1902: 'Moore, who saw an article of this boy's says it is preposterously clever.' There was truth in Joyce's criticism. At this juncture, Moore needed Ireland far more than Ireland needed (or wanted) him, both as a source of narrative and a locale of frictions, conditions necessary to his artistic output. As he said in a letter to Maurice in November 1901: 'Ireland is interesting because it is in the process of making, but at present ignorance is everywhere, and intellectually the country is unwashed, that is why it is interesting; green fruit is more interesting than red, though not so sweet to the taste.'[3] George Moore's responses to the gauntlet thrown down by the young man were *The Untilled Field* and *The Lake*, works that in turn influenced Joyce. It is interesting that Joyce chose *Vain Fortune* as 'fine original work'. He borrowed Moore's ending, where a couple's intimacies are over-shadowed by a suicide, in 'The Dead'. The fact that *Vain Fortune* satirises theatre critics was not lost on Joyce. Gabriel Conroy was a part-time newspaper critic. Moore would acknowledge this flattery years later when claiming that 'The Dead' was the only story in *Dubliners* worth reading.[4]

In *The Lake* Moore acknowledges the accuracy of Joyce's criticism, and accepts the inevitable 'changing of the guard' when he has Fr. Gogarty reminisce about Joycetown House.

Joycetown House was the last link between the present time and the past. In the beginning of the century a duellist lived there; the terror of the countryside he, for he was never known to miss his man. For the slightest offence, real or imaginary, he sent seconds demanding redress...

The story runs how Joyce, knowing that the feeling of the country was against him, tried to keep the peace. But the blood fever came on him again, and he called out to his nearest neighbour, Browne of the Neale, the only friend he had in the world. Browne lived at Neale House, just over the border, in County Galway, so the gentlemen arranged to fight in a certain field near the mearing. It was Browne of Neale who was the first to arrive. Joyce having to come a dozen miles, was a few minutes late. As soon as his gig was seen, the people, who were in hiding, came out, and they put themselves between him and Browne, telling him up to his face there would be no fighting that day! And the priest, who was at the head of them, said the same; but Joyce, who knew his countrymen paid no heed, but stood up in the gig, and looking round him, said, 'Now, boys, which is it to be? The Mayo cock or the Galway cock?' No sooner did he speak these words than they began to cheer him, and in spite of all the priest could say they carried him into the field in which he shot Browne of the Neale.[5]

When one takes into account Moore's previous form, his choice of the name Oliver Gogarty for his protagonist, and Joyce's criticism in *Day of the Rabblement*, then it seems possible that this section is a metaphorical recognition of the literary power and confrontational attitude of his younger contemporary. Joyce, too, recognised the Roman rather than the Sassenach as the tyrant of the islanders.[6] It may be significant that the wishes of the priest are ignored by Joyce and Browne of the Neale, and that Joyce arrived late to the scene. Luke Gibbons has suggested the significance of Gogarty swimming to Joycetown to embark on a new way of life.[7] However, he doesn't attach significance to the passage quoted above. The allusions are subtle, but are there nonetheless.

While Moore was writing *The Lake*, Joyce famously shared accommodation with Oliver St. John Gogarty for a brief period,[8] a friend of Moore and regular visitor to 4 Upper Ely Place. Gogarty shared Moore's talent for witty repartee and his taste for gossip to be moulded into urban folklore. The Joyce family's pretentions to grandeur were no secret in Dublin. James's father, John Stanislaus, claimed descent from the Joyce family of Mervue, prosperous Catholic gentry, and one of the fourteen tribes of Galway. The Joyce coat of arms, a double-headed eagle with the motto, *Mors Aut Honorabills Vita* (Death before Dishonour) accompanied John and his family through many changes of address as they slipped rung by rung down Dublin's social ladder. No matter how precarious the family's financial situation became, these items were never sold. James continued this tradition, and the coat of arms was lugged to Trieste, Zurich and Paris as he pursued his literary ambitions. In *Portrait of the Artist*, Steven invites Davin to 'come with me to the office of arms and I will show you the tree of my family'.[9] Some thirty pages further in the narrative, Stephen's pedigree is again discussed when Temple says to him: 'I know all the history of your family, too.' Two sentences on, Temple says: '*Pernobilis et pervesta familia.*'[10] This is the opening salutation of the 1790 pedigree of Gregory Joyce, meaning the illustrious and ancient family of Joyce.

James Joyce did have an ancestral link to the Mervue Joyces, though it is tenuous. According to Gordon St. George Mark,[11] the two families share common descent from the Joyces of Ardrahan, who arrived in Ireland as followers of Maurice Fitzgerald in circa 1235. By the time the Galway Joyces established themselves as a wealthy merchant family, the Joyces of Ardrahan had split a number of times due to various disputes.[12] Looked at from this perspective, Joyce's hostility towards the revivalists appears to have a more complex genesis than mere artistic integrity. Status anxiety played a part in shaping his attitude towards his more well-connected contemporaries. Having grown-up observing the decline in his family's social standing, it would be natural for Joyce to envy, and indeed resent, the cultural, economic and social capital available to artists whom he considered inferior to himself. In 1912, this simmering resentment bubbled to the surface in Joyce's poem, *Gas from a Burner.* Referring to Moore's play *The Apostle*, Joyce writes, 'Written by Moore, a genuine gent / that lives on his property's ten per cent.'

Joyce had no problem utilising the capital of these cultural elites when it was made available to him, be it through a letter of introduction or financial assistance. This hypocrisy would not have been lost on Moore, always alert to double standards. The subtlety of the literary jibes at Joyce contained within *The Lake* imply a respect for Joyce's talent that contradicts the attitudes attributed to Moore by Hone and others. However, no compliment of George Moore was delivered without a barb in its tail. This compliment is no different. It underlines Joyce's insecurity regarding his pedigree. The fact that Moore makes Joyce the Mayo cock rather than the Galway cock is no accident, for the former had far greater claim to the title of Galway cock, being directly descended from at least four of the Galway tribes. His great-great-grandmother was Jane Lynch-Athy, his grandmother, Louisa Browne, and his mother, Mary Blake. The fact that he uses the name Browne may be a gesture towards Moore's kinsman, Jim Browne, who inspired a young George to travel to Paris and study art. Or it may be a recognition that of all the tribal families, the Moore family had at least two direct connections to the Browne family. Indeed, it is true to say that Moore was more closely related to the tribal Joyces than James was.[13] According to Major Walter Joyce, the founder of the Joyce family of Merview was Marcus Joyes, a rich merchant who bought land in Mayo during the reign of James I,[14] hence the Mayo cock. There were Joyces of Oxford, in the barony of Clanmorris, and of Joycegrove, near Tuam. When Catholics returned to Galway during the reigns of Charles II and James II, among those granted the freedom of the city was John Joyes, who is most likely the John Joyce included in the ensuing pedigree, a pedigree that by this stage, excluded James Joyce's predecessors, who may have been the Joyces of Joycegrove. This branch of the Joyce family went bankrupt in 1850 and sold the estate to the Brownes of Tuam, who renamed the property Brownsgrove.[15] Perhaps Joyce of Joycetown had good reason to shoot Browne of the Neale.

The question remains as to whether or not George Moore was aware of this history. As it happens, a number of letters are extant that confirm the complex interconnected genealogy of the Moore/Brown/Blake families. The research was conducted by three cousins who corresponded regularly: Martin J. Blake of Dublin, Dominick Browne of Christchurch, New Zealand, and Maurice Moore of Moore Hall, Co Mayo. George Moore himself received a number of letters concerning his family's pedigree from Browne and Blake in the 1890s.[16] While Moore worked on *The Lake*, he rekindled his interest in the history of the families around Lough Carra and his correspondence with Maurice from this period is full of queries about local history and folklore.[17]

Joyce took an active interest in *The Lake* when it was published. On 4 December 1905, he wrote to his aunt Josephine from Trieste asking her to 'send a critique from a Dublin paper on Moore's novel in which Fr O. Gogarty appears'.[18] In a letter to his brother Stanislaus, posted from Rome on 19 August 1906, he calls Oliver St. John Gogarty an Irish imitator of Wilde before going on to request that a copy of *The Lake* be posted to him.[19] By 31 August, Joyce told Stanislaus that he had 'bought and read *The Lake*: and will send it when I know where to send it so that you may tell me what you think of it'. Joyce goes on to discuss what *The Times* calls 'a prose poem' and his tone is sarcastic throughout. He pokes fun at some of the descriptions employed by Moore, in particular, the moon shining on Fr. Gogarty's 'firm erect frame and grey buttocks'.[20] Joyce makes a snide reference to a reputed history between George Moore and Lady Ardilaun, 'whose lily-white hand he lingered over some years back', before he disparages Moore's breeding, 'George Moore, out of George Henry Moore and a Ballyglass Lady.'[21] Was this prickliness partly a reaction to Fr. Gogarty's meditation on Joyce of Joycetown?

Curiously, Joyce pokes fun at the perceived pretension of the preface in French dedicated to Edouard Dujardin, but displays no knowledge of the French author, and fails to make the connection between Dujardin and the character, Mr. Ralph Ellis. Since Joyce is reputed to have purchased a copy of *Les Lauriers sont coupés* at a Parisian railway station in February 1902, it seems unusual that he doesn't express an opinion on Moore's friend. He refers to Ellis as 'one of Moore's literary men, you can imagine what, second silent cousin of that terribly knowing fellow, Mr Harding'.[22] Characteristically, this letter ends with a request for funds, and Joyce uses the opportunity to poke fun at *The Lake* one last time; 'Already the moon is threatening to shine on my grey buttocks and I wish somebody would send me a pair of Fr Oliver's small-clothes that he hid among the bulrushes.'[23]

On 6 September, *The Lake* was sent to Stanislaus, with instructions to 'send me your opinion of it', along with an article by Ibsen.[24] Yet again, Joyce pokes fun at Moore's preface, when he writes 'Méme jeu (as G.M. would say)'. Though it is difficult to evaluate Joyce's exact feelings towards Moore, there is one certainty; *The Lake* was a significant irritation.

There is one further curiosity contained in Joyce's correspondence from the period that connects him to *The Lake*. Joyce tells Stanislaus that his aunt Josephine had sent him copies of the Rev. Thomas Connellan's pamphlet, *The Catholic*. This is just one of a number of times Joyce mentions Fr. Connellan in his correspondence from this period. John Kelly and others have claimed that *The Lake*'s protagonist was based on Fr. Jeremiah O'Donovan,[25] understandable, given O'Donovan's circumstances,[26] and the fact that his novel *Father Ralph* (1913) was similar in some ways to *The Lake*. However, it was this earlier absconder that served as the inspiration for Fr. Oliver Gogarty.

A former Catholic curate, Fr. Thomas Connellan was a remarkable character, and resided in Dublin at this time. It is possible that O'Donovan introduced Moore to Connellan's story but given his interests at the time, he could not have lived in Dublin and not had an awareness of Connellan's activities.

In the Dublin of 1903, the ultra Catholic legacy of Cardinal Cullen and Irish Ireland propaganda of D.P. Moran didn't have it all its own way. Ultra Protestantism and militant Unionism were far from negligible forces at the turn of the century. This strand of Anglo-Irish politics, which refused to accept the decline of the Ascendancy in the aftermath of the Land War and strongly resisted Home Rule, was represented by the Irish Unionists Association's *Notes from Ireland* and the news sheet of Patrick Trench, Third Baron Ashdown, *Grievances from Ireland*. In The *Long Gestation*, Patrick Maume describes this Protestant evangelical fervour:

> Lord Ashdown was part of an ultra-Protestant sub-culture still preaching modernisation through Protestant evangelisation and speaking for groups effected by the breakdown of traditional structures of Anglo-Irish ascendancy. In the eighteen-nineties this sub-culture was visibly represented in Dublin by missionary groups, such as that headed by the former Catholic priest Thomas Connellan, publisher of a monthly called *The Catholic*.[27]

The Rev. Thomas Connellan was, as this excerpt implies, a notorious figure in Dublin. Born in Geevagh, County Sligo in 1854, Connellan's happy childhood was disrupted, at age thirteen, by 'being placed in the charge of a religious brotherhood in a neighbouring town'.[28] He was ordained a priest for the Diocese of Elphin in 1880 and was by all accounts a curate of exceptional ability. He officiated in the Bishop's palace at Sligo for four years, before moving to Strokestown, Co Roscommon, Roscommon Town, then on to St. Peter's, Athlone.[29]

Connellan's birthplace is the home of Kilronan Abbey. In *The Lake*, Fr. Gogarty's 'baptism' occurs within sight of Kilronan Abbey. Connellan published an account of his early life in The *Irish Ecclesiastical Record*.[30] Like Fr. Oliver Gogarty, he was an avid local historian, and well capable of turning a phrase. Disillusioned with a church he had been coerced into joining in the first place, Fr. Thomas Connellan faked his own death in Lough Ree and absconded to England. In his memoir, *Hear the Other Side*, he recalls the experience.

Tuesday, September 20th, 1887, was my last day on the Shannon.

... After breakfast my parish priest had a talk with me about certain schools of which I had charge, and then I walked out of St Peter's forever. I had sent a Gladstone bag containing a secular suit of clothes to the boat, and determined at any risk to have done with my old life. ... [Having] deposited my secular clothes in some underwood, and pushed into the river[,] I then undressed, dodged a fisherman for a little, and having plunged into the water swam ashore ... No baptism by water had ever wrought a more wonderful regeneration than had that plunge into the sunlit Shannon.[31]

Following his 'baptism' and 'death', Fr. Thomas Connellan was born again as the Rev. Thomas Connellan. In an act of supreme audacity, Connellan returned to Ireland to convert his former brethren in 1889, establishing his evangelical mission at 51b Dawson St, less than half a mile from Moore's residence at 4 Upper Ely Place. Published in the same year, *Hear the Other Side* was a widely read memoir. The twelfth 'revised and illustrated' edition lists 'One Hundred and Seven Thousand' copies. Connellan's caustic depictions of his former colleagues would not look out of place in *Parnell and his Island*. He recalled the more dedicated seminaries at Maynooth: 'The sanctimonious scoundrel, with face expressive as a time-worn tombstone; with eyes fixed upon the ground as if eternally measuring six feet for a grave; with hypocrisy personified in his gait, and speaking in his voice – he will be a success, not alone in Maynooth, but in his afterlife as a priest.'[32]

The charismatic leader of a collaborative circle of converts that included his brother, Connellan even went so far as to revisit Athlone in 1892 as part of his evangelical tour of the Irish countryside. With converts like the Rev. Thomas Connellan based in Dublin, it was little wonder that Moore's 1903 conversion to Protestantism fell short of causing the furore he had hoped for.

Perhaps Moore became aware of the story through his friendship with Fr. Jeremiah O'Donovan, who, as a priest on the verge of leaving the priesthood, had reason to be interested in Connellan. It is certain that Moore read *The Catholic*, and probably *Hear the Other Side* or *Roads from Rome*, a series of personal narratives compiled by the Rev. Charles Stuteville Isaacson and published in January 1903 by the Religious Tract Society. There are many parallels between the true-life story of Connellan and the fictional story of Fr. Gogarty. In the preface to *Roads from Rome*[33] the Rev. Thomas Connellan is introduced as somebody who is carrying on a remarkable work for the evangelisation of Ireland. It is Connellan's narrative that opens the collection. There are no sales figures available for the publication, but it was in its third edition by July 1903.

Connellan also worked his way into the consciousness of Joyce. In *Ulysses*: 'Mr Bloom turned at Gray's confectioner's window of unbought tarts and passed the reverend Thomas Connellan's bookstore, *Why I left the Church of Rome*? Birds' nest women run him.'[34] As a reaction to all of this evangelical activity, The Catholic Association was founded in 1903, with the aim of protecting Catholic business interests against a perceived imbalance of Protestant economic power. 'Catholics are three fourths of the people, the protestants are three fourths of the upper classes.'[35] Like Moore, Connellan was quick to poke fun at the new association, which was chaired by Edward Martyn. Its puritan philosophy – excluding indiscreet Catholics and drunkards – and clandestine nature left the Catholic Association open to ridicule. Connellan wrote a series of articles about the association in the *The Catholic*, which was sent to Joyce by his aunt, Josephine. Connellan maintained that if they were excluding indiscreet Catholics and drunkards, they would have a difficult time recruiting members in rural Ireland. Maurice Moore offered to write an article on the Catholic Association for *Dana*, following requests from Moore to contribute to the periodical in February 1904. Having read the handbook of the Association, Moore was shocked to say the least: 'Did you notice the proposal that there should be dinners in the presence of priests in order that drunkenness may be avoided? Who wrote this handbook?'[36]

Connellan's was the type of story in which George Moore revelled; full of individuality, rebelliousness and integrity. Initially, Moore saw *The Lake* as a story to be included in *The Untilled Field*, but he recognised that it had the potential to be more than a short story. However, though the climax of Connellan's story – the 'baptism' of the lake – was a stimulus to the creation of Fr. Oliver Gogarty, Connellan's psychological journey lacked the inner conflict Moore required for his protagonist. Connellan had been cynical towards Catholicism from the beginning. His defection from the church was as inevitable as it was dramatic. Moore's difficulty lay in creating a credible protagonist who would journey from devout Catholicism to a realisation of the paralysis this Catholicism instilled in an impressionable individual.

An event occurred in George Moore's life during 1902 that would go some way towards solving this difficulty. In February, fatigued by bickering with Yeats and the Coole circle and disillusioned by the apathy of the Gaelic League and others towards him, Moore went to Paris to visit with Edouard Dujardin at his home in the former Impressionist stomping ground of Fountainebleau. The timing was fortuitous as Dujardin's recent experiments with *le monologue intérieur*[37] inspired Moore to adopt a variation of the method in his depiction of the psychological 'inner life' of his protagonist. Moore himself admitted that 'To none have I given so ardent an ear as I have to Edouard Dujardin. I have harvested most profitably in Dujardin's work.'[38] In *Salve*, Moore recalls long theological discussions with Dujardin "til one in the morning',[39] and he appropriated the title of Dujardin's *La Source du Fleuve Chrétien* for the book written by Ralph Ellis[40] in *The Lake*, a character based on Moore's Parisian collaborator. Joyce too harvested profitably from Dujardin's work. Whether Moore was a conduit to this is difficult to ascertain. Joyce claimed to have discovered Dujardin's method of interior monologue separately but as we've seen, the letter to his brother sent after reading *The Lake* does not allude to any prior knowledge of the French author.

Richard Ellman believed that Joyce took the idea of secular baptism from *The Lake*,[41] but there are far more significant connections to be teased out. Moore, referring to *Portrait of an Artist* as a book entirely without distinction, an inferior version of *Confessions of a Young Man*, tells us that Moore was either being facetious, hadn't actually read Joyce's novel, or both. To take this statement seriously, as many have done, is to do Moore an injustice. Moore, even after a cursory reading of *Portrait*, or a summary from an acquaintance that had actually read it, would have recognised that *Portrait* owed more to *The Lake* than it did to Confessions. The fact that Moore made this statement shortly after completing an extensive revision of *The Lake* makes it especially intriguing.

There are similarities between *Confessions* and *Portrait*, not least of all the titles and general premise of both books. The chief character in both novels is a literary persona that gradually develops towards the present mentality of the respective authors, both coming to within two years of their ages when they began writing. There is a continental flair to the styles, or multiple styles, utilised in each novel, and though thirty years separates the two, both were published when the authors were thirty-four years old. While *Confessions* was published almost immediately upon completion, it took some time before

Portrait was serialised in *The Egoist* (1914/15) and eventually published in book form by New York publishers B.W. Huebsch in 1916.

In January 1904, Joyce submitted his essay/story 'A Portrait of the Artist' to *Dana* only to have it rejected. In February of that year, reportedly on his birthday, he began work on *Stephen Hero*, the novel that would eventually become *A Portrait of the Artist as a Young Man*. It is surely significant that he sought out and read *The Lake* when he was still working on early drafts of what would become *Portrait*, following the rejection of his piece by a journal with which Moore was associated. In a letter to his brother on 31 August 1906, Joyce is harshly critical of any Irish writing he happens upon, so his critique of *The Lake* should be assessed bearing this in mind. After writing of articles he read in *Dialogues of the Day* and *The Irish Catholic*, Joyce rants about the literary success enjoyed by Francis Sheehy-Skeffington, Thomas Kettle and

> ... even Dr O.S. Jesus Gogarty. And here I am (whom their writings and lives nauseate to the point of vomiting) writing away letters for ten hours a day like the blue devil on the offchance of pleasing three bad-tempered bankers and inducing them to let me retain my position while at the same time (as a luxury) I am allowed to haggle for two years with the same publisher, trying to induce him to publish a book for which he has an intense admiration. *Orco Dio!*

The Lake is more than a novel concerning the psychological awakening of a prodigal priest. It is a *bildungsroman*, epistolary novel, stream of consciousness, treatise of naturalist philosophy, a Big House novel, a parable, a love story and a beautifully crafted critique of Catholic Ireland. If one looks at the wider social and cultural contexts within which Moore composed *The Lake*, it becomes apparent that the novel was a literary articulation of the cultural milieu in which Moore found himself in Dublin at the *fin de siècle*. Most importantly, both *The Lake* and *A Portrait of the Artist* depict the gradual awakening of an artistic consciousness by carefully mapping the evolving mindscapes of Oliver Gogarty and Stephen Dedalus respectively. Established literary techniques are used by Moore and Joyce as entry points into the more radical realm of interior monologue. Moore utilises the epistolary form to provide a basic framework for the narrative while Joyce introduces Stephen's thoughts as entries into his secret diary. Both protagonists develop from a position where they idealise religion only to become disillusioned, a condition they combat through asceticism before eventually casting off restraints they realise are self-imposed.

In *The Image*,[42] Irish novelist John McGahern suggested that to look closely at one's own life is not only a kind of reading but it may also become a kind of writing, a way of seeing, of creating one's own private world. McGahern echoes Fr. Gogarty's meditation when he defines 'The Vision, that still and private world that each of us possesses and which others cannot see.' It is this unique perspective that is at the heart of an individual artist's vision of reality. For Gogarty, his epiphany occurs when he wakes up to himself, having been paralysed within the world of family, work and tradition. *The Lake* traces the internal journey to a way of seeing the external world through Gogarty's own life. The difference between life and art concerns order or unity. Life is transformed into the central vision of the artist. It is a reflection of the real world seen through a personality, a reflection from the lake in every man's heart.

The defining difference between Fr. Oliver Gogarty and Stephen Dedalus is that of class. Fr. Oliver Gogarty belonged to what Moore considered the new gentry, a gentry every bit as parasitic as the one it had replaced. As his artistic consciousness evolved, he recognised the psychological paralysis this position necessitated and gradually thought his way out of a labyrinth he himself had fashioned. Fr. Gogarty and Stephen Dedalus would cross the water in order to spread their wings and discover life and art. In one final delicious coincidence, Gogarty made his climactic swim to Joycetown in June 1904.

In many ways George Moore deserted the gentry, though as Joyce pointed out in 1912, he still had his property's ten per cent. Joyce, despite an illustrious name and prestigious coat of arms, was never in a position to separate from the gentry. Stephen did have an opportunity to join the new gentry of the Irish clergy, but rejected the awful power available to a priest of God. Like Moore, Joyce too would leave for continental Europe, but rather than being accompanied by a valet and maintained by an estate income, he had his young lover and was close to penniless. Joyce no doubt recognised that his artistic integrity may have been compromised had he possessed the privilege enjoyed by Moore, Lady Gregory and other revivalists, but as the expressed resentment in many of his letters to friends and family illustrates, he would have appreciated the opportunities afforded by having some capital at his disposal. In fairness to Moore, he had sent his valet home. One gets the impression that James Joyce, of the illustrious and ancient family of Joyce, might not have done.

NOTES

1. Joseph Hone, *The Life of George Moore* (London: Victor Gollancz, 1936), p.229.
2. Richard Ellman, *James Joyce* (Oxford: Oxford University Press, 1959).
3. Letter from George Moore to his brother Maurice (NLI MS: 2646).
4. Linda Bennett, 'George Moore and James Joyce: Story-Teller Versus Stylist', *An Irish Quarterly Review*, Vol. 66, No. 264 (Winter, 1977), pp.275–91. In *Memories of George Moore*, Nancy Cunard recalled Moore commenting that ' "The Dead" seemed to me perfection … I regretted I was not the author of it.'
5. George Moore, *The Lake* (London: William Heinemann, 1905, 1906, 1921).
6. James Joyce, *Stephen Hero*, edited by John J. Slocum and Herbert Cahoon (London: Paladin, 1991) p.57.'The Roman, not the Sassenach, was … the tyrant of the islanders.'
7. Luke Gibbons, 'Famished Ghosts: Bloom, Bible Wars and "U.P. up" in Joyce's Dublin', *Dublin James Joyce Journal 2009* (Dublin: UCD, 2009).
8. Martello Tower in Sandycove, ref: Oliver St. John Gogarty *As I Was going Down Sackville St* (Dublin: O'Brien Press 1995 [Originally published 1937]).
9. James Joyce, *A Portrait of the Artist as a Young Man* (London: Penguin, 1996), p.230.
10. Ibid., p.262.
11. Gordon St. George Mark, 'The Joyces of Merview', *The Irish Genealogist*, Vol 8, No 3 (1992).
12. Ibid. (It appears that the Connemara Joyces were a separate branch of the Ardrahan family from that which became the Galway tribe.)
13. As James Hardiman states in his *History of the town and County of Galway* (1820): 'The tribes frequently intermarried', and 'had a singular friendship and attachment to one another'.
14. See Gordon St. George Mark, *The Irish Genealogist*, vol.8, no.3 (1992).
15. There is another relevant exchange of title. In 1792, the year Moore of Alicante returned to Mayo, Walter Joyce of Merview (1763–1853) sold his Mayo lands to Isidore Blake of Towerhill for £4,100 (NLI: MS. 10,789).
16. There are a number of letters extant from both Dominick Browne and Martin J. Blake to George and Maurice Moore concerning the Moore/Browne/Blake family history. They trace the family back to Sir Thomas More (NLI: Maurice Moore Papers, MS: 10,566).
17. Letter (ALS) from George Moore to his brother Maurice (NLI, MS: 2646).
18. Richard Ellman (ed.), *Letters of James Joyce: Volume Two* (London: Faber and Faber, 1966).
19. Ibid., p.152.
20. Ibid., p.154.
21. Ibid., p.154.
22. Mr. Harding was a literary persona employed by George Moore in a number of early works.
23. See Ellman, *Letters of James Joyce: Volume Two*.
24. Ibid., p.157.
25. W.B. Yeats in John Kelly and Ronald Schuchard (eds), *Collected Letters: Vol IV* (Oxford: Oxford University Press, 2005), p.1002, n.3.
26. Fr. Jeremiah O'Donovan is a good entry point to any discussion of *The Lake*, and indeed to any discussion concerning the complexities attached to cultural nationalism in Ireland during this period. Administrator of Loughrea parish in County Galway, O'Donovan was active in the Gaelic League and the Irish Agriculture Organisation Society. He was committed to the promotion of Irish crafts and had lectured to the Irish Literary Society on 'Native or Foreign Art' on 5 March 1901. He almost certainly inspired *The Window* and served as a model for the idealistic priests in *The Way Back* and *In the Clay*. True to his ideals, O'Donovan commissioned work by Sarah Purser, Jack B. Yeats and other Irish artists in the construction and decoration of St. Brendan's Cathedral, Loughrea. O'Donovan became disillusioned with the hierarchy of the Catholic Church, left the priesthood in 1904, and travelled to London to become a literary figure. In 1903, he was one of the few subjects upon which W.B. Yeats and Moore agreed fully. Yeats thought of him as 'cultured and intelligent, the best priest I know', while Moore, with typical hyperbole, championed him

as the 'most intelligent man in Ireland'. O'Donovan was a regular visitor to 4 Upper Ely Place.

27. Patrick Maume, *The Long Gestation: Irish Nationalist Life 1891–1918* (Dublin: Gill & Macmillan, 1999), p.93.
28. Rev. Charles Stuteville Isaacson (ed.), *Roads from Rome* (London: Religious Tract Society, 1903).
29. See Gibbons, *Dublin James Joyce Journal* 2009.
30. *Irish Ecclesiastical Record* [of Dublin from 1865–1922], (Dublin: John F. Fowler).
31. Rev. Thomas Connellan, *Hear The Other Side*, 12th ed. (Dublin: Office of 'The Catholic',1889).
32. Ibid., p.13.
33. Isaacson, *Roads from Rome*, Preface written by Right Rev. Hanley C.G. Moule DD, Lord Bishop of Durham.
34. James Joyce, *Ulysses*, Modern Library edition, (New York: Random House, 1961), p.178.
35. Catholic Association Handbook (1903).
36. Letter from George Moore to his brother, Maurice (NLI, MS: 2646).
37. Adrian Frazier, *George Moore 1852–1933* (New Haven and London:Yale University Press, 2000), p.323.
38. George Moore, *Conversations in Ebury Street* (New York: Carra, 1922–24), p.176.
39. George Moore, *Hail and Farewell*, edited by Richard Allen Cave and Colin Smythe, (Buckinghamshire: Colin Smyth, 1976), p.320.
40. Walter Poole in the 1921 edition.
41. Ellman, *Letters of James Joyce: Volume Two*, p.243.
42. John McGahern, 'The Image', in Stanley Van Der Ziel (ed.), *Love of the World – Essays* (Faber and Faber, 2009), p.5.

CHAPTER ELEVEN

Moore and Hemingway

STODDARD MARTIN

There are three or four occasions in *Green Hills of Africa* when Hemingway breaks off from the minutiae of a big-game hunting safari to discuss literary matters. The attempt is to record or simulate chat as it would naturally come up in the course of cocktail rumination after a spate of tracking and shooting. One or two of Hemingway's interlocutors have some literary knowledge and views, but in general it is he who is applied to for pronouncements or, on one occasion,[1] 'literary anecdotes'. Hemingway offers four examples of this phenomenon, all banal. First is of a dinner he had with James Joyce in Paris the night before setting out for Africa; they got drunk and ate a pheasant Hemingway had shot in the Sologne earlier that day. Second is general mention of many occasions of eating and drinking with Ezra Pound during his earlier Paris years. Third comes this:

'Ever heard of George Moore?'

'Chap that wrote "But before I go, George Moore, here's a last long health to you?"'

'That's him.'

'What about him?'

'He's dead.'

'That's a damned dismal anecdote. You can do better than that.'

'I saw him in a book-shop once.'

'That's better. See how lively he can make them?'

'I went to call on him once in Dublin,' P.O.M. said. 'With Clara Dunn.'

'What happened?'

'He wasn't in.'

'By God. I tell you the literary life's the thing,' Pop said. 'You can't beat it.'

'I hate Clara Dunn,' I said.

'So do I,' said Pop. 'What did she write?'.

'Letters,' I said. 'You know Dos Passos?'

And so on to a fourth 'anecdote', or send-up of such.

What's remarkable about this sequence is the place – indeed, presence – of Moore in it. Joyce was Hemingway's most admired contemporary, as he often said. Pound had been his mentor and would remain, despite all, a cared-for friend. Dos Passos, like Pound a compatriot fellow-writer during his first years in Europe, but, unlike Pound, of the generation and a stylistic innovator in prose rather than poetry, was possibly the contemporary to whom he felt closest, famous association with Scott Fitzgerald (unmentioned here) notwithstanding. But Moore? He alone of the four was no personal friend, yet he gets more lines of 'anecdote' than the others. So what, if anything, did Hemingway know of this patrician Anglo-Irish aesthete or his work that Moore should be mentioned in such a wildly improbable locale: a book about big game hunting?

Various possibilities exist. First, *Green Hills of Africa* is an extreme effort in naturalism, as its author/narrator notes,[2] and the onetime disciple of Zola would have been known to Hemingway as pioneer and great prior practitioner of that mode in English – father-figure or rival in the Harold Bloom sense that the ever-competitive young American may have felt he had to 'beat'. Second, *Green Hills* is a self-conscious attempt at novelistic memoir, a genre of which Moore would also have been known as a great inceptor/precursor, not least in *Hail and Farewell*, which Hemingway recommended to young writers and colleagues, *Salve* of its volumes being a special favourite to him.[3] Third, literary asides and vignettes dropped over afternoon beer or around evening's campfire often veer back to the author's apprentice years in Paris,[4] and Moore's *Confessions of a Young Man* would still have been seen as groundbreaking work in that mode in English, a fact Hemingway could not have missed. Fourth, less important, but perhaps as telling: the layout of *Green Hills* and section-head drawings deemed essential to it share in the aesthetic mode of later novels of Moore, notably those of the '20s which Hemingway's first wife read in Paris while he was learning his craft – she was especially taken by *Héloïse and Abélard*, writing to a friend that it 'is a book to set you dreaming. Love is so lovely when it's like that.'[5] Fifth, a concern expressed with sufficient emphasis as to seem thematic is about what happens to male writers as they age,[6] and Moore could have entered Hemingway's mind here not only since he had recently died but also because it is a type of concern he had often rehearsed. Sixth, there is chat about writing as an end in itself,[7] which is what it self-evidently became for Moore in later decades, probably more so than for any major writer in recent memory, at least in English; it is a concept Hemingway seems especially sensitive to at a time when he himself was embarked on the second great experimental phase of his career, daring after the relative failure of *Death in the Afternoon* further loss of status as the great commercial highbrow of his generation. Seventh – and here I indulge in a most tenuous link – *Green Hills*, though set wholly in Africa, ends with the narrator and his party sitting by the Sea of Galilee, an extrinsic locale which might evoke for those who know it the most ambitious outing of Moore's post-*Hail and Farewell* career, *The Brook Kerith*, a book replete with a species of the pastoral power Hemingway seeks out and celebrates during his otherwise apparently predatory pilgrimage.

These possibilities come to mind, and there is not nothing in them, though they fail to pinpoint how extensively Hemingway may have read Moore or rated his work. One *could* downplay allusion in *Green Hills* as an aside lampooning an old buffer famed for rumination, or paying cost-free homage to one lately departed or damning by faint praise a literary approach recognised as having distant kinship to the author's own. All this may be so in part, but it does not preclude the probability that Hemingway paid close attention to Moore during the phase of his early career when his wife was praising *Héloïse*. What might he have been likely to have picked up then, and from whom? Regarding Joyce, Hemingway not only admired and did favours for this Irish master during the time of publication of *Ulysses*, but he also talked extensively to and about him, trading gossip and views on the revolution his book augured. This would have involved reference to traditions Joyce had emerged from, which Joyce himself may have batted away with blarney and an acolyte in Hemingway's position would not have pursued face-to-face without couching it in deference and obliquity; but in discussion with others no such restriction would have applied. Take Sylvia Beach, for example. Both writers were in constant contact with her, Joyce as the 'star' whom she was moving heaven and earth to publish and promote, Hemingway as the hopeful for whom her bookshop – which doubled as lending library – was the salon. What views and tips might she have passed during numerous chats while the Hemingways checked out such titles as *Héloïse* and *Hail and Farewell*? Or take Ford Madox Ford, for whom Hemingway deputised on *transatlantic review*, arguably his most significant job of the era. 'Fordie' would have exhorted him with typically expansive views not only about Joyce and whatever else was new in naturalism and style in the novel, of which he too was a leading if somewhat under-recognised light, but also about predecessors whom any aspirant ought to go to school to. In an essay written in the *Ulysses* year, 'A Haughty, Proud Generation', Ford ranks Moore as 'one of the four or five British novelists of the first flight',[8] others being his onetime collaborator Conrad, his friend the not-long deceased Henry James and the soon-to-die though long inactive as a novelist Thomas Hardy. Hemingway paid close attention to the first two of these, as to European masters whom Moore had known and/or gone to school with, notably D'Annunzio,[9] as well as native mentors like Sherwood Anderson, to whom he owed introduction to his other influential literary preceptor of these years: Gertrude Stein. If Moore came up in conversation with Miss Stein, which seems likely, she would have assayed him not only as a prose stylist, but in relation to his early phase as art student, his friendship with Manet and the Impressionists and his lifelong interest in art, especially French art. Arguably Moore's attempt to use painterly techniques in prose was pathfinding for an author who not only collected the next generation of French painters and knew them well, but tried to adapt Cubism to hers. This synaes-thetic urge – to adapt painterly technique to writerly art, specifically French painterly technique – is one which Hemingway, via Stein, shares with Moore, though in his case Cézanne replaces Manet as exemplar, a fact demonstrated in early chapters of the book he worked on most painstakingly throughout his first decade as writer, *A Farewell to Arms* – a book which when published in 1929 marked the culmination and end-point of his apprenticeship phase of inno-vation in literary naturalism.

Hemingway's dinner with Joyce the night before embarking for Africa in 1933 included discussion of his ambition to write a new kind of book, a novelistic memoir. If he had not already noted resonance of Moore in this, Joyce must have. By then less concerned to cover tracks of his own literary inspiration, Joyce had recently paid Moore the tribute which he signally hadn't at the time of *Ulysses*, when he had famously attributed inspiration to Moore's pal Dujardin[10] without mentioning the more obvious Irish precursor. We know from Joyce's wife that the apparent freedom and scope of Hemingway's *Green Hills* plan triggered envy in an author then tangled up in his own ultimate literary experiment, yet to be titled.[11] Fortified by pheasant and 'the Queen's urine' might Joyce have expressed a regret that he had not gone in a more Moore-ish direction? Did he praise the old buffer; offer faint praise laced with lampoonery; allude to him at all? It would be delicious to think that proximity of recollection of this dinner to the unexpected mention of Moore in *Green Hills* incorporates some echo of some exchange that went on, but we can't say so. Nor can we know exactly what Hemingway had absorbed of Joyce's debt to the previous Irish giant in Paris, even if Joyce may have become less diffident in speaking of it. Joyce, however, was far from the sole figure in Hemingway's Paris to provide a potential, or even principal, conduit to Moore.

He had been friendly with Nancy Cunard since 1922. At the moment when his wife was making the remarks about *Héloïse* quoted above, he was writing to Pound to arrange a visit to Rapallo, his chief worry being that Ezra might skive off to Calabria 'to pursue some horizontal pleasures with Nancy Cunard'.[12] Ezra's pleasures were adulterous: he was married to Yeats's first beloved's daughter but made no bones about faithlessness to her, a fact well-known in the *demimonde* young Ernest was trying to enter; Nancy's sexual vagaries were well-whispered about the *quartier* at this time too. Whether the aspirant author fancied her himself, or even enjoyed a spot of horizontal pleasure with her, is unknown; if so, it might explain the note of rivalry in banter with his elder, Pound, who certainly was her lover and an important one.[13] What we do know is that Hemingway found Nancy's flat in the Île St. Louis 'a convenient stepping off place' on his way home from work at the *Transatlantic Review* to spartan suppers with his wife.[14] These *cinq-à-septs* would have involved literary chat, which must have included allusion to Moore, who was visiting Nancy in this phase and corresponding with her regularly. That taste was moving from Moore's generation to another's would never prompt Nancy to slacken in her devotion to him: her Eure Press – one of a handful of Anglo expat operations to which Pound, Hemingway and the whole 'published in Paris' crew were linked – would bring out a deluxe edition of his *Peronnik the Fool* in 1928.[15] Nancy's later memoirs reveal that in those days 'G.M. was delighted to talk of Turgenev and reminded me of his insistence ... that I should read *Torrents of Spring* and *A Sportsman's Sketches*, two of the finest books ever written.'[16] As every reader of *A Moveable Feast* knows, Turgenev was *ne plus ultra* among models for young Hemingway as he worked in café and garret on his first two books, one a volume of stories inspired by *Sportsman's Sketches*, the other a parodic novella entitled *The Torrents of Spring*. Conclusion? Moore, via Nancy, was Hemingway's invisible tutor and, by way of taste, if not example, perhaps more influential even than the modernist Joyces and Steins.

Why did Hemingway never state this? To the generation of the '20s, however unfairly, septuagenarian Moore must have seemed Jamesianly neuter, passé, having little in common with the apache mores of contemporary *vie bohème*, let alone its aesthetics, which he was pleased to deride, possibly out of annoyance over Nancy's romps with Pound, or even contemporaneous snubbing by Joyce;[17] but gossip re Moore's relation to Nancy may have modified the impression. Rumours of her American expatriate mother's decades-long friendship with a literary giant of the previous generation, and possible pregnancy by him, must have been current in the milieu, going some way to explain why an *outré* young woman should want to pass time with a relic while simultaneously bedding the capo of the Modernists, and share his ideas and encourage reading of his books. That the tyro from suburban Oak Park, Illinois, whose mother had recently run off with a lesbian lover and father would shoot himself partly in consequence, was in this era (and would continue to be) fascinated by unconventional mores is beyond doubt: one need not go into contortions about gender and masculinity such as have bent Hemingway studies in recent years to assert this, only plumb origins of the name of his first hero, Jake Barnes – Natalie *Barney* and Djuna *Barnes*, as prominent among anglophone lesbian writers in the *quartier* as Miss Stein, both lived in Rue Jacob[18] – and consider the twist of his sexual fate – Jake's war wound disables him from making love in other than a sapphic manner – and you can see how they worked on the young writer's psyche. *En passant* note too that the female adventuress who is object of Jake's unfulfillable longings, Brett Ashley, is taken by many to be a portrait of Cunard as much as the oft-cited Duff Twysden.[19]

My point is that Moore may have struck Hemingway as an intriguing precursor on other than merely literary grounds. Mores were of major importance to both, in life as in art. That said, the greater link remains in aesthetic practice, chiefly the painterly mentioned – Manet in one case, Cézanne in the other: poise in the prose of early Moore, angularity of it in early Hemingway.[20] In *Vale* Moore spends pages comparing the two, pages which Hemingway may have found useful in confirming his taste for an artist whom Moore characterises as exercising 'the art of the trowel rather than of the brush' – i.e., elemental and crude in contrast to urban and sophisticated, or just the sort of values a determined young masculinist like Hemingway might find reassuringly primal and frill-less. 'We all have models,' Moore writes in a nearby passage, on portrait painting in words; 'and if we copy the model intelligently, a type emerges'.[21] Regarding the tactic of novelistic memorising, when we set *Hail and Farewell* against *Green Hills*, both works of transit from mid-career, the conclusion is similar. These two devoted naturalists, both figures for whom 'the visible world exists',[22] are nonetheless supreme stylists, neither content journalistically just to record, but compelled to 'render', to intrude a Jamesian term: that is, heighten, daub, enhance, remove, pare down, background and foreground – *aestheticise*, though not in so cumbersome a psychological manner as James (Hemingway's forays into Jamesian prolixity, evident in *Death in the Afternoon*, did not go far). Care for such rendering has a tendency in both cases towards the implication that literary endeavour may be aimed less to convey content for its own sake than to do so beautifully, artistically, in more ideal form; or, if it proves resistant to that, satirically. The antagonistic element in this process is similar for both: demands of a society or civilisation which interrupt the grander melody, the more profound natural picture or arrangement, operating like a figurative 'person from Porlock'; so that even if society/civilisation is the ostensible topic – as often in, say, *Hail and Farewell* – it is, as value, inferior to it. If one doubts this, consider how after *Hail and Farewell* Moore moved on to *The Brook Kerith*, the pastoral chasing the societal as sharply as it would in Hemingway's valedictory *Old Man and the Sea*.[23] Here, the focus on natural existential struggle contrasts with the irritable social positioning that consumed characters in *To Have and Have Not*, a novel set in similar milieu and the final work from this middle phase of experimentation to which *Green Hills* is central.

As a foray into the genre of Moore-ish memoir, *Green Hills* is not a ringing success; triumph had to wait for *A Moveable Feast*, the 'memoir of [his] dead life' published shortly after Hemingway's own suicide. But its urge to experiment, as in other outings, shows Hemingway's sympathy with Moore's restlessness amid genres and his tendency to travel in a similar direction when trying out new ones. Avoiding the cul-de-sacs entered by more famous mentors – Hemingway almost never followed paths blazed by Joyce or Stein, and his homages to them are in this sense lip-service – he might find in Moore an eminently *serviable* model, always making new departures worth considering. As experimenter, he shared in Moore's instinct always to keep one foot on the ground of readability; whatever elitism he felt, he never jettisoned comprehensibility à la *Finnegans Wake* or *The Making of Americans*, even if he typed the latter for Stein during nights at *Transatlantic Review* and imitated snatches of it in early tales. The sensibility of Moore was simply closer. We can see this in both writers' development of dialogue, where actual conversations come to seem less important than 'rendered' ones, rendered ones to morph into imaginary ones and imaginary ones into those with the self. The process could become faintly alarming in Hemingway, as in the great novel he wrote when coming out of his middle phase: *For Whom the Bell Tolls* occasionally mixes hero's and author's and omniscient narrator's tenses and referents and even identities in ways that can seem otiose and/or unconscious. With Moore an analogous development proceeds with characteristic lightness of touch, causing the reader less worry as to whether incipient psychological damage may be at work in the author. But then the *homme moyen sensuel* did not torment himself with alcoholic, sexual, physical and behavioural excesses such as runaway celebrity increasingly imposed on his American successor.

One could go further and assess parallels in both writers' techniques of digression, moral observation and other devices rarely if ever used in later works of Joyce or Stein, or even of Hemingway's friend and fellow experimenter Dos Passos. However, a dance on the head of a pin should not carry on *ad absurdam*. On the other hand, to shy away from it – as this case, I think, shows – is to risk overlooking some of the more tantalising relations buried in literary histories.

NOTES

1. Ernest Hemingway, *Green Hills of Africa* [1936] (New York: Scribner's, 1954), pp.190–2.
2. Ibid., p.28.
3. Fraser Sutherland, *The Style of Innocence* (Toronto: Clarke, Irwin & Co, 1972), p.83. Mention of *Salve* comes in a letter to Max Perkins, 14 February 1927, and of the high rank of *Hail and Farewell* among memoirs in one to Scott Fitzgerald, 22 or 29 October 1929 (Carlos Baker (ed.), *Selected letters of Ernest Hemingway* [New York: Scribner's, 1981], pp.246, 309).
4. *Green Hills*, pp.19, 75, etc.
5. Michael Reynolds, *Hemingway: The Paris Years* (Oxford: Blackwell, 1989), pp.99–100.
6. *Green Hills*, p.30.
7. Ibid., p.32.
8. See Adrian Frazier, *George Moore 1852–1933* (London: Yale University Press, 2000), pp.421, 570.
9. D'Annunzio's innovative novel *Nottorno* appeared in French in the *Ulysses* year and was reviewed favourably by Pound in *The Dial*. My essay on Hemingway's interest in the Italian appeared in *Quarterly Review* (Autumn 2011). Moore's interest in D'Annunzio I discussed at a British Victorian Literature Association conference at Salford (September 2007), a lecture at St. Catherine's College Oxford (May 2008) and the Moore conference at Hull (September 2008). Others of Hemingway's European masters/models included his beloved Turgenev, of whom I speak further on, and the 'true Penelope' of Flaubert (Pound's formulation).
10. His famous inclusion of Dujardin at the luncheon Sylvia Beach held to celebrate publication, on the basis that Dujardin's pioneering use of *monologue intérieur* in *Les Lauriers sont coupé* (1886) inspired the method of *Ulysses*. One would have thought an equally, if not more, obvious inspiration came from the wanderings of Moore around Dublin in *Salve* (Vol. 2 of *Hail and Farewell* [1912]) including not only the geography of the novel but some of its glimpsed inhabitants, such as Æ, Oliver St. John Gogarty and John Eglinton.
11. Brenda Maddox, *Nora: A biography of Nora Joyce* (London: Minerva, 1988), p.329. 'One night when they were dining with the Hemingways, Joyce marvelled at Hemingway's African adventures and worried aloud that perhaps his books were too suburban. "Ah, Jim could do with a spot of that lion-hunting," Nora told Hemingway. The very thought terrified Joyce. He protested that he would be unable to see the lion. Nora replied, "Hemingway'd describe him to you and afterwards you could go up and touch him and smell of him. That's all you'd need."' This may be the dinner to which Hemingway refers in *Green Hills*. See also Carlos Baker, *Ernest Hemingway: A Life Story* (New York: Scribner's, 1969), p.247.
12. See note 5, above.
13. Lois Gordon in *Nancy Cunard: Heiress, Muse, Political Idealist* (New York: Columbia University Press, 2007) suggests that the affair began in 1921 and lasted sporadically through Pound's Paris years, probably until he met Olga Rudge. Her chapter 'In Love with the Artist-God' (99–106) includes partial quotation from Nancy: 'The "sharp/straight flame" of Pound's love "is silent", although "like a saint" it performs its ministrations and lends her "a steadfast radiance"'. Moore must have been aware of the affair and possibly deplored it; Nancy's mother surely would have; and one might extrapolate that some of Moore's invective vs *vers libre* and modernist aesthetics to Nancy in 1922 (Frazier, p.427 etc.) had an origin in jealousy, envy and or paternal ire. An intriguing sidelight to this is that it was Pound who in 1916 persuaded Lady Cunard to persuade the British authorities to award Joyce a grant on which to subsist in order to carry on writing *Ulysses*, persuasions that were witnessed by Moore and Nancy from another part of the famed Emerald's London salon.
14. See Kenneth Lynn, *Hemingway* (New York: Simon & Schuster, 1987), p.238.
15. See Joseph Hone, *The Life of George Moore* (London: Victor Gollancz, 1936), p.423–4.
16. Hugh Ford (ed.), *Nancy Cunard: brave poet, indomitable rebel* (Chilton Book Company, 1968), p.12. *A Sportsman's Sketches* was a book Hemingway borrowed from Sylvia Beach 'time and again' (Lynn, 154).
17. See note 7 above, cf. Frazier, p.427.
18. Lynn, *Hemingway* p.323.
19. Gordon, *Nancy Cunard*, p.126.
20. Moore's opinion on Cézanne, notably in comparison to Manet, can be found in *Vale* (Vol. 3 of *Hail and Farewell* [1914], London: Heinemann, 1947, pp.109–10): 'I thought of Manet, and we congratulated ourselves on the advancement of our taste, forgetful that the next

generation may speak of Cézanne's portraits as the art of the trowel rather than of the brush.' That Moore was painting versions of Manet portraits in words, especially in these memoirs, can be in little doubt.

21. Ibid., pp.147–8.
22. A phrase Moore's friend Arthur Symons frequently quoted from Gérard du Nerval.
23. Where did Hemingway get his most famous title? Could he have possibly remembered, subconsciously or not, a sentence in *Vale* (p.81) describing in decline the painter friend of Moore's Paris youth, Lewis Hawkins? 'An old man from the sea, I said, whom I cannot shake off.' Hemingway's marlin 'cannot shake off' the hook Santiago puts into him; nor in turn can Santiago 'shake off' his melancholy struggle with the sea and the fish, fate and the elements.

CHAPTER TWELVE

The Dandyism of George Moore

MELANIE GRUNDMANN

The figure of the dandy first appeared in the early nineteenth century in England at the court of the prince regent George IV. The dandy was marginalised in the following, morally austere reign of Queen Victoria. In France, however, the dandy was discovered and refined by artists in the 1830s and after. Towards the end of the Victorian era, the dandy was reintroduced into the English cultural movement through artists such as Oscar Wilde and Max Beerbohm. George Moore, however, is hardly to be found in the annals of dandyism, even though Jacques-Émile Blanche called him 'le plus grand dandy des Batignolles'.[1] Moreover, Théodore Duret once described Moore as 'a golden-haired fop',[2] an aesthete long before Wilde became infamous. Finally, Moore imagined himself as a 'blasé roué … rotten with literature and art'.[3] Both, the fop and the roué, were predecessors of the dandy dating back to the eighteenth century.[4] These imputations and self-attributions clearly position Moore in the tradition of dandyism. In this chapter, I would like to investigate the dandyism of George Moore, a man who had been active in promoting French writers, artists, and styles in English culture since the 1880s. The constant remodelling and masking of his persona throughout his life and works, which becomes most apparent in Moore's multiple autobiographies – from his *Confessions of a Young Man* (1886), to the *Memoirs of my Dead Life* (1906) and the three volumes of *Hail and Farewell* (1911–1914) – suggest a dandyistic self as much as Moore's devotion to art and artistic representation of life.

In his sartorial satire *Sartor Resartus* (1833) Thomas Carlyle outlined the public image of the dandy as 'a clothes-wearing man'.[5] However, dandyism first and foremost is an intellectual phenomenon. The dandy acts as the preserver of aristocratic values in what he perceives as a time of cultural demise, that is, an era of a rising bourgeoisie and democracy. Confronted with a new morality that focuses on utilitarianism, equality, assimilation and respectability, the dandy aims for individuality, superiority and eccentricity. The dandy's claim for originality leads to opposition to bourgeois society. A dandy asserts his originality by stylising himself into a work of art. Ultimately, the dandy is a utopian figure. Single representatives of this class only approximate this mythical figure and will all look different while sharing some of the key characteristics: vanity, egotism, nonconformity, sarcasm, wit, an ambiguous sexuality, ennui, estrangement, aestheticism, impertinence, dilettantism, oppositional behaviour, and, of course, fashionable appearance. These aspects have been gathered by a comparative reading of the two first and most influential works on dandyism, Charles Baudelaire's essay 'The Dandy'[6] (1863) and Jules Barbey d'Aurevilly's *On Dandyism and George Brummell* (1845).[7] There is no definite proof that Moore had read either one of these works, but he was very well acquainted with French realistic and naturalistic literature in general, as well as with the works of Baudelaire, whose *Fleurs du Mal* (1857) influenced Moore's own *Flowers of Passion* (1878). George Brummell was no stranger to Moore. He paradoxically called Brummell 'one of Nature's triumphs'.[8]

GEORGE MOORE AS A DANDY

The most superficial yet defining aspect of dandyism is a fashionable appearance. Moore admitted not being good at clothes,[9] Édouard Manet spoke of his 'somewhat eccentric appearance'.[10] Susan Mitchell claimed he was the only man in Dublin 'that walked fashionably', in fact, the only 'man of fashion' in Ireland at all.[11] Nancy Cunard remembered Moore 'smartly dressed: a top hat, a white or grey waistcoat, a pair of dove-coloured gloves in one hand'.[12] Mostly, his suits were 'quiet, well-cut if sometimes rather crumpled, darkish and of good quality. Often, to be sure, he had a rich silk tie on, and sometimes a very high, very stiff white collar. Above all, what a personality there was in those slow-moving, critical, appraising hands, often in long, soft shirt-cuffs done up so tightly.'[13] The quiet quality of his clothes is reminiscent of the most famous of all dandies, Beau Brummell, whose conspicuous inconspicuousness set new standards in male fashion. The elaborately draped 'stiff white collar' was the dandy's most visible trademark. When Brummell fled the British Island from his creditors, he left a note saying 'Starch is the thing',[14] thus answering the open question of how he had managed to create his trendsetting stiff, white collars. Finally, the emphasis on his 'personality' accentuates that, ultimately, it is not what you wear, but how you wear it that matters most, or, as Baudelaire wrote: 'Contrary to what many thoughtless people seem to believe, dandyism is not even an excessive delight in clothes and material elegance. For the perfect dandy, these things are no more than the symbol of the aristocratic superiority of his mind.'[15] In his memoirs of his time in France, though, Moore admits: 'hours were spent at the tailors considering different patterns; at the hosiers turning over scarves, neckties and shirts of many descriptions, frilled and plain ... to be ridiculous has always been *mon petite luxe*'.[16] Moore had been familiar with this material side of dandyism from early childhood. His father's toilet-table had been 'covered with cut-glass phials of macassar oil, pots of bear's grease, many kinds of ivory brushes, tortoise-shell combs of all sorts and sizes, some destined for the hair of the head, some for the whiskers, relics of the days of his dandyhood, for he must have been a great dandy'.[17] Despite his youthful fancy in clothing,[18] Moore came to prefer simplicity in dress because he had discovered 'that whosoever adorns himself will soon begin to adorn his verses, so robbing them of that intimate sense of life which we admire in Verlaine'.[19] This conviction was probably inspired by Manet, whom Moore quotes as saying that 'a serious writer cannot be expected to put on fancy dress'.[20] Dress impacts the artistic faculty of its wearer. The intellectual superiority of the dandy is externalised in an elegant yet accentuated attire. Moore is said to have fascinated less by his fashionable appearance, than by his 'charmingly, courteous manner'.[21] He repeatedly managed to appear 'the most distinguished person present',[22] thus proving to be well-versed in how to wear his clothes.

ELOQUENCE AND WIT

The dandy's fascination not only emanates from his fashionable appearance but also from his witticisms. It is through sarcasm, paradoxes, and witty remarks that the dandy astonishes, entertains, and irritates. In this way he exercises power over people. Moore was a passionate discourser. Cunard primarily remembered his mode of speaking, the tone of his voice, the French verbiage and Moore's gestures: 'no one spoke at all like him, no one else's mind worked like his in all its paradoxical, individual Irish brilliance',[23] and 'whatever he told, he told with style'.[24] Moore loved to talk art and literature until early in the mornings. His writings entertained, less because of expertise than style.[25] He possessed the rare gift of writing about nothing in an exquisite style. Moore was characterised as 'playful, garrulous, an aggressive socialiser, and an exasperating wit'.[26] Cunard saw him as curious and eccentric: 'he was full of mischief and a tease',[27] and 'extremely witty'.[28] He was known for his naive sentences, his sarcasm, provocative tirades, and his 'delight in shocking'.[29] Moore himself soberly remarked: 'if there were nobody to shock, our trade would come to an end',[30] following Baudelaire who had stated that the dandy's doctrine is 'the pleasure of causing surprise in others, and the proud satisfaction of never showing any oneself'.[31] Moore indeed possessed the cold sovereignty of the dandy. He could utter the most violent remarks in a cold-blooded manner.[32] Moore polarised – so much so, that no one was indifferent towards him.[33] Accordingly, Moore's conversation was interspersed with taboo topics which guaranteed a shocking effect:

> He was a beautiful conversationalist. Yet the subjects, the subjects! Was it really permissible to go on so much, for instance, about Catholicism, in such a flippant vein? Such queries were often silenced by the hostess who pointed out that George Moore was the life and soul of the party; he must not, she said, be taken so seriously as all that, do you not see how he exaggerates, some of it is pure childishness![34]

The sincerity of Moore's remarks is downplayed by the hostess in order to rebut Moore's provocative assertions. This indicates a transgression of accepted cultural norms which is constitutive of the dandy's performative behaviour. Transgressions of this kind pervade many of Moore's literary works as well. It is through the portrayal of taboo topics such as rape (*A Mere Accident*, 1887), homosexuality (*A Drama in Muslin*, 1886; 'Hugh Monfert' in *Celibate Lives*, 1927), suicide (Mike Fletcher, 1889), or emancipation (*Evelyn Innes/Sister Theresa*, 1898/1901; 'Mildred Lawson' in *Celibates*, 1895) that Moore as narrator provokes and fascinates his readers at the same time.

AMBIGUOUS SEXUALITY

The dandy does not act on impulses but after due consideration. According to Baudelaire, the dandy must 'strengthen the will and school the soul'.[35] He abhors the instinctual masses and glorifies a cultivated mind. His disdain of the contemporary state of civilisation easily leads to the refusal of reproduction and the willing acceptance of celibacy. Women are often seen as the embodiment of nature and instincts. 'Woman is the opposite of the dandy,' declared Baudelaire, because she is 'natural/instinctive'.[36] Thus, the dandy appears as artificial and spiritual. This dichotomy is central in many of Moore's works, especially in the stories revolving around John Norton.[37] Moore himself rejected marriage. To him, it meant routine, a life devoid of surprises and mysteries. Marriage was degrading to an individual. A dandy would only marry for money, hence the topos of the rich widow in the dandyistic discourse. Indeed, Moore once courted a Miss Rose but soon gave up on this after he realised that she had a mere eight hundred pounds per annum at her disposal.[38] Moore also refrained from procreation. He did not intend to increase 'the great evil of human life'.[39] In his disdain for the state of contemporary society and in his striving to turn himself into a piece of art which can only be everlastingly beautiful when it is dead, the dandy is inevitably driven to suicide, a recurring theme in Moore's literary characters from Mike Fletcher to Lewis Seymour, from Evelyn Innes to Lady Helen. Moore asserted that he refrained from suicide himself because he wanted to act as a worthy example to others to refrain from love. The worst crime was putting a child into this world.[40]

So, strong self-control can be detected in Moore. The artistic self that he presented to the world preferred erotic adventures on a discursive level rather than on practical terms.[41] Indeed, the dandy is spiritually minded. Sexual impulses are inconsistent with the self-control of the dandy. Furthermore, the sexual act destroys the ideal that had been evoked by the aesthetic mind. The recurring topic of celibacy in his novels reflects Moore's own tendency towards abstinence. Further, it symbolises his eagerness for independence, which he saw threatened by any kind of fixation, such as women, business, society, religion. This egotism is characteristic of the dandy, as Baudelaire remarked when he called dandyism 'a kind of cult of the ego which can still survive the pursuit of that form of happiness to be found in others, in woman for example, which can even survive what are called illusions'.[42]

AESTHETICISM

The dandy stylises himself to become a work of art to protest against a bourgeoisie that preaches uniformity, compliance, and utilitarianism. From childhood on, Moore had developed a passion for art. He never conceived a common occupation. As an artist, he would be independent of rules and regulations. Moore aimed to develop a unique personality. Accordingly, his artistic formation did not take part in any academy but in the cafés of Paris. Art enabled the dandyistic formation of this unique personality: 'The work of the great artist is himself.'[43] Similarly, Baudelaire had stated that dandies 'have no other status but that of cultivating the idea of beauty in their own persons'.[44] The artist remains unaffected by dogmas, beliefs and arguments. Education is the antithesis to art, according to Moore, because it brings everyone to a single level. Education and democracy destroy individuality by making people equal. Moore postulated self-education through art. Art originates in the artist's individual expression of external influences: 'Art is a personal rethinking of life from end to end, and for this reason the artist is always eccentric.'[45] Art is the perfect tool for the formation of the dandy's unique personality because it is singular rather than commonplace. For the dandy, life becomes art and art becomes life. Accordingly, Moore stated that art was his life and outside of art he had no life.[46]

He was never interested in nature, unless it was art's sake. The dandy aestheticizes because art offers an escape from 'the animality of human existence,[47] which the dandy is eager to emancipate from. The dandy's striving for independence first and foremost requires him to overcome natural impulses, that is independence from his own nature. He creates his ownpersona which is artistic and consequentially artificial. This creation of an ideal, independent self explains Moore's rejection of any kind of fixation such as marriage, which would lead him into duties and habits that would destroy his independence.

ESTRANGEMENT

The mediocrity and vulgarity of a democratic people caused Moore to feel convinced of his own intellectual superiority. Moore fits Baudelaire's description of dandies, who 'all share the same characteristic of opposition and revolt; all are representatives of what is best in human pride, of that need, which is too rare in the modern generation, to combat and destroy triviality'.[48] Moore viewed modern civilisation as decadence instead of progress. He lamented the demise of handcraft in favour of mass production and machinery. The dandy's originality needed to be asserted in times of mass-market commodities. To Moore, the malady of democracy was the assimilation of the weak and the strong. He preferred the subsistence of an elite and thus an ideology of strength, grandeur and glory. This coincides exactly with Baudelaire's view on dandyism as 'the idea of establishing a new kind of aristocracy, all the more difficult to break down because established on the most precious, the most indestructible faculties, on the divine gifts that neither work nor money can give. Dandyism is the last flicker of heroism in decadent ages.'[49] Only a world of irregularities and injustices would avert the boredom of mediocrity. However, the dandy's ideals were lost. Surrounded by numb masses, 'we, the great ship that has floated up from the antique world',[50] is doomed to sink. Heroic times of the past, such as Antiquity or the Middle Ages, are important reference points for the dandy. Moore himself was born into feudalism and deeply rooted in the spirit and traditions of the eighteenth century.[51] He was aware of belonging to the class of landlords, the basis of whose superiority was disappearing; that intensified his feeling of estrangement. Antiquity, too, affected him more than the present age, due to its elegance, art of conversation and aesthetic achievements.[52] The dandy fled the contemporary age of democratisation because it led to conformity and ennui. Furthermore, aesthetic and cultural values were lost because the burgeoning masses dictated a taste that was vulgar and coarse. What was left in these times was snobbery: 'the snob is now the ark that floats triumphant over the democratic wave; the faith of the old world reposes in his breast, and he shall proclaim it when the waters have subsided'.[53] When comparing this sentence of Moore with a phrase from Baudelaire's essay on the dandy, it becomes clear that Moore is using the word 'snob' for the idea of dandyism: 'But alas! the rising tide of democracy, which spreads everywhere and reduces everything to the same level, is daily carrying away these last champions of human pride, and submerging, in the waters of oblivion, the last traces of these remarkable myrmidons.'[54] Both writers use an imagery of floating and sailing. While Moore was positive about a return of the dandy, Baudelaire appeared rather pessimistic. However, he added: 'Here in France, dandies are becoming rarer and rarer, whereas amongst our neighbours in England the state of society and the constitution ... will, for a long time yet, leave room for the heirs of Sheridan, Brummell and Byron, always assuming that men worthy of them come forward.'[55] I would like to argue that Moore viewed himself as one of these heirs.[56]

OPPOSITIONAL BEHAVIOUR

According to Baudelaire, dandyism 'is, above all, the burning desire to create a personal form of originality, within the external limits of social conventions'.[57] Moore's originality is as paradoxical as the myth of the dandy demands. His early works were heavily influenced by French writers; which, on first sight, proves rather unoriginal. However, in puritan England, where these works were condemned and hardly accessible, Moore achieved the intended effect of entertaining and surprising the audience, as much as in his more original later works. As Barbey d'Aurevilly demanded: 'one of the consequences of Dandyism, one of its principal characteristics – or rather its character in more general terms – is always to produce the unexpected. For this the mind that toils under the yoke of logical rules is unprepared.'[58] Moore loved to shock. His brother Maurice lamented: 'It's a great pity that you always set yourself in opposition to all received ideas.'[59] Moore admitted deliberately choosing disconcerting topics for his writings that would irritate the public.[60] He put on the mask of the *enfant terrible* of English literature and repeatedly taunted the audience about his 'perverse mind'.[61] However, serious convictions motivated this rather bombastic masquerade. Moore demanded absolute liberty for the artist, thus paving the way for realism and naturalism in England. He accepted no taboos and self-censorship. Moore was too haughty to compromise and after heavy disputes with the circulating libraries, publishers and critics decided to publish his books to subscribers only. He deliberately addressed a select audience, as other dandies did before him, and was consciously writing for 'the few',[62] as Stendhal had written for the happy few. Moore's directness and his detailed narrations of human nature were considered to be immoral and coarse. He was called one of the most courageous writers of his time,[63] because he dared to challenge the artistic traditions of England. Back in Ireland, Moore supported the Irish independent theatre movement to show 'the strange, the unknown, the unexpected'[64] in a largely taboo-ridden society. Obviously, Moore was on the very limits of social conventions. He confirms Barbey d'Aurevilly's view on dandyism which 'plays games with the rules while continuing to respect them. It suffers from their constricting effects and takes its revenge, tolerating them all the while. It invokes them even as it breaks free from them. It governs them and is governed by them in its turn.'[65] From early childhood on Moore had felt the urge to rebel against authorities of any kind.[66] He fought literary censorship, puritanism and Catholicism, all of which suppress the individual. Throughout his life Moore was looking for likeminded, independent personalities. He was an elitist, detaching himself from the 'common herd',[67] just as Brummell had done. He did not act according to conventions, but followed his own rules. English society, and Irish society too, seemed sterile to Moore. Thus Moore could say: 'I was born, I live, I shall die a peculiar man. I couldn't be commonplace were I to try,'[68] affirming Baudelaire's dictum that 'a dandy can never be a vulgar man'.[69]

NOTES

1. M. Delbourg-Delphis, *Masculin singulier. Le dandysme et son histoire* (Paris: Hachette, 1985), p. 17.
2. See M. Elwin, 'George Moore: The Comedy of a Card' in M. Elwin, *Old Gods Falling* (Freeport and New York: Books for Libraries Press, 1971), p. 57.
3. J. Hone, *The Life of George Moore* (New York: Macmillan, 1936), p. 188.
4. The French roué was a seducing libertine without virtue and principles, see D. Stanton, *The Aristocrat as Art* (New York: Columbia University Press, 1980) p.55–56. The British fop was a rather effeminate progenitor of the dandy with a strong focus on theatricality and performativity, see M. Miller, *Slaves to Fashion: Black Dandyism and the Styling of Black Diasporic Identity* (Durham and London: Duke University Press, 2009), p. 8.
5. H. D. Traill (ed.), *The Works of Thomas Carlyle* (Cambridge: Cambridge University Press, 2010), p. 217.
6. C. Baudelaire, 'The Painter of Modern Life. IX. The dandy.', in C. Baudelaire, *Selected Writings on Art and Artists* (Cambridge: Cambridge University Press, 1972), pp. 419–422.
7. J. Barbey d'Aurevilly, 'On Dandyism and George Brummell', in G. Walden, *Who is a Dandy?*(London: Gibson Square Books, 2002), pp. 63–175.
8. G. Moore, *Hail and Farewell!*, vol 1 (New York: Appleton, 1925), p. ix.
9. See G. Moore, *Hail and Farewell!*, vol. 2 (New York: Appleton, 1925), p. 58.
10. T. Gray, *A Peculiar Man: A Life of George Moore* (London: Sinclair-Stevenson, 1996), p. 87.
11. Ibid.
12. N. Cunard, *Memories of George Moore* (London: Hart-Davis, 1956), pp. 25–26.
13. Ibid., p. 26.
14. S. Vincent, *The Anatomy of Fashion: Dressing the Body from the Renaissance to Today* (Oxford: Berg, 2009), p. 29.
15. Baudelaire, 'The Painter of Modern Life', p. 420. Similarly Barbey d'Aurevilly: 'People who see things from a narrow perspective have got it into their heads that it was above all a question of dress, of external elegance - that Dandies were merely dictators of fashion, bold and felicitous masters of the art of making one's toilet. It is most certainly that, but it is other things besides. [...] Dandyism is a whole way of being.' (Barbey d'Aurevilly, 'Of Dandyism and of George Brummell', pp. 78–79.)
16. Moore, *Hail and Farewell!*, vol. 2, p. 198.
17. Ibid., p. 405.
18. Moore remembers himself in Paris, 'a magnificent, young Montmartrian, with a blond beard *à la Capoul*, trousers hanging wide over the foot, and a hat so small that my sister had once mistaken it for her riding-hat' (Moore, *Hail and Farewell!*, vol. 1, p. 9).

19. Ibid., p. 42.
20. G. Moore, *Confessions of a Young Man* (London: Heinemann, 1928), p. 247.
21. Cunard, *Memories of George Moore,* p. 50.
22. Hone, *The Life of George Moore,* p. 125.
23. Ibid., p. 29.
24. Ibid., p. 172.
25. B. Rascoe, 'George Moore. The Man of Letters' in B. Rascoe, *Titans of Literature, from Homer to the Present* (New York: G. P. Putnam's Sons, 1932), pp. 474–75.
26. H. Gerber (ed.), *George Moore in Transition. Letters to T. Fisher Unwin and Lena Milman, 1894–1910* (Detroit: Wayne State University Press, 1968), p. 25.
27. Cunard, *Memories of George Moore,* p. 24.
28. Ibid., p. 28.
29. Ibid, pp. 26–27.
30. G. Moore, *Hail and Farewell!,* vol. 1, p. 47.
31. Baudelaire, 'The Painter of Modern Life', p. 420.
32. See J. Abthorne, *The Opinions of John Abthorne on the Arts and Living* (London: Heinemann, 1920), p. 115.
33. Cunard, *Memories of George Moore,* p. 27.
34. Ibid., pp. 29–30.
35. Baudelaire, 'The Painter of Modern Life', p. 421.
36. C. Baudelaire, *Intimate Journals* (London and New York: Syrens, 1995), p. 31. In contrast, Barbey d'Aurevilly says, 'a Dandy has something of the woman about him' (Barbey d'Aurevilly, 'Of Dandyism and of George Brummell', p. 137), which illustrates the paradox structure of the dandy figure. With Mildred Lawson Moore portrays a woman who comes very close to being a *femme dandy*. Mildred ultimately fails as a dandy because she never succeeds in realizing her true inner self, that is, she cannot emancipate from her very nature.
37. *A Mere Accident* (1887); 'John Norton' in *Celibates* (1895); 'Hugh Monfert' in *Celibates Lives* (1927).
38. Hone, *The Life of George Moore,* pp. 58–59. See also the patronage of Lewis Seymour by Mrs. Bentham and Seymour's marriage to the rich and influential Lady Helen in George Moore's *A Modern Lover* (1883) and *Lewis Seymour and Some Women* (1917), as well as Mike Fletcher's unexpected inheritance that was willed to him by a rich widow in Moore's novel *Mike Fletcher* (1889).
39. Moore, *Confessions of a Young Man,* p. 185.
40. Ibid., p. 198.
41. Moore 'is happiest when sex is polymorphous: that is, when it is transferred from genital intercourse to touch and talk, sight and speculation, to future prospects or long retrospection, where it can be indefinitely prolonged through thought. Sex that is only speculative, speculations that are sexualized, he preferred to the brief deed of procreation.' (A. Frazier, 'On His Honor: George Moore and Some Women' in *English Literature in Transition, 1880–1920,* vol 35, (4/1992), p. 428.
42. Baudelaire, 'The Painter of Modern Life', p. 420.
43. Moore, *Hail and Farewell!,* vol. 2, p. 269.
44. Baudelaire, 'The Painter of Modern Life', p. 419.
45. Moore, *Hail and Farewell!,* vol. 2, p. 271.
46. Burton, 'George Moore: The Man of Letters', p. 475.
47. Moore, *Confessions of a Young Man,* p. 141.
48. Baudelaire, 'The Painter of Modern Life', p. 421.
49. Ibid., p. 421.
50. Moore, *Confessions of a Young Man,* p. 119.
51. G. Moore, *Conversations in Ebury Street* (New York: Boni and Liveright, 1924), p. 201.
52. G. Moore, *Avowals* (New York: Boni and Liveright, 1919), p. 292.
53. Moore, *Confessions of a Young Man,* S. 144.
54. Baudelaire, 'The Painter of Modern Life', p. 422.
55. Ibid.
56. Moore's estrangement was not only of a temporal kind, but also spatial. His native country, Ireland, he abhorred, due to the dominant forces of Catholicism. His intellectual home was France.
57. Baudelaire, 'The Painter of Modern Life', p. 420.
58. Ibid, p. 80.

59. Moore, *Hail and Farewell!*, vol. 2, p. 37.
60. Ibid, p. 244,
61. Ibid, p. 88; see also Moore, *Confessions of a Young Man*, p. 48 ('I am feminine, morbid, perverse. But above all perverse, almost everything perverse interests, fascinates me.')
62. Moore, *Conversations in Ebury Street*, p. 216.
63. See F. Reid, 'The Novels of George Moore' in *The Westminster Review* 172 (August 1909), p. 200.
64. G. Moore, *Impressions and Opinions* (New York: Bloom, 1972), p. 240.
65. Barbey d'Aurevilly, 'Of Dandyism and of George Brummell', p. 81.
66. See Moore, *Hail and Farewell!*, vol. 1, p. 210.
67. Moore, *Confessions of a Young Man*, p. 157.
68. Gray, *A Peculiar Man*, p. 1.
69. Baudelaire, 'The Painter of Modern Life', p. 420.

REFERENCES

Abthorne, J., *The Opinions of John Abthorne on the Arts and Living* (London: Heinemann, 1920).
d'Aurevilly Barbey, J., 'On Dandyism and George Brummell', in G. Walden, *Who is A Dandy?* (London: Gibson Square Books, 2002), pp.63–175.
Baudelaire, C., 'The Painter of Modern Life. IX. The dandy.', in C. Baudelaire, *Selected Writings on Art and Artists* (Cambridge: Cambridge University Press, 1972), pp.419–422.
Baudelaire, C., *Intimate Journals* (London and New York: Syrens, 1995).
Cunard, N., *Memories of George Moore* (London: Hart-Davis, 1956).
Delbourg-Delphis, M., *Masculin singulier. Le dandysme et son histoire* (Paris: Hachette, 1985).
Elwin, M., 'George Moore: The Comedy of a Card', in M. Elwin, *Old Gods Falling* (Freeport, New York: Books for Libraries Press, 1971), pp.46–76.
Frazier, F., 'On His Honor: George Moore and Some Women', in *English Literature in Transition, 1880–1920*, Vol. 35, (4/1992), pp.423–445.
Gerber, H. (ed.), *George Moore in Transition. Letters to T. Fisher Unwin and Lena Milman, 1894–1910* (Detroit: Wayne State University Press, 1968).
Gray, T., *A Peculiar Man. A Life of George Moore* (London: Sinclair-Stevenson, 1996).
Hone, J., *The Life of George Moore* (New York: Macmillan, 1936).
Miller, M., *Slaves to Fashion. Black Dandyism and the Styling of Black Diasporic Identity* (Durham and London: Duke University Press, 2009).
Moore, G., *Avowals* (New York: Boni and Liveright, 1919).
Moore, G., *Conversations in Ebury Street* (New York: Boni and Liveright, 1924).
Moore, G., *Hail and Farewell*, Vol. 1 (New York: Appleton, 1925).
Moore, G., *Hail and Farewell*, Vol. 2 (New York: Appleton, 1925).
Moore, G., *Confessions of a Young Man* (London: Heinemann, 1928).
Moore, G., *Impressions and Opinions* (New York: Bloom, 1972).
Rascoe, B., 'George Moore. The Man of Letters', in B. Rascoe, *Titans of Literature, from Homer to the Present* (New York: G.P. Putnam's Sons, 1932), pp.472–477.
Reid, F., 'The Novels of George Moore', in The Westminster Review, 172 (August 1909), pp.200–208.
Stanton, D., *The Aristocrat as Art* (New York: Columbia University Press, 1980).
Traill, H.D. (ed.), *The Works of Thomas Carlyle* (Cambridge: Cambridge University Press, 2010).
Vincent, S., *The Anatomy of Fashion: Dressing the Body from the Renaissance to Today* (Oxford: Berg, 2009).

CHAPTER THIRTEEN

George Moore's Correspondence as Social Practice

ELIZABETH GRUBGELD

The letters of George Moore have been edited and annotated in many different volumes, from the *Letters from George Moore to Ed. Dujardin,* published with his encouragement in 1929, to Helmut E. Gerber's 1988 *George Moore on Parnassus.* These diverse compilations have supported biographical portraits and interpretations of Moore's development as a writer and the issues that preoccupied him during specific periods of his life. In *George Moore and the Autogenous Self* (1994), I offered an analysis of his correspondence less concerned with its content than its generic properties as a form of life writing. Drawing from the newly emergent field of epistolary theory, I examined Moore's epistolary autobiography in light of four issues: the development of a consistent authorial persona and his concerns about the reception of that persona if and when his letters might be published;[1] his compulsion to occupy a position of dominance in almost every correspondence; and the manner by which his letters employ narratives by relating stories within themselves, producing storylines to be enacted in the world to which he wrote and engendering further letters which, read together, would in themselves tell a story. Finally, I discussed the way his epistolary narratives provide points of recollection from which the speaker reflects on the most pervasive themes of the letter as a genre: the sorrow of absence, the unfulfilment of desire, the passage of time, and the inevitability of death.[2]

Theorisation of the letter has since turned from its internal properties to its function within epistolary communities and the historical and material conditions surrounding its production. Many studies have analysed correspondence as practiced among very specific groups and, in some cases, argued that key epistolary preoccupations traverse such social contexts. Others have explored the inscription of gendered identities within correspondence, the formative influence of prescriptive guides like the letter-writing manuals that served a rapidly expanding middle class, and the relationship between letter-writing and historical changes such as the development of postal services or the needs of the ever-expanding British Empire and the American frontier. Additionally, several studies have considered the material aspects of epistolary production, such as the transformation of autograph documents into edited, published collections and the recent manifestation of the letter as email, texting, tweeting, Facebook, and the blog, the latter a form Philippe Lejeune has described as 'une synthèse du journal et de la correspondance' in being simultaneously both expressive and transactional, constructing an audience of both the 'alter ego' and readers with embodied as well as virtual lives.[3]

Electronic mail, blogging, and social media may seem far removed from the letters of George Moore, although several important analyses of nineteenth-century correspondence draw parallels between past and present forms of epistolarity.[4] The workings of email and texting resemble the impulsive, spontaneous qualities of many of Moore's letters, his often anxious wait for a reply and expression of impatience when the reply failed to come at once, and his later preference for what we might now call virtual eroticism. The phenomenon of the blog recalls his need for audience and his preference to extemporise at length about his enthusiasms and convictions in a communicatory rather than privately diaristic venue. Moore apparently never kept a diary or journal, and the audience of another appears to have been a requisite factor in his thinking and writing. Exploring the protocols of social media could potentially illuminate the flurries of letters that would spread rumour and innuendo among his friends, especially in Dublin. The social nature of those communications calls our attention to Moore's letters as social acts, as well as autobiographical ones. How did his letters participate within established rhetorics of correspondence and communities of epistolary exchange, and how does seeing his correspondence work as a social practice alter our readings of his letters?

From the outset, his letters reveal a sense of the form's inherent malleability, and throughout his life he continues to use the letter as a vehicle for experimentation in style and voice. Even as a child, he was ready to adjust voice and authorial positioning to gain his point.

Appalled at his son's atrocious grammar, punctuation, and spelling, George Henry Moore required young George to write letters home from school in an effort to improve his control over the English language. The extant letters from this experiment reveal a boy who through craft or ignorance repeatedly manipulates the terms of the injunction to what he hopes will be his own advantage. To his 'dear Papa', he declares, 'I did not willfully disobey your commands about writing you three pages of note paper. I could not as it was impossible for me to do it every day if you will only try it for a week or two you will find it more difficult that you expect just you write me three pages every day you will soon get puzzled about [what] you would say to fill up to three pages.' A few days later he continues to instruct his father on the hardships of the task to which he has been set: 'I am sure that we by acting in concert will do a deel [sic] more good than by scolding me. And as for the three pages a day I think I have made you understand that it is not so easy as you might suppose ... I am sure we will do much good if you will only follow out the advice of this letter.' Although such reluctant epistles cleverly attempt to usurp the role of instructor in their admonitions and wheedling logic, they exhibit none of the usual rituals of letter writing – the standard salutations, inquiries, and closures. In the same letter, the young Moore suggests that were he to 'get a book of those every day letters I could write one out every day and send it to you', but people of his class did not generally use manuals of correspondence.[5] The life-and-letters biographies and histories which undoubtedly filled the extensive library at Moore Hall would have contained correspondences immune from the rigid formulations evident in letters of the emergent classes, were the youthful Moore even to have read them, and there is no evidence and little reason to believe he did. His attempt to bargain his way out from under his father's authority in these letters and claim the role of teacher for himself figures as an early sign of the way he would later grasp for dominance in an epistolary situation with similar audacity and strangely beguiling offensiveness, but it is also a sign of how tractable he found the form.

In adulthood, Moore was either oblivious to the letter's obligation to its addressee or wilfully rejected expectations that the letter should adapt its language and subject matter to the needs of its reader. Thus during the summer of 1877 he writes to his mother about his intrigues with married women, and at the turn of the century sends his brother Colonel Maurice Moore, who was then in the midst of combat in

South Africa, letters railing against the injustice of the war against the Boers. This pattern must derive from temperament rather than ignorance of convention, as he repeatedly apologises for his epistolary behaviour, and in a letter of 1893 offers Maurice a half-hearted apology for having 'written you a long letter all about myself', followed immediately by an sentence of which only the beginning is legible: 'The superficial think that such a letter...'[6] Although the rest of the sentence is unfortunately illegible, Moore appears to retract the apology he had just offered. In another letter to Maurice written during the height of pro-Boer agitation in Ireland, Moore again half-offers, then retracts, an apology: 'But my dear brother ... it is very painful for me to write to you – the circumstances of the war are so painful that I cannot overcome my reluctance ... You will not think me neglectful for you know me well.' As a postscript, he adds, 'On reading over this letter I see it is not the right kind of letter to write. I ought to have written a cheerful gossipy letter. But we do not do what we like.'[7] Apparently the force of what he often called his 'instinct' overwhelms the convention of writing letters of good cheer to a soldier, as well as any effort to alter his tone or content in light of his brother's position as his addressee, because again in a later letter he confesses, 'I feel it to be wrong to write to you in this strain for you are a soldier engaged in a campaign, but I can neither write or speak to anyone without telling him my opinions on this subject.'[8]

With women, particularly those in whom he felt sexual interest, Moore enjoyed replicating the stylistic features of published love letters, and his usual preoccupations with politics or art might take second place to a display of style meant to signify intimate emotion. Although he admired what he called the naturalness and spontaneity of the letters of Mariana Alcoforado, in practice he understood, as Elizabeth Cook points out in her study of epistolary fiction, that 'texts are always more complexly mediated than we first take them to be and ... this is particularly likely to be true of texts that invoke epistolary tropes of immediacy, intimacy, and authenticity.'[9] Mediation, in Moore's case, is more explicit and self-conscious than in many other practitioners of the love letter as he discusses the epistolary styles that charm him within the very letters in which he imitates them, especially the published love letters of the Portuguese nun, Balzac and Evelina Hanska, and Wagner and Mathilde Wesendonck. To imitate these letters was to signal an emotional state of tenderness and absolute sincerity, although paradoxically this apparent state of nature was indicated by the self-conscious flaunting of a literary style. Linda Kauffman notes that in French culture, even in the late twentieth-century, 'to write "a la Portugaise" became a veritable code for a certain style of writing-to-the moment, at the height of intensity and anguish'.[10] Just as Ralph Waldo Emerson and his circle admired what they believed to be passionate letters from Bettina von Armin to Goethe and circulated copies of this published correspondence among their friends, Moore was so enamoured with the letters of Wagner to Mathilde Wesendonck ('I have just read Mathilde's letters and I have read them with tears in my eyes') that he sent a copy to his friend Lord Howard de Walden and dashed off a long, effusive, metaphor-laden love letter to Maude Cunard modelled after what he had been reading.[11] The William Ashton Ellis translation Moore would have known labours under its heavy purple prose, invocations of abstract entities, 'thees' and 'thous', repetitive interjections like 'ah!' and 'alas!,' and mincing allusions to the little dog Mathilde sent to Wagner. Although his letters to Lady Cunard remain effusive to the end, he indulged in such literary mannerisms only during his first infatuation with the famous correspondence; the style is thus very clearly an artifice meant to communicate great sincerity.

On several occasions, Moore attempted to entice female friends to collaborate with him in the production of literary correspondences for publication. Two years after the Wagnerian letter, he suggests to Maude Cunard that they 'begin a correspondence with a view to some possible publication later on. For this correspondence to be interesting it must be sincere and it must be complete; you must confess your frailties and I will answer that my love is above all trans-gressions on your part. … The correspondence will be affectionate, amorous, and literary; each letter should be at least as long as a leading article in *The Times*.'[12] To become involved in such a correspondence, with a scripted content and an assumed, if easily decoded, identity, surely seemed to her socially dangerous and potentially humiliating. Even more to the point, the overt artificiality of the project runs counter to the naïve convention of the amorous letter as a token of another's mind, heart, and body. The 'view to some possible publication later' also belies assumptions about the letter's privacy. As has been well-documented, personal letters in earlier historical periods were rarely private unless they hid some secret; Moore's plan harkens back to the plots of eighteenth-century fiction and that intermediary realm between public and private in which correspondence then resided. By 1907, however, a 'sincere' exchange of letters would carry expectations of privacy, not the public readership that Moore intended.

In a much later series of titillating letter exchanges with various young women, the elderly Moore is even more willing to allow the letter to simulate passion that the body need not perform and to imagine intimate correspondence as destined for public consumption. Although, for instance, he had promised the flirtatious correspondent known as 'Gabrielle' in August 1904 that he would refrain from writing the romantic comedy he had planned to base upon their correspondence, the next month he reported to Edward Dujardin that he was doing just that.[13] Moore speaks in *Hail and Farewell* of 'having so often heard young women say they fear they never can be really in love, because of a second self which spies upon the first, forcing them to see the comic side even when a lover pleads',[14] and accordingly, if the love letter is a form learned by the reading of love letters, no wonder that the writer-self spies upon the self-that-speaks according to the amorous script until finally even the pretence of representation and sincerity falls away and a fictionalised theatrical adaptation is next on the writer's agenda. Moore often declared himself a man of the eighteenth century, when epistolary fiction and collections of love letters, like those of the Portuguese nun and *Héloïse and Abélard*, enjoyed a wide readership and effusive praise for the intimacy and sentiment displayed on their pages. His own participation in a stylised and potentially very public notion of an amorous correspondence also indicates how thoroughly he saw himself as an intermediary figure between an older world that he increasingly valorised and the newer world of market value that he also understood astutely. The intimate could be public, and even produced for public consumption, while simultaneously the fact of the printed page exposes the sensation of privacy between correspondents as an illusion. Elizabeth Cook suggests that such literary correspondences popular during the eighteenth century 'articulate their readers' own experience of the transition from the habits and thought forms of a pre-typographical world – the world Alvin Kernan describes as that of "polite or courtly letters ... primarily oral, aristocratic, amateur, authoritarian, court-centered" – to a culture shaped by the technology and logic of print and the democratised open market of the burgeoning publishing industry. The letter-narrative figures this historical moment between manuscript and print, private correspondence and published text.'[15]

Moore's concept of the amorous familiar letter derives from eighteenth-century models of fictionalised letter-narratives in book form, presenting yet another adaptation of a genre he had seen as infinitely adaptable since his childhood letters to his father and his only partially apologetic expostulations to his brother.

Although models for letter writing rarely produce the self-conscious repudiation of representational claims of sincerity that Moore offers in his amorous correspondence, models for writing do shape the expectations of particular groups of writers and addressees. No one has yet examined the epistolary communities to which Moore belonged. No study of British letters as a literary genre or a cultural practice looks later than the mid-Victorian period analysed in Catherine J. Golden's 2009 *Posting It: The Victorian Revolution in Letter Writing*, and her focus on the effects of the penny post necessarily draws her away from letter writing among people with education and literary propensities. Studies of the letters of individual literary figures like Yeats and Joyce treat correspondence as an adjunct to biography or to their poems, plays, or fictions rather than as an distinct genre, and there exist at present no analyses of letter writing in Ireland as a distinct cultural formation. Yet there is rich material for a culturally based genre analysis of Irish literary correspondences. It would be necessary to ask of these letters some of the same questions one would ask of any discourse community: what sorts of writing personas emerge? How do letters within a community create textual and extratextual narratives about that community? What discourse protocols are common within a group and interpreted in common? And how does individual voice interact with broader cultural practices?

Although, as I have suggested, even an ostensibly private letter with a single addressee adapts its rhetoric from its author's literary and social experience, epistolary acts that are intentionally public and directly involve a larger community are even more revelatory of the ways a speaking self constructs its voice in dialogue with others. The letters Moore wrote to the press in protest of Queen Victoria's planned visit in the spring of 1900 reflect the terms of Moore's participation in a community discourse. Since the spring of 1899, English newspapers had attempted to rally national support for military action that would eventually annex the gold-rich Transvaal Republic to other areas controlled by Great Britain. Dublin, in contrast, experienced what was called at the time, 'Boer Fever',manifesting itself in street rallies, public exhibitions, and letters and articles in the nationalist press. Irish newspapers that had paid little attention to other colonial questions saturated their pages with stories, speeches, editorials, and letters protesting the escalating war against the Boers and even applauding British defeats.[16] When Queen Victoria proposed to visit Ireland in the spring of 1900, with the official purpose of thanking Irish soldiers for their efforts in the war, the projected visit sparked one of many moments in modern Irish history when, as Lucy McDiarmid explains of Irish conflict more generally,

> Large forces explode in a small site. They do not usually cause transformations, but they make visible social change as it is in the process of occurring. And because controversies tend to happen in border areas, unlegislated zones not definitely controlled by any single authority, their conflicts are often decided, if they are decided at all, by bluff and bravado, by performative skills and improvisational flair.[17]

Those in positions of power or influence could not agree as to how Ireland should respond to the Queen's visit or whether the visit was a political ploy, a recruitment effort, or the personal gesture of gratitude it claimed to be. Nationalist response was as mixed as the official response and that of the general public. Although the visit itself passed without major disruption – in part because of the well-organised repression of planned counter-demonstrations – the exchange of views leading up to the occasion displays the hyperbolic verbal performances and theatrical gestures of which McDiarmid speaks. Some insisted that good manners required a civil welcome to an aged woman, while others – like Moore – called for a 'chill politeness', and more activist opposition leaders called for boycotts and protests, some of which took place. During the months preceding the Queen's April visit, letters to the editors of such newspapers as the unionist *Irish Times*, the moderate *Freeman's Journal*, or Arthur Griffiths's advanced nationalist *United Irishman* display a common focus on the Queen as an elderly woman, whether as 'an aged and gracious lady' (*The Irish Catholic*), 'the senile relic of Royalty' (George Lyons), or one 'in her dotage' (Arthur Griffiths) and 'in the decrepitude of her eighty-one years' (Maud Gonne).[18] While her defenders argue that her visit was without political motive and should be accepted as a personal gesture of goodwill, those who wrote letters opposing the visit on the grounds of religious and political defiance, support for the Boers, or a combination of these positions, seize upon the very personalisation invoked by her defenders.

When in March 1900 Moore voices his opposition to the war through letters protesting the Queen's visit to Ireland, he too draws upon the characterisation of her gender and age that appears in the letters of others and that figures as a dominant feature of public discourse regarding the Queen more generally. Moore characteristically brings to this shared language the satiric reductionism with which he was to confront many serious questions of politics, aesthetics, ethics and religion just a few years later in *Hail and Farewell*.[19] The first of his two letters appears March 14 in *Freeman's Journal* and was reprinted days later in other Irish papers. The newspaper vigorously supported the Boer cause but called for a 'courteous' reception of Queen Victoria. After a quick summary of events and quotation of recent statistics that show greater mortality among Irish and Scottish troops than among the English, Moore alters his diction from mere reportage to a hyperbolic comparison between English efforts to 'extend her commercial empire' into the Transvaal and the vandals who sacked Rome. Like those who defended the Queen's intentions or merely called for courtesy, Moore repeatedly invokes her gender and eighty-one years: she is 'aged and venerable' and the Irish, whom he claims (with what conviction?) are known for 'chivalry to women', must admire the 'fortitude of this woman'. Having established this admirable trait of fortitude to which those who oppose him would presumably assent, Moore then suggests that it lies in being so dutiful that she would cross the water at the bidding of the men who actually govern England. She comes, he taunts, 'with the shilling between her forefinger and thumb and a bag of shillings at her girdle'. 'No shilling,' he declares, 'should be found missing from the bag which hangs at the Queen's girdle.' In his satire, Victoria's femininity and age become the ruse for a scheme of bribery organised by men who exploit her attractions for their own purposes. With the repeated reference to her 'girdle', Moore draws attention to the belt at her waist and by extension, her body, even further reinforcing his implication that the Queen functions as a female lure in a con game run by the men at home in Westminster. Moore's second letter to *Freeman's Journal* on April 16 makes little reference to the Queen herself but continues to attack through metaphors of embodiment, offering in its conclusion a call for Irish landlords to be disloyal to the Queen in the interest of saving themselves:

But can the Irish landlord learn to be disloyal? I am afraid not. His loyalty is a sheer Atavism. It is a curious survival: it is so disinterested that it may be called an abstract virtue, existing of, and through, itself, it is like certain plumes and appendages in birds and animals which abide in them long after the use of them has passed away.[20]

Although reducing the monarch of the British Empire to a con man's strumpet and political positions to a residual stub of tail, Moore's letters lack the venom of some nationalist utterances, most infamously Maude Gonne's article 'The Famine Queen', which appalled even those who agreed with her views in its representation of Queen Victoria as what James H. Murphy calls 'a mythic hybrid of ghoul and witch'.[21] His depiction of his Boer fever in *Hail and Farewell* incorporates ugly class and racial stereotypes (although placed in the mouths of his English friends), but his letters to the papers avoid the racist hysteria of those who blamed British involvement on a conspiracy of Jewish financial interests and mocked the black Africans who fought with the Imperial Army. Having seen a draft of his first letter on March 12, Augusta Gregory notes in her diary that the caricature therein was 'not in the best taste, but restrained for him'.[22] Despite their satiric attacks, Moore's letters were mild by nationalist standards, and echoed in thought if not in expression some of the positions held by moderate nationalists and liberal unionists.

However, if Moore wanted to offend, he apparently succeeded. Adrian Frazier remarks that 'the "Queen letters" of Yeats and Moore were judged by many … to be outside the bounds of decency, somewhere between very bad manners and treasonous disloyalty', and Augusta Gregory records on March 14 that she 'is rather afraid to face' Lady Layard over lunch 'because of G. Moore's letter about the Queen's visit'. Moore apparently understood and anticipated the reaction his first letter received. Gregory's diary entry on the March 12 relates that having shown her the letter he intended to send, Moore 'wanted to know if I was shocked by anything in it – I said it did not shock me, but wd no doubt shock many people over here— but that he says he does not mind.' Yeats reports that as a result of his letters to the press, 'Moores [sic] "smart" friends are cutting him. He is in fine spirits as a result.'[23] On one hand, it would be inaccurate and unfair to suggest that Moore cared more for causing commotion than he did the issues about which he wrote. He was seriously disturbed by the patriotic bombast of the British press and by the sufferings of innocent people. In a letter to Maurice Moore – who fought in South Africa very reluctantly and wrote frankly to his brother about the mistreatment of Boer prisoners and civilians – he expresses sorrow that his anti-war views are separating him from his friends, although he quickly turns his argument in defence of his actions. The autobiographical narrator of *Hail and Farewell* appears remorseful at his 'obsession' with the war and the 'love of cruelty' that compelled him to torment his English friends over the issue.[24] Still, he never shrank from controversy and, as Yeats suggests, even enjoyed it. In many ways, the letter was for Moore not only a vehicle of literary experimentation and the expression of strong opinions but the stage for an actor's performance and an arena for competitive sports.

The provocation of controversy is however less a stage monologue than a phase within a dialogue, and the letter – whether primarily self-reflecting, self-consciously literary, or intentionally provocational – invites exchange with a world beyond the self. Free to exploit the stylistic possibilities of a form whose conventions he invoked or ignored at will, Moore borrows from the stylised discourses of the published love letter and from the reductive satire of the political caricature to produce an effect in the recipient who lies beyond the text.

As such, the letter constitutes more than dialogue with oneself or an act of self-construction such as autobiography. Liz Stanley, the editor of Olive Schreiner's voluminous epistolarium, invites readers to see correspondences as systems of exchange, and her exploration of editing letters in light of the early twentieth-century French sociologist Marcel Mauss's concept of 'the gift' has much to offer a reading of Moore's correspondence. In his major work on the subject, *The Gift: Forms and Functions of Exchange in Archaic Societies*, Mauss contends that giving is by nature reciprocal and the circulation of gifts produces a social relationship whose importance far exceeds the nature or value of the gift itself. 'In the *epistolary* form of gift exchange', Stanley argues,

> What is circulated are the letters sent and replied to. ... There is the gift of the letter itself, but more importantly, there is what it metonymically stands for and symbolises about the ongoing social bond between writer-giver and addressee-receiver ... such exchanges occur because they are the material expression of connection and continuing relationship – and this is, of course, the foundation of sociality and the social. [25]

Even the most contentious correspondences, then, represent a form of engagement. Just as Moore repeatedly expresses indifference to the letter as a material object, the contents of a letter may also have been of much less importance to him than the social interaction it represents.[26] In contrast to the diary or even a published work of fiction, the letter specifies and requires a readership and presumes that the reader will respond. In this way, Moore's letters consist of more than, as I once argued, a means of 'writing the life in dialogue'. Whether designed to provoke, insist, impress, seduce, or express a new-found fascination with an epistolary style, Moore's letters are not only autobiographical self-construction: they are always designed to engage. They affirm the undeniable reality of another and in so doing affirm the social basis of his literary life.

NOTES

1. Moore voiced such concerns frequently, despite his assertion to Nancy Cunard that 'no more do I think of posterity in my letters than in my books'. Moore to Nancy Cunard, in C. Burkhart, 'The Letters of George Moore to Edmund Gosse, W.B. Yeats, R.I. Best, Miss Nancy Cunard, and Mrs. Mary Hutchinson', Ph.D. diss., University of Maryland, 1958, p.330.
2. E. Grubgeld, *George Moore and the Autogenous Self: The Autobiography and Fiction* (Syracuse, NY: Syracuse University Press, 1994), pp.174–99.
3. P. Lejeune, 'Le moi électronique', August 2004. See http://www.autopacte.org (accessed 01/06/2012).
4. Several studies of nineteenth-century letters detail the many similarities between the emergence of inexpensive and rapid postal services and the rise of electronic communications. See particularly W. Decker, *Epistolary Practices: Letter Writing in America Before Telecommunications* (Chapel Hill, NC: University of North Carolina Press, 1998; D. Henkin, *The Postal Age: The Emergence of Modern Communications in Nineteenth-Century America* (Chicago, IL: University of Chicago Press, 2007); and C. Golden, *Posting It: The Victorian Revolution in Letter Writing* (Gainesville, FL: University Press of Florida, 2010).
5. Moore to G.H. Moore, in R. Becker, 'The Letters of George Moore, 1863–1901', Ph.D. diss., University of Reading, 1980, pp.91–2, 93.
6. Moore to Maurice Moore, in S. MacDonncha, 'Letters of George Moore (1852–1933) to His Brother, Colonel Maurice Moore, CB (1857–1939)', Ph.D. diss., National University of Ireland, Galway, 1972–3, p.29. MacDonncha identifies the sentence as unreadable, and I have been unable to examine the original.
7. Ibid., p.79.
8. Ibid., p.96.
9. E. Cook, *Epistolary Bodies: Gender and Genre in the Eighteenth-Century Republic of Letters* (Stanford, CA: Stanford University Press, 1996), p.vii.
10. L. Kauffman, 'Not a Love Story: Retrospective and Prospective Epistolary Directions', in A. Gilroy and W.M. Verhoeven (eds), *Epistolary Histories: Letters, Fiction, Culture* (Charlottesville, VA: University of Virginia Press, 2000), p.198.
11. Moore to Maude Cunard, in R. Hart-Davis (ed.), *Letters to Lady Cunard 1895–1933* (London: Rupert Hart-Davis, 1957), pp.40–43; Moore to Lord Howard de Walden, in J. Hone, *The Life of George Moore* (New York: Macmillan, 1939), pp.258–9.
12. Moore to Maud Cunard, in Hart-Davis, p.54.
13. On 1 August 1904, Moore assures Gabrielle that 'if you do not wish the Comedy written I will not write it'. In D. Eakin and R. Langenfeld (eds), *George Moore's Correspondence with the Mysterious Countess* (Victoria, BC: University of Victoria, 1984), p.66. His letter to Dujardin

is dated 23 September of the same year. In J. Eglinton [W.K. Magee] (ed.), *Letters from George Moore to Ed. Dujardin 1886–1922* (New York: Crosby, Gaige, 1929), p.54.

14. G. Moore, *Hail and Farewell* (Buckinghamshire: Colin Smythe, 1985), p.114.
15. Cook, *Epistolary Bodies*, p.2.
16. Detailed discussions of the role of newspapers in shaping and expressing Irish opinion on the war are given in S. Potter (ed.), *Newspapers and Empire in Ireland and Britain: Reporting the British Empire, c. 1857–1921* (Dublin: Four Courts, 2004).
17. L. McDiarmid, *The Irish Art of Controversy* (Ithaca NY: Cornell University Press, 2005), p.7.
18. *The Irish Catholic* is quoted in D. Lowry, 'Nationalist and Unionist Responses to the British Empire in the Age of the South African War' in Potter, p.175. Lyons, Griffith and Gonne are quoted in D. McCracken, *Forgotten Protest: Ireland and the Anglo-Boer War* (Belfast: Ulster Historical Foundation, 2003), pp.67–9.
19. To my knowledge, the earliest mention of what would become *Hail and Farewell* occurs in a letter to Filson Young in October, 1905, only five years after Moore's letters of protest against the Queen's visit. In H. Gerber (ed.), *George Moore on Parnassus: Letters (1900–1933) to Secretaries, Publishers, Printers, Agents, Literati, Friends, and Acquaintances* (Newark, DE: University of Delaware Press, 1988), pp.123–5.
20. Moore to The Editor, *Freeman's Journal*, 14 March 1900; 16 April 1900.
21. J. Murphy, 'Broken Glass and Batoned Crowds: Cathleen ni Houlihan and the Tensions of Transition', in D.G. Boyce and A. O'Day (eds), *Ireland in Transition: 1867–1921* (London: Routledge, 2004), p.120.
22. A. Gregory in J. Pethica (ed.), *Lady Gregory's Diaries, 1892–1902* (New York: Oxford University Press, 1996), p.255.
23. Adrian Frazier, *George Moore, 1852–1933* (New Haven, CT: Yale University Press, 2000), pp.290–91. Pethica, 256, 255; Yeats to Augusta Gregory, in W. Gould, J. Kelly, and D. Toomey (eds), *The Collected Letters of W.B. Yeats: Vol. 2* (Oxford: Clarendon, 1997), p.506.
24. Moore to Maurice Moore, in MacDonncha, p.96; G. Moore, *Hail and Farewell*, pp.220, 221.
25. L. Stanley, 'The Epistolary Gift, the Editorial Third-Party, Counter-Epistolaria: Rethinking the Epistolarium', *Life Writing*, 8, 2 (2011), pp.140, 41.
26. My analysis of Moore's letters includes a discussion of his indifference to the letter's materiality. See 'Writing the Life in Dialogue: Letters, Epistolary Novels, and Imaginary Conversations' in Grubgeld, *George Moore and the Autogenous Self*, pp.174–99.

REFERENCES

Becker, R., 'The Letters of George Moore, 1863–1901', Ph.D. diss., University of Reading, 1980.
Burkhart, C., 'The Letters of George Moore to Edmund Gosse, W.B. Yeats, R.I. Best, Miss Nancy Cunard, and Mrs. Mary Hutchinson', Ph.D. diss., University of Maryland, 1958.
Cook, E., *Epistolary Bodies: Gender and Genre in the Eighteenth-Century Republic of Letters* (Stanford, CA: Stanford University Press, 1996).
Decker, W., *Epistolary Practices: Letter Writing in America Before Telecommunications* (Chapel Hill, NC: University of North Carolina Press, 1998).
Frazier, A., *George Moore, 1852–1933* (New Haven, CT: Yale University Press, 2000).
Golden, C., *Posting It: The Victorian Revolution in Letter Writing* (Gainesville, FL: University Press of Florida, 2010).
Gregory, A., *Lady Gregory's Diaries, 1892–1902*, J. Pethica (ed.), (New York: Oxford University Press, 1996).
Grubgeld, E., *George Moore and the Autogenous Self: The Autobiography and Fiction* (Syracuse, NY: Syracuse University Press, 1994).
Henkin, D., *The Postal Age: The Emergence of Modern Communications in Nineteenth-Century America* (Chicago, IL: University of Chicago Press, 2007).
Hone, J., *The Life of George Moore* (New York: Macmillan, 1938).
Kauffman, L., 'Not a Love Story: Retrospective and Prospective Epistolary Directions', in A. Gilroy and W.M. Verhoeven (eds), *Epistolary Histories: Letters, Fiction, Culture* (Charlottesville, VA: University of Virginia Press, 2000), pp.198–224.
Lejeune, P., 'Le moi électronique', August 2004. See http://www.autopacte.org (accessed 01/06/2012).
Lowry, D., 'Nationalist and Unionist Responses to the British Empire in the Age of the South

African War', in S. Potter (ed.), *Newspapers and Empire in Ireland and Britain: Reporting the British Empire, c. 1857–1921* (Dublin: Four Courts, 2004): pp.159–76.

MacDonncha, S., 'Letters of George Moore (1852–1933) to His Brother, Colonel Maurice Moore, CB (1857–1939)', Ph.D. diss., National University of Ireland, Galway, 1972–3.

McCracken, D., *Forgotten Protest: Ireland and the Anglo-Boer War* (Belfast: Ulster Historical Foundation, 2003).

McDiarmid, L., *The Irish Art of Controversy* (Ithaca NY: Cornell University Press, 2005).

Moore, G., To the Editor, *Freeman's Journal*, 14 March 1900; 16 April 1900.

Moore, G., *Letters from George Moore to Ed. Dujardin 1886–1922*, J. Eglinton [W.K. Magee] (ed.), (New York: Crosby, Gaige, 1929).

Moore, G., *Letters to Lady Cunard 1895–1933*, R. Hart-Davis (ed.), (London: Rupert Hart-Davis, 1957).

Moore, G., *George Moore's Correspondence with the Mysterious Countess*, D. Eakin and R. Langenfeld (eds), (Victoria, BC: University of Victoria, 1984).

Moore, G., *Hail and Farewell* (Buckinghamshire: Colin Smythe, 1985).

Moore G., *George Moore on Parnassus: Letters (1900–1933) to Secretaries, Publishers, Printers, Agents, Literati, Friends, and Acquaintances*, H. Gerber (ed.), (Newark, DE: University of Delaware Press, 1988).

Murphy, J., 'Broken Glass and Batoned Crowds: Cathleen ni Houlihan and the Tensions of Transition', in D.G. Boyce and A. O'Day (eds), *Ireland in Transition: 1867–1921* (London: Routledge, 2004), pp.113–28.

Potter, S. (ed.), *Newspapers and Empire in Ireland and Britain: Reporting the British Empire, c. 1857–1921* (Dublin: Four Courts, 2004).

Stanley, L., 'The Epistolary Gift, the Editorial Third-Party, Counter-Epistolaria: Rethinking the Epistolarium', *Life Writing*, 8, 2 (2011), pp.135–52.

Yeats, W.B., in W. Gould, J. Kelly, and D. Toomey (eds), *The Collected Letters of W.B. Yeats: Vol. 2* (Oxford: Clarendon, 1997).

CHAPTER FOURTEEN

Innovations and Limitations: George Moore's use of the Romantic Epiphany in his Victorian Novels

JAYNE THOMAS

This chapter looks at George Moore's use of the literary, or romantic, epiphany in his Victorian novels, a technique he had inherited from William Wordsworth. Moore's use of the romantic epiphany in these novels both develops the form he had inherited and reveals the limitations of that form in the Victorian period. In both senses, his work reflects cultural changes that had an impact on the epiphany as a literary technique. Moore had specifically used the romantic epiphany in these early novels as part of his quest to render the interiority or 'under life' of character,[1] a technique that came to fruition later in his career with works like *The Lake* of 1905. Critics have often read Moore's experimentation with epiphany in his Victorian novels as part of his experimentation with Huysmanesque and Wagnerian methods of rendering character,[2] paying little heed to its links to the romantic epiphany. However, many of these early epiphanies conform more to the romantic paradigm than to Continental forms. It is this form that James Joyce was to re-work in the early twentieth century in his own version of epiphany, albeit in the language of Aquinas. Rather than locating Moore's epiphanic style within Huysmanesque and Wagnerian symbolism, therefore, this chapter ties it distinctly to the romantic epiphany. Moore reveals the form's potential as well as its limitations.

William Wordsworth is credited with inaugurating the romantic epiphany. He re-shaped the theological epiphany for secular use, although other romantic poets, like Percy Bysshe Shelley and Samuel Taylor Coleridge, also made use of it as a poetic tool. Wordsworth explicitly based his use of epiphany on Kant's epistemology, in which the mind, plays a creative role in the act of perception. Kant saw the mind as actively imposing its own forms on the objects of perception, in that we can 'know *a priori* of things only what we ourselves put into them',[3] and which he intimately linked to imagination.[4] In 'Lines composed a few miles above Tintern Abbey, on revisiting the Banks of the Wye during a Tour. July 13, 1798', Wordsworth gave such ideas a poetic idiom and wrote of how the eye and ear 'half create' what they perceive: 'Therefore am I still / A lover of the meadows and the woods, / And mountains; and of all that we behold / From his green earth; of all the mighty world / Of eye, and ear, both what they half create, / And what they perceive.'[5] Predicated on this Kantian belief in the mind's creative role in sense perception – of its ability to 'half create' what it perceived – works like *The Prelude* saw the mind gain domination over the world of sense, which resulted in moments of transcendental awareness and temporal suspension, or 'spots of time'.[6] These suspended moments were 'scattered everywhere',[7] and were based on 'ordinary sight',[8] like that of the 'visionary dreariness'[9] of a 'Girl who bore a Pitcher on her head',[10] but could equally be experienced amongst the grandeur of the Simplon Pass[11] or on the top of Mount Snowdon.[12] Emotion, and occasionally memory, was also involved in producing these random 'spots of time'; involuntary memories from the past often resulted in epiphanic significance in the present, for instance. However, as Rajan correctly explains, the romantics did not advance the eighteenth-century understanding of representation; they regressed from it: 'Romantic theory, with its reabsorption of imagination into perception and its claims for the fusion of subject and object in the act of perception, reveals itself as regressive in relation to the understanding of representation that emerged in the eighteenth century.'[13] In simply fusing subject and object in the act of perception, and of similarly equating language with the thing described, romanticism is 'a conservative and sentimental attempt to revive a Renaissance or hermetic system of correspondences, in a world which has already been revealed as discontinuous'.[14] In the romantic epiphany, language related to referent, as subject related to object.

Critics like Morris Beja and Robert Langbaum have defined the Wordsworthian romantic epiphany by its adherence to several formalist criteria. Beja names this the Criterion of Incongruity, because the epiphany is not strictly relevant to whatever produces it.[15] A second aspect of the Romantic epiphany Beja calls the Criterion of Insignificance, because the epiphany is triggered by a trivial object or incident.[16]

He also differentiates between dream-epiphanies and the two major types of epiphany that derive from memory: the retrospective epiphany, and that of the past recaptured.[17] The retrospective epiphany is 'one in which an event arouses no special impression when it occurs, but produces a sudden sensation of new awareness when it is recalled at some future time'.[18] Robert Langbaum adds four more criteria to the definition of the modern literary epiphany: the Criterion of Psychological Association, in which the epiphany, rather than an incursion of God from outside, is a psychological phenomenon arising from a real sensuous experience, either present or recollected; the Criterion of Momentaneousness, where the epiphany only lasts a moment, but leaves an enduring effect; the Criterion of Suddenness, in which a sudden change in external conditions causes a shift in sensuous perception that sensitises the reader for epiphany, and the fourth, the Criterion of Fragmentation or Epiphanic Leap, where the text never quite equals the epiphany.[19] He also went on to define all epiphanies as involving the shock of recognition – 'recognition of the self in the external world'.[20] These criteria have become parts of the working definition of the romantic, or literary, epiphany.

The romantic epiphany was appropriated in the Victorian period by poets and novelists alike. Alfred, Lord Tennyson, Robert Browning, Dante Gabriel Rossetti, all made use of the form, whether in the form of stilled moments of time like Rossetti,[21] or the 'infinite moment' like Browning.[22] Novelists as disparate as Charles Dickens, George Eliot and Thomas Hardy made use of heightened moments of awareness, based on the Wordsworthian model, although this was in an intermittent, rather tentative fashion. George Moore, however, perhaps more than any other novelist in this period, helped to develop the romantic epiphany in novelistic form. As early as the 1888 *Spring Days*,[23] one of Moore's 'transitional' novels, in which he experimented with Huysman's method of rendering character through analogy and symbol, Moore began to employ the romantic epiphany as a vehicle with which to render the 'under life' of his characters. Novels like *Evelyn Innes*[24] and *Sister Teresa*,[25] as well as the other experimental novels of the 1880s, like *A Mere Accident* (1887),[26] and *Mike Fletcher* (1889),[27] also contain significant epiphanic moments, as does *Vain Fortune* (1891).[28] Rather than simply being part of a general experiment with Huysmanesque and Wagnerian methods of rendering character, these epiphanies have a clear Wordsworthian root, and fit most, if not all, of the formalist criteria established above.

The culmination of Moore's epiphanic technique in the Victorian period was Hubert Price's epiphany at the close of *Vain Fortune*. According to Richard Ellmann, James Joyce is known to have re-fashioned some of Moore's material in terms of plot and theme for 'The Dead', the final story of his collection of short stories, *Dubliners*.[29] If we look at the ending, however, we see that, rather than Huysmanesque, or even Wagnerian symbolism,[30] the epiphany is a Wordsworthian composite of emotion, perception, and memory, as the mind converts an object of sense into meaning. Here, Moore, it seems, is making full use of the romantic, or literary, epiphany to elucidate character. The novel tells the story of Hubert Price, a somewhat unsuccessful dramatist, who inherits not only a large sum of money from his uncle, but also his uncle's young ward, Emily. He soon becomes the object of the young Emily's affections. He himself, meanwhile, falls in love with Emily's chaperone, Julia. Price and Julia eventually marry; Emily, denied Hubert's affections, commits suicide. The epiphany occurs shortly after Hubert has learnt of Emily's suicide. He wakes suddenly, and shivers in the 'chill room'.[31] He looks at his wife, and finds her 'very beautiful' whilst she sleeps.[32] He goes to the window, and looks out at the breaking day. Moore continues:

> He looked at his wife and quailed a little at the thought that had suddenly come upon him. She was something like himself – that was why he had married her. We are attracted by what is like ourselves. Emily's passion might have stirred him. Now he would have to settle down to live with Julia, and their similar natures would grow more and more like one another. Then, turning on his thoughts, he dismissed them. They were morbid feverish fancies of an exceptional, of a terrible night. He opened the window quietly so as to not awaken his wife. And in the melancholy greyness of the dawn he looked down into the street and wondered what the end would be.
>
> He did not think that he would live long. Disappointed men – those who have failed in their ambitions – do not live to make old bones. There were men like him in every profession – the arts are crowded with them. He had met barristers and soldiers and clergymen, just like himself. One hears of their deaths – failure of the heart's action, paralysis of the brain, a hundred other medical causes – but the real cause is lack of appreciation.
>
> He would hang on for another few years, no doubt; during that

time he must try to make his wife happy. His duty now was to be a good husband, at all events, there was that.[33]

The Wordsworthian component is overt here – the 'object' of his wife as she sleeps, and the emotion of the night's suicide – induce in Hubert the sudden realisation of why he had married his wife. The epiphany, in addition, is both analeptic and proleptic, as it involves a direct perception of the present and a memory which has a particular significance in the present, complementary versions of the Wordsworthian epiphany. Something that has occurred in the past – Hubert's decision to marry – suddenly has significance in the present. The epiphany also meets several of Beja's and Langbaum's criteria for the romantic epiphany: it is precipitated by a trivial event (the image of Julia as she sleeps), is psychological rather than from an external source, lasts for a moment only, is sudden, and realises the self in the world. But whereas Wordsworth's epiphanies had resulted in moments of transcendence and joy, here they result in a sense of entrapment and despair, as Hubert realises his own lack of escape. Wordsworth's epiphanies stem from despair, but result in joy; here, Moore's epiphany stems from despair and results in despair, as he aims to give a truthful account of Hubert Price's moral and emotional awakening.

Robert Browning had begun to use the romantic epiphany to render character in his poetry from this period,[34] but Moore uses it here to successfully render character in novelistic form. The epiphany is mediated through a third-person narrator. The narrator reveals Hubert Price's inner thoughts to the reader. Nonetheless, Moore moves at times onto a free indirect style here, as he captures the workings of Hubert's thoughts. He writes of how Hubert 'looked at his wife and quailed a little at the thought that had suddenly come upon him'. *She was something like himself – that was why he had married her* (my italics), and goes on to write of how Hubert 'would hang on for another few years, *no doubt*'; during that time he must try to make his wife happy. 'His duty now was to be a good husband, *at all events, there was that*' (emphasis added). Moore, therefore, both uses, and extends the use of, the Wordsworthian epiphany, as he strives to shape it to his own narrative form. Joyce was to echo several aspects of Moore's work in the epiphany that closes 'The Dead': the triangular emotional relationship between Gretta, Michael Furey and Gabriel Conroy; the symbolic window. Interestingly, he was also to employ Moore's free indirect narrational style to help render Gabriel's epiphany.[35] The romantic epiphany as developed by Moore was the precursor for this, as he re-moulded what was essentially a poetic form for his own novelistic purposes.

A similar effect had been achieved with *Spring Days* (1888), the only comic novel Moore published in this period. The novel has three narrative strands, one of which concerns Frank Escott, the heir to an Irish estate, who is attracted to both the middle-class Maggie Brooke and the working-class Welsh barmaid of the Gaiety Theatre. At one point in the novel, Lizzie Baker, the barmaid, experiences an epiphany that allows her to see her 'self' in the world, a key aspect of the Wordsworthian epiphany, as we have seen, and which, again, meets other of Beja's and Langbaum's critieria for the romantic epiphany: trivial, psychological, momentary, sudden. Moore writes:

> Lizzie dipped her arm to the elbow, and rejoiced in the soft flowing water. The river rose up into what beautiful views and prospects. The locks, the sensation of the boat sinking among the slimy piles with Frank erect holding her off with the boat hook, or the slow rising till the banks were overflowed, and the wonderful wooden gates opened, disclosing a placid stream with overhanging boughs and a barge. And the charming discoveries they made in the water world, the moorhen's indolence, and the watchful rat swimming for its hole; each bend was a new picture. How beautifully expressive of the work of the field were the comfortable barns. If life is never very fair, a vision of life may be fair indeed, and once the tears came to the bar-girl's eyes, for she, too, suddenly remembered her life of tobacco and whisky; long weary hours of standing, politeness, washing glasses, and listening to filthy jokes. Would there be no change? If she might live her life here! She thought of the morning light, and the home occupations of the morning, and then the languid and lazy afternoons in this boat, amid the enchantments of these river lands.[36]

Emotion, perception, and memory – key aspects of the Wordsworthian epiphany – combine to produce a new sense of awareness of the self in the world; as Lizzie says, 'Would there be no change?' Lizzie realises both how her life is, and how it will seemingly be. However, the epiphany is analeptic rather than proleptic despite the use of memory, using Langbaum's definition of the Wordsworthian epiphany, as the present scene, with its 'soft flowing water', 'beautiful views' and 'watchful rat', impress themselves on her mind to create the epiphany. And again, the epiphany is mediated through the third-person, although

Moore attempts to blend this with a putative free indirect discourse, in an attempt to capture Lizzie's mental processes. As he writes, '*Would there be no change? If she might live her life here!*' This exclamatory sentence seems to stem directly from Lizzie's mind. In departing from his Wordsworthian model, however, Moore again offers an epiphany of entrapment rather than transcendence. In attempting to offer an honest account of Lizzie's inner thoughts, Moore eschews moments of joy in favour of moments of seeming entrapment.

These two examples are evidence of Moore's innovations and amendments involving the Wordsworthian epiphany. Both involve conversions of the external world, objects of sense, by an intuitive mind; both involve perception, memory, sensation, emotion. But both are shaped by Moore's desire to offer a truthful account of the mind's real-isation of itself in the world. Wordsworth was content for the mind to 'half create' what it saw, to create fictions of itself in effect. Moore is more concerned with the mind creating a 'true' picture of itself.

In making these changes, however, Moore's innovations reflect changes to the notion of the self that occurred during the Victorian period.[37] The romantic epiphany had grown out of Cartesian dualism: personal consciousness became the locus of knowledge. The mind was separated from the world, as formalised in Descartes's famous formula, *cogito ergo sum*, 'I think, therefore I am.'[38] In the Victorian era, however, the self was placed within society, history, and politics in forms like the dramatic monologue. Such forms consciously challenged the notion of the discrete, Cartesian self. In them, the self is deliberately seen as 'as part of an open system' rather than a 'discrete whole'.[39] Unlike the lyric, where the speaker is assumed to be discrete, uniform, self-enclosed, often male, and yet universal,[40] the speaker of the dramatic monologue exists, as W. Slinn puts it, 'not as a separate entity, but as a part of human history',[41] located 'with other persons, times, cultures'.[42] Robert Brown-ing's dramatic monologues, for instance, through irony, 'expose both the limits to point of view and the uncertain boundaries of selfhood'.[43]

Like the dramatic monologue, epiphany as a form in *Spring Days* and *Vain Fortune* reflects changes to the Cartesian self that occurred in the Victorian period. The Cartesian 'I' of these epiphanies in Moore's novels becomes part of history and the world, rather than remaining discrete like the 'I' of the Wordsworthian romantic self. Still based on the personal consciousness of the experiencing 'I', the post-Cartesian 'I' of Moore's experiencing subject cannot remain separated from the world. Wordsworth's epiphanies were rarefied experiences, available for the artist only to enjoy,[44] despite being based on perceptions of the ordinary. Like the subjective self of the dramatic monologue, however, the epiphanists of Moore's Victorian novels are part of history, and this involves the epiphany itself in a complex role with history and the world.

This shift to the post-Cartesian self is in evidence in Moore's Victorian epiphanies, like those of *Spring Days* and *Vain Fortune*. Lizzie Baker's epiphany in *Spring Days*, for instance, is inflected by Lizzie's economic and social position. It is an epiphany of a 'self' situated in history, and that self is not of the Wordsworthian artistic elite, but of the ordinary: Lizzie Baker is a working-class barmaid. Rather than gaining transcendence, or liberation, through her moment of awareness, Lizzie's economic and social position both inform her epiphany and entrap her within it. The transcendence any epiphany offers, as Langbaum has emphasised, is of a momentary nature only. The 'I' of the epiphany is involved in history, and the epiphany provides temporary suspension from that history only. It does not allow Lizzie Baker to permanently transcend her social circumstances. In the novel that follows *Spring Days* – *Mike Fletcher* – Lizzie marries Frank Escott, and thus escapes her social circumstances, but the epiphany in *Spring Days* does not occasion this. She remains the bar-girl, trapped in a life of washing glasses and weary hours of standing. Thus, if post-Cartesianism opens up the 'I' of epiphany to history and sociology, it is also possible that it reinforces the prevailing class system, or ideology, at the same time.[45] Lizzie Baker's epiphany, whilst positioning her within society, also traps her within it. According to postmodern theory, epiphanies are ideological constructs, vehicles designed to perpetuate the prevailing ideology.[46] The temporal stasis occasioned by the epiphany is matched by ideological stasis. The post-Cartesian epiphany is, therefore, both liberating and limiting.

This innovation, nevertheless, saw the Wordsworthian epiphany re-shaped for a new purpose. No longer a discrete and privileged self that creates an imaginative fiction of itself, the self of Moore's epiphanies is actively involved in the world, and sometimes trapped by it. If Wordsworth's epiphanies had been of the ordinary by the elite, here in Moore they are of the ordinary by the ordinary. Such innovations helped shape the epiphany for use by the modernists like Joyce who followed Moore. In *Dubliners*, Joyce writes epiphanies of the 'ordinary'. The ideological implications of the new post-Cartesian epiphany remained unsolved, however.

During this period Pater had re-fashioned the romantic epiphany. Pater's privileged moments celebrated the moment for the moment's sake only, without reference to epistemological meaning: 'Not the fruit of experience, but experience itself, is the end.'[47] For Pater, 'A counted number of pulses only is given to us of a variegated, dramatic life', and 'success in life' was to 'maintain this ecstasy' and 'to burn with a hard, gemlike flame'.[48] Art gave the highest quality to these moments as they passed, and 'simply for those moments' sake'.[49] Dramatic poetry, for instance, produces 'ideal instants', 'exquisite pauses in time',[50] where time stands still.

In formulating the 'privileged moment', Pater challenged the Kantian premises on which the romantic epiphany had been based: the confluence between subject and object, language and referent. In 'The Function of Criticism at the Present Time',[51] Matthew Arnold had urged an objectivist account of perception, based on 'seeing the object as it really is'. In 'The Preface' to *The Renaissance*, however, Pater privileged a subjectivist account of reality, of knowing 'one's impression as it really is': 'the first step towards seeing one's object as it really is, is to know one's own impression as it really is, to discriminate it, to realise it distinctly'.[52] Pater, in effect, reduced meaning to a purely subjective impressionism. This had the concomitant effect of reducing selfhood to a series of impressions, of a 'self constantly re-forming itself on the stream',[53] which results in 'that strange, perpetual weaving and unweaving of ourselves'.[54] Similarly, Pater's work saw the relation between language and its referent attenuated. In Pater's work, a 'form of nominalism produces the symbol with a disappearing referent, a sign whose meaning is behind and beyond the word. Meaning does not lie between words and world but *beyond* them'.[55] For Pater, therefore, representation is at a remove from what it represents, as language begins to be dissociated from its referent.

George Moore was heavily influenced by Pater's work, both in terms of subject matter and style. In *Confessions of A Young Man*,[56] Moore had recounted the – autobiographical – journey of a young Paterian aesthete in Paris, charting his devotion to living a life devoted to living for the moment, of burning with a 'gemlike flame'. The eponymous Evelyn Innes, a Wagnerian opera singer and protégé of Sir Owen Asher, devotes her life to the art for art's sake movement, until she rejects the aestheticism to which Asher has introduced her and seeks solace in a higher power. And in *Mike Fletcher*, Moore had described a life devoted to the kind of decadence to which Pater's 'The Conclusion' had given rise. In these early Victorian novels, Moore had paid explicit homage to Pater, listing, for instance, in *A Mere Accident* John Norton's choice of Paterian reading material.[57] Pater's influence also extended to Moore's use of the privileged moment. However, Moore does more than simply echo Pater. Rather than attenuating the link between subject and object as Pater does, Moore severs the link between impression and object, language and referent. The mind fails to link impression and object, and language fails to connect to its referent. These failures have profound effects on how the epiphanist is able to 'create' the self in the world. For the romantic, the mind's valorisation of mind over sense results in knowledge of the self in the world, as we have seen. Impressionism, whereby the object is placed in subordination to the perceiving mind, results in Moore in occasions where the mind is unable to link to the object at all. The self fails to find its 'self' in the world.

At several points in *Evelyn Innes*, for instance, Evelyn fails to make the link between impression and object. The results are 'failed epiphanies'. Moore had styled several epiphanic moments in *Evelyn Innes* on Pater's impressionism, even transcribing Pater's linguistic phrasing at one point in the novel, writing of Evelyn's 'intense consciousness' of the present on viewing Asher for the first time,[58] which is a verbatim account of Pater's 'exquisite pause in time' in *The Renaissance*.[59] On returning to London after her initially disastrous elopement to the Continent with Sir Owen Asher, however, Evelyn searches the London street scene for 'answers' to her distress. Whereas the Wordsworthian epiphany would have provided its epiphanee with a sense of epistemological meaning, of itself in the world, based on the mind's conversion of objects of sense, here there is no such transcendence of the world, and no such sense of the self's place in the world either. The disconnection between subject and object begun by Pater is taken to its extreme. Moore writes:

> The sun glanced through the foliage, and glittered on the cockades of the coachmen and on the shining hides of the horses. It was the height of the season, and the young beauties of the year, and the fashionable beauties of the last decade, lay back, sunning themselves under the shade of their parasols. The carriages came round the square close to the curb, under the waving branches, and, waiting for an opportunity to cross, Evelyn's eyes followed an unusually beautiful carriage, drawn by a pair of chestnut horses. She did not see the lady's face, but she wore a yellow dress, and the irises in her bonnet nodded over the hood of the

carriage. This lady, graceful and idle, seemed to mean something, but what? Evelyn thought of the picture of the colonnade in the gallery.[60]

Evelyn is unable to convert the object of her impression into meaning. The graceful and idle lady seems to mean something, but Evelyn, relying purely on her impressions rather than the object of those impressions in a Wordsworthian or Arnoldian sense, is unable to make them signify. Equally, she is unable to rely on memory – a staple of the Wordsworthian epiphany – to render the present meaningful as a result of a past event. She thinks of the picture of the colonnade in the gallery she had viewed earlier, but memory is unable to connect to a present perception as it does in Wordsworth's *The Prelude*, for instance, to create meaning. Similarly, Evelyn cannot 'half create' what she sees in order to create a sense of meaning and of self in the world. The disconnection between subject and object introduced by Pater is taken to its logical extreme here, as the mind fails to create any synergy between itself and the world. Harold Bloom has written – insightfully – of Pater's contribution to the development of the epiphany: 'Pater's strange achievement is to have assimilated Wordsworth to Lucretius, to have compounded an idealistic naturalism with a corrective materialism. By de-idealising the epiphany, he [Pater] makes it available to the coming age, when the mind will know neither itself nor the object but only the dumbfoundering abyss that comes between.'[61] It seems as if Evelyn is indeed floundering in that abyss between subject and object here. Language loses track of its referent, as the lady's 'yellow dress' and the 'irises in her bonnet' seem to mean something – but, as Moore writes, 'what'? Knowledge of the self in the world breaks down.

A similar non-epiphanic moment occurs later in the novel, as Evelyn continues to try to make sense of her place in the world. Again, the romantic epiphany is elided, as the mind is unable to convert objects of sense in the world, or to 'half create' meaning from its surroundings. Evelyn sits by a window, and gains a sense of the world's infinity, but as she turns 'to the enigma of her own individuality' – the essence of the literary epiphany, after all – her 'brain seemed to melt in the moonlight'.[62]

> She was aware that she lived. She was aware that some things were right, that some things were wrong. She was aware of the strange fortune that had lured her, that had chosen her out of

millions. What did it mean? It must mean something, just as those stars must mean something – but what?

Opposite to her window there was an open space; it was full of mist and moonlight; the lights of a distant street looked across it. She too had said, "'Tis hard upon me, I love my folk above all things, but a great longing seizes me.' That story is the story of human life. What is human life but a longing for something beyond us, for something we shall not attain? Again she wondered what her end must be. She must end somehow, and was it not strange that she could no more answer that simple question than she could the sublime question which the moon and the stars

Propounded […] That breathless, glittering peace, was it not wonderful?[63]

Again, Evelyn is unable to convert the objects of sense – the mist and the moonlight and the distant street – into meaning. Such objects fail to provide epiphanic awareness, as the link between object and perceiving subject is broken. Moore's choice of nebulous imagery – mist and moonlight and the lights of a distant street – seem to echo Evelyn's nebulous ability to use her mind's capacity to convert an object into meaning. Similarly, the fact that her brain seems to melt away reinforces the mind's inability to perform the kind of creative acts that Wordsworth had himself performed. Rather, mind and object fail to connect in a textual example of what Gerard Manley Hopkins had come to fear: the complete dispersal of subject and object as a result of Paterian impressionism.[64]

By using Pater's version of the romantic epiphany in such a way, Moore pushes the form to limits which Pater himself had not reached, but which are its logical conclusion. In so doing, Moore, rather than simply copying Pater's style, extends and challenges the form of the romantic epiphany.

Moore would go on, however, to use the romantic epiphany to help render interior moments of consciousness to great effect, most noticeably in *The Lake* of 1905, where he combined such moments with a prototype stream of consciousness technique; the putative free indirect discourse of *Spring Days* and *Vain Fortune* transmutes into a full stream of consciousness in the rendering of the epiphanic moment. Moore's use of the Victorian version of the romantic epiphany is the seed-bed for this; his work reflects the form's potential as well as its limitations. Moore's innovations, like the use of free indirect discourse as a descriptive tool in the rendering of epiphany, were to be copied by James Joyce in 'The Dead'. And Joyce's *Dubliners* themselves, like Moore's Lizzie Baker, were ordinary people rather than an artistic elite. For Joyce, in the moment of illumination, the mind discovers the soul of the commonest object, as the object achieves its own epiphany.[65] Moore's romantic epiphanies inform such modernist epiphanies that were to follow.

NOTES

1. G. Moore, 'Since the Elizabethans', *Cosmopolis*, October 1896, p.57. In this essay, Moore describes this 'under life' as the 'true humanity', where 'we find the wonder and mystery of life', p.57. He also praises Tolstoi (*sic*) for having refined a method of rendering the subconscious by which he enables us to know 'the real life', the 'life of the ages', p.57.
2. Richard Allen Cave, for instance, writes at length on Moore's epiphanies in these early novels, but does so in the context of Moore's experiments with Huysmanesque and Wagnerian symbolism, without mentioning their connections to the romantic epiphany, from which they inevitably stemmed. See R. A. Cave, *A Study in the Novels of George Moore: Irish Literary Studies 3* (Buckinghamshire: Colin Smythe, 1978).
3. E. Kant, *The Critique of Pure Reason*, translated by Norman Kemp Smith (London: Macmillan, 1933), p.23.
4. Kant, *The Critique of Pure Reason*, p.144.
5. T. Hutchinson (ed.), *Wordsworth: Poetical Works, revised by Ernest de Selincourt* (London, New York, Toronto: Oxford University Press, 1974), pp.164–5, ll.102–7.
6. W. Wordsworth, *The Prelude, or Growth of a Poet's Mind*, edited from the manuscripts, with introduction and textual and critical notes by Ernest de Selincourt (London: Oxford University Press, 1959), p.437, XII. II. 208–25.
7. Ibid., XII. I. 224.
8. Ibid., XII. I. 254.
9. Ibid., XII. I. 256.
10. Ibid., XII. I. 251.
11. Ibid., VI. II. 621–40.
12. Ibid., XIV. II. 28–62.
13. T. Rajan, *Dark Interpreter: The Discourse of Romanticism* (Ithaca and London: Cornell University Press, 1980), p.260.
14. See Rajan, *Dark Interpreter*, p.207. Rajan points out that not all romantics reverted to pre-eighteenth-century aesthetics. Coleridge and Shelley, for instance, are 'careful not to claim this naïve fusion of image with thing', p.207.
15. M. Beja, *Epiphany in the Modern Novel* (London: Peter Owen, 1971), p.16.
16. Ibid., p.16.
17. Ibid., p.15.
18. Ibid.
19. R. Langbaum, 'The Epiphanic Mode in Wordsworth and Modern Literature', in R. Langbaum (ed.), *The Word From Below: Essays on Modern Literature and Culture* (Madison: University of Wisconsin Press, 1987), p.40.
20. Langbaum, 'The Epiphanic Mode in Wordsworth and Modern Literature', p.54.
21. See poems like 'Silent Noon' in D.G. Rossetti's collection, *The House of Life*, where time seems suspended in a stilled moment. D.G. Rossetti, *The House of Life*, with an introduction and notes by Paul Franklin Baum (Cambridge, Mass.: Harvard University Press, 1928), pp.92–3.
22. Robert Browning celebrated the 'infinite moment' in many poems, including 'By the Fireside', from collections like *Men and Women*, where the lovers of the poem are in the 'moment, one and infinite'. See I. Jack (ed.), *Men and Women, in Browning: Poetical Works 1833–1864* (London: Oxford University Press, 1970), pp.580–9, III. l. 208. For some interesting comments on Browning's use of the infinite moment, see, for instance, A. Nichols, *The*

Poetics of Epiphany: Nineteenth-Century Origins of the Modern Literary Moment (Tuscaloosa: University of Alabama Press, 1997), pp.107–43. Also see J. Hillis Miller, *The Disappearance of God: Five Nineteenth-Century Writers* (Cambridge, Mass., London: The Belknap Press of Harvard University Press, Oxford University Press, 1963), pp.81–156.

23. G. Moore, *Spring Days: A Realistic Novel* (London: Vizitelly & Co., 1888).
24. G. Moore, *Evelyn Innes* (London: T. Fisher Unwin, 1898).
25. G. Moore, *Sister Teresa* (London: T. Fisher Unwin, 1901).
26. G. Moore, *A Mere Accident* (New York and London: Garland Publishing, Inc., 1978).
27. G. Moore, *Mike Fletcher* (New York and London: Garland Publishing, Inc., 1977).
28. G. Moore, *Vain Fortune* (London: Walter Scott, 1895).
29. R. Ellmann, *James Joyce* (New York: Oxford University Press, 1959), pp.259–60. See J. Joyce, 'The Dead', in J. Johnson (ed.), *Dubliners* (Oxford: Oxford University Press, 2008), pp.138–176.
30. Cave reads the epiphany, for example, as 'having the power and density of implication of one of Wagner's monologues', and which comes 'very close' to 'Symbolism'. For Cave, the Symbolists had been attracted to Wagner because of his belief 'that ideas or thoughts are but images of the perceptions of the senses'. See R. Cave, *A Study in the Novels of George Moore*, pp.113–146.
31. See Moore, *Vain Fortune*, p.270.
32. Ibid.
33. Ibid., pp.270–72.
34. See Nichols, *The Poetics of Epiphany*, p.109.
35. J. Joyce, 'The Dead', pp. 138–176. Joyce writes, for instance: 'The time had come for him to set out on his journey westward. Yes, the newspapers were right: snow was general all over Ireland', p.176. This 'Yes' seems to stem directly from Gabriel rather than the narrator. It is possible, of course, to ascribe this method simply to Joyce's overall use of idiom in the collection.
36. See Moore, *Spring Days*, p.154.
37. E. Warwick Slinn, 'Dramatic Monologue', in Richard Cronin, Alison Chapman and Anthony H. Harrison (eds), *A Companion to Victorian Poetry* (Oxford: Wiley-Blackwell, 2007), p.89.
38. R. Descartes, *Rules for the Direction of the Mind*, in Elizabeth S. Haldane and G.R.T. Ross (trans), *Descartes/Spinoza* (Chicago: University of Chicago Press, 1952), p.4.
39. Slinn, 'Dramatic Monologue', p.89.
40. Ibid.
41. Ibid.
42. Ibid.
43. Ibid.
44. P. Maltby, *The Visionary Moment: A Postmodern Critique* (Albany: SUNY, 2002), p.41. Maltby has some interesting things to say about how Wordsworth's 'spot of time' is the most 'eloquent testimony' to the artistic sensibility.
45. From a postmodern perspective, the romantic epiphany, and indeed the high modernist, epiphany are seen as an escape from the political and sociological history. See Maltby, *The Visionary Moment*, p.121.
46. Ibid., p.36.
47. W. Pater, *The Renaissance: Studies in Art and Poetry* (London: Macmillan and Co., Ltd., 1920), p.236.
48. Ibid.
49. Ibid., p.239.
50. Ibid., p.150.
51. M. Arnold, 'The Function of Criticism at the Present Time', R.H. Super (ed.), *The Complete Prose Works*, Vol. 3 (Ann Arbor: University of Michigan Press, 1960–77), p.258.
52. See Pater, 'Preface', *The Renaissance*, p.viii.
53. See Pater, *The Renaissance*, p.236.
54. Ibid.
55. I. Armstrong, *Victorian Poetry: Poetry, Poetics and Politics* (London and New York: Routledge, 1996), p.383.
56. G. Moore, *Confessions of A Young Man* (London: William Heinemann, 1917).
57. See Moore, *A Mere Accident*, pp.65–8.
58. See Moore, *Evelyn Innes*, p.15.
59. Pater, *The Renaissance*, p.150.

60. See Moore, *Evelyn Innes*, p.103.
61. H. Bloom, 'Walter Pater: The Intoxication of Belatedness', *Yale French Studies*, 50, Intoxication and Literature (1974), 163–189 (p.172).
62. See Moore, *Evelyn Innes*, p.233.
63. Ibid., p.224.
64. Armstrong, *Victorian Poetry*, p.421.
65. J. Joyce, *Stephen Hero: Part of the First Draft of 'A Portrait of the Artist as a Young Man'*, edited with an introduction by Theodore Spencer, revised by John J. Slocum and Herbert Cahoon (London: Jonathan Cape, 1963), p.218.

REFERENCES

Armstrong, I., *Victorian Poetry: Poetry, Poetics and Politics* (London and New York: Routledge, 1996).

Arnold, M., 'The Function of Criticism at the Present Time', in R.H. Super (ed.), *The Complete Prose Works*, Vol. 3 (Ann Arbor: University of Michigan Press, 1960–77).

Beja, M., *Epiphany in the Modern Novel* (London: Peter Owen, 1971).

Bloom, H., 'Walter Pater: The Intoxication of Belatedness', *Yale French Studies*, 50, Intoxication and Literature (1974), pp.163–189.

Cave, R.A., *A Study of the Novels of George Moore: Irish Literary Studies 3* (Buckinghamshire: Colin Smythe, 1978).

Descartes, R., *Rules for the Direction of the Mind*, in Elizabeth S. Haldane and G.R.T. Ross (trans), *Descartes/Spinoza* (Chicago: University of Chicago Press, 1952).

Ellmann, R., *James Joyce* (New York: Oxford University Press, 1959).

Jack, I. (ed.), *Browning: Poetical Works 1833–1864* (London: Oxford University Press, 1970).

Joyce, J., *Stephen Hero: Part of the First Draft of 'A Portrait of the Artist as a Young Man'*, edited with an introduction by Theodore Spencer, revised by John J. Slocum and Herbert Cahoon (London: Jonathan Cape, 1963).

Joyce, J., 'The Dead', in J. Johnson (ed.), *Dubliners* (Oxford: Oxford University Press, 2008), pp.138–176.

Kant, E., *The Critique of Pure Reason*, translated by Norman Kemp Smith (London: Macmillan, 1933).

Langbaum, R., 'The Epiphanic Mode in Wordsworth and Modern Literature', in R. Langbaum (ed.), *The Word From Below: Essays on Modern Literature and Culture* (Madison: University of Wisconsin Press, 1987), pp.33–57.

Maltby, P., *The Visionary Moment: A Postmodern Critique* (Albany: SUNY, 2002).

Miller, J. Hillis., *The Disappearance of God: Five Nineteenth-Century Writers* (Cambridge, Mass.; London: The Belknap Press of Harvard University Press; Oxford University Press, 1963).

Moore, G., *Confessions of A Young Man* (1886; London: William Heinemann, 1917).

Moore, G., *A Mere Accident* (1887; New York and London: Garland Publishing, Inc., 1978).

Moore, G., *Spring Days: A Realistic Novel* (London: Vizitelly & Co., 1888).

Moore, G., *Mike Fletcher*, (1889; New York and London: Garland Publishing, Inc., 1977).

Moore, G., *Vain Fortune* (1891; London: Walter Scott, 1895).

Moore, G., *Evelyn Innes* (London: T. Fisher Unwin, 1898).

Moore, G., *Sister Teresa* (London: T. Fisher Unwin, 1901).

Moore, G., *The Lake* (London: Heinemann, 1905).

Nichols, A., *The Poetics of Epiphany: Nineteenth-Century Origins of the Modern Literary Moment* (Tuscaloosa: University of Alabama Press, 1997).

Pater, W., *The Renaissance: Studies in Art and Poetry* (London: Macmillan & Co. Ltd., 1920).

Rajan, T., *Dark Interpreter: The Discourse of Romanticism* (Ithaca and London: Cornell University Press, 1980).

Rossetti, D.G., *The House of Life: A Sonnet Sequence*, with an introduction and notes by Paul Franklin Baum (Cambridge, Mass.: Harvard University Press, 1928).

Slinn, E.W., 'Dramatic Monologue', in Richard Cronin, Alison Chapman and Anthony H. Harrison (eds), *A Companion to Victorian Poetry* (Oxford: Wiley-Blackwell, 2007), pp.80–98.

Wordsworth, W., *The Prelude, or Growth of a Poet's Mind*, edited from the manuscripts, with introduction and textual and critical notes by Ernest de Selincourt (London: Oxford University Press, 1959).

CHAPTER FIFTEEN

'Albert Nobbs and Company': Introduction to an Unpublished Reprint of Celibate Lives

ADRIAN FRAZIER

Irish writer George Moore (1852–1933) had a particular interest in people who did not fall into the category of married-with-a-family heterosexuals.[1] He called them 'celibates', literally meaning unmarried persons. That was technically his own condition, though Moore never passed a year of his adult life without a sexual entanglement, and from 1894 he conducted a long-lasting if sporadic extramarital relationship with a London society-hostess, Lady Cunard. To borrow the idiom of Mrs Pat Campbell, Moore preferred the hurly burly of the chaise lounge to the deep deep happiness of the double bed. His interest in celibates was not so much in those people who get satisfaction from a member of the opposite sex, but in those who do not.

A common Victorian view was that all goodness, all normality, is to be found in the family, and the state was the enemy of those individuals who did not belong in a marriage; they were to be thought of as odd, or perverse, possibly even criminal. The nine-teenth-century English novel principally concerned a man and a woman who get married at the end. But the life of persons who do not get married, whether because they are homosexual, prolifically sexual, sexually phobic, or not sexual at all, seemed to Moore a literary subject of great poignancy – lonely, dangerous, and hemmed about by private shame and public scandal. 'Only weaklings,' Freud believed, 'have submitted to such an extensive encroachment upon their sexual freedom' as required by the twin compulsions of hetero-sexuality and monogamy, but when the matrimonial state was so strong, many had little choice but to be weak.[2]

Out of twenty-six works of prose narrative in his complete works, Moore dealt with unmarried and un-marrying persons in fourteen. *Confessions of a Young Man* (1888), *Memoirs of My Dead Life* (1906), and *Hail and Farewell* (1914) are autobiographies often explicitly concerned with the vagaries of his own love life. *A Mere Accident* (1887) and *Mike Fletcher* (1889), two in his 'Don Juan Trilogy', deal respectively with an inactive homosexual and a crudely active heterosexual. *Evelyn Innes* (1898) and *Sister Teresa* (1901), two novels with a single heroine, concern a beautiful and passionate opera-singer who immures herself in a convent. *Héloïse and Abélard* (1921) explores a heroine of similarly sensuous and spiritual psychology in an historical romance. *The Lake* (1905) narrates the stream-of-consciousness of an Irish priest who, troubled by his attraction to a local schoolmistress, removes his collar and embraces the natural life, while *The Brook Kerith* (1914) is an epic rendering of the archetype of all Christian celibates, Jesus of Nazareth. Finally, Moore published four collections of stories that concern sexual refusal: *Celibates* (1895), *A Story-Teller's Holiday* (1918), *In Single Strictness* (1922), and *Celibate Lives* (1927).

The relationships between these four short-story collections are tricky, and for a detailed account of them, *A Bibliography of George Moore* by Edwin Gilcher must be consulted. The first forerunner of *Celibate Lives* (1927) was *Celibates* (1895), written immediately after Moore's critically-admired bestseller, *Esther Waters* (1894). The nature and style of the book may be gathered from a December 1894 letter from Moore to Sybil, Lady Eden:

> The story ['Agnes Lahens'] I am working on is rather good – the subject is interesting. Briefly, it is this: A girl of 17 is brought home from a convent school by a priest. Her mother has a lover and very disorderly people (society roughs) frequent the house. The husband is a complacent husband of an exceptional kind and yet he is natural. He has lost all his money and lives in his wife's house as a sort of servant. He insists on giving up his room and sleeping in one of the servants' rooms; he wears the butler's clothes. But now that his daughter has come home he wants his wife to give up her lover. The girl interrupts a very violent scene between the husband and the wife. This opens her eyes. One of the society roughs makes love to her very unpleasantly – she rushes to her room and overhears a terrible conversation between her mother and her mother's lover – she learns that it is she who has created all the trouble and many

other things. So she goes to the priest, asks him to inform her father that her mother has a lover and finally is taken back to the convent by the priest. Life is submitted to the girl's judgment and she decides that she will not accept life.

As Moore turned the tale, it became as much an expression of the inadequacy of the education of girls as of the moral failures of the contemporary middle classes. 'Life,' as understood in this story, is the working out of sexual instinct in the field of social custom, and Agnes Lahens has by her convent upbringing been unprepared for life. She is, to borrow Tennyson's phrase, a 'linnet born within the cage / That never knew the summer woods' and counts as a blest future never to plight her troth, but to 'stagnate in the weeds of sloth' (*In Memoriam*, xxvii).

According to Moore's explanation of the book's style, the characters were 'merely indicated', a painter's term for giving expression to a thing by token brush-strokes (as in the painting of Manet), rather than by the full representation through drawing, shading, and perspective. In later years, Moore continued the practice of this swift, indicative mode of narration in later stories, but altered the tone by making the narrator something of an oral storyteller, sometimes addressing a listener implied or even named within the narrative itself. Dropping the use of quotation marks, Moore removed the print distinctions between direct discourse or dialogue and free indirect discourse (in which the storyteller uses the language and speech patterns of the character without using the first person). Expressions of a character's state of mind give way to descriptions of that mental state, and those in their turn give way to indications of setting or time. This melting of discursive types does not go, of course, as far as the ultimate oral narrative, Molly Bloom's four vast unpunctuated sentences in the last chapter of *Ulysses* (1922). It is a literary evocation of ancient storytelling, rather than an avant-garde manifesto of the modern. Moore called the style 'the melodic line,' and the stories in *Celibate Lives* are one of its best expressions.

'Agnes Lahens', was not reprinted, nor was a second story in *Celibates*, 'John Norton'. It is a condensation of Moore's 1887 novel *A Mere Accident*. Both are life studies of the Irish playwright and patron of the arts, Edward Martyn, a devout Catholic who 'hated women', and loved young boys, though evidently from a moral distance. Moore made a third try at the depiction of the Catholic homosexual in 'Hugh Monfert',' published in *In Single Strictness*, a 1922 collection of stories. Unlike John Norton, Hugh Monfert finally admits to himself and others that he loves men.[3]

> Ideas, principles, beliefs, he said, are lashed into us by our mothers, our fathers, by priests, schoolmasters, and our lives are spent going through our tricks, our antics, in fear and trembling, till the original wild instinct breaks out in us and we fall upon our trainers and rend them.

This is a beautiful and brave statement of male–male desire as innate and unalterable, but it is also one of the only natural pieces of writing in a very artificial story, which Moore was correct to drop from *Celibate Lives*.

One story from *Celibates* reappears, though in altered form and under a different title, in both *In Single Strictness* and *Celibate Lives*. It is called 'Mildred Lawson' in the first collection and 'Henrietta Marr' in the last, but in both it is a detailed reflection on Moore's disappointed pursuit of the novelist Pearl Craigie (1867–1906; penname: John Oliver Hobbes), one of only two women he ever considered marrying. In the first four months of 1894, she gave him many reasons to believe that she regarded him as a highly eligible suitor – letters, invitations, compliments, professions of affection, confidences – never, however, sexual favours of the wet variety. Then suddenly she broke off with him and gave no explanation. Moore's pain and bewilderment were profound. There is an element of literary revenge in the lacerating portrait he paints in this story of a cold-hearted flirt, a liar, a wealthy idle woman, and an artist without impulse or talent. It is, frankly, a character assassination of Pearl Craigie.

But it is more than that, too. The novelist lets us see that as a single woman with a man's ambition for fame, his heroine is blocked at every turn by contemporary restrictions on a woman's freedom. Should she give up her virginity, she will have paid out all her social capital to another, and Henrietta wants to know what she will get in return. She wants to use men to get what she wants, but what she wants is not the joy of bodily love; men do not attract her that way, they frighten her. The 1895 version ends with Mildred Lawson crying out, 'Give me a passion for God or man, but give me a passion.'[4]

By making his heroine an artist rather than, as Craigie was, a novelist, Moore was able to draw upon his own extensive knowledge of painting in London and Paris. The portrait of 'Davau' in Chapter 6 of 'Henrietta Marr' is based on Rodolphe Julian, in whose academy of painting Moore himself had studied in the 1870s, and to whose profitably extended network of studios many Englishwomen came to paint in the 1890s. Chapters 8 through 10 give a faithful account of the social history of Impressionist painting in Barbizon from the 1860s to the 1880s, when Millet, Corot, Monet, Rousseau, and others painted landscapes there.

In rewriting the 'Mildred Lawson' of 1895 as the 'Henrietta Marr' of 1927, Moore cut a third of the opening narrative (a rather good pen portrait of Karl Marx and his daughter Eleanor), and he changed the ending from a cry out of the void of desire on the part of the heroine, to her sudden suicide. Strangely enough, the change was the result of events in Pearl Craigie's life since the first version was printed.

In 1902, Pearl Craigie went to India with her friend Mary Leiter Curzon and Lord Curzon, then Viceroy. Prior to his marriage, Lord Curzon had evidenced some interest in Pearl, a pretty, millionaire American debutant, and in those respects, just like his eventual choice, Mary Leiter. Several close acquaintances (Moore included) believed that Pearl Craigie entertained a continuing hope in becoming the wife of the Viceroy. This was a possible ambition because Mary Leiter Curzon was not a well woman. Indeed, Mary died in July 1906, and Pearl's father then observed to his daughter that Lord Curzon had become available. But on 12 August 1906, Pearl was found dead in her bed – by cardiac arrest, according to the doctor; by suicide according to Moore's story. Her hopes of a great marriage having been dashed by a rebuke from Lord Curzon, she could see no other choice.[5]

It seems strange that an author should amend a completed work of literary fiction to match subsequent events in the life of the person on whom a character was modelled. But it was Moore's creed as a novelist in the tradition of Balzac, Flaubert, and Zola that nature is the greatest novelist of all. In nature, it is – as he liked to say – always the improbable, even the unimaginable, that occurs in the life of an individual. It is for the writer to submit to the intricacies of what truly passes in human lives, and to render life's ironies and surprises without shame or apology. For a rich meditation on this subject, read Moore's preface to *Hail and Farewell*, 'Art without the Artist.'[6]

As Moore's fiction is often drawn from his acquaintances, and its models are the famous artists and intellectuals of the era, such parallels have a certain interest in their own right. However, the literary value of 'Henrietta Marr' lies elsewhere. If Moore's other stories of 'celibates' are fundamentally rendered in a style of pity – cold pity, but pity nonetheless – the tale of the frigid woman is frigid itself; the narrative is bitter male frustration in the act of being spent. It is an indictment of sexual 'virtue' as actually immoral and emotionally promiscuous. After Moore first read the story to his acquaintances, male friends – Arthur Symons, Edward Martyn, and Frank Harris – loved it, and female friends shrunk from it as an unpleasant story about an unpleasant person by an unpleasant person.[7] That is surely understandable, as is the limited appetite of male readers for tales of a woman who dies of a broken heart as a result of her lover's cruelty, the stock plotline that Moore transgenders in 'Henrietta Marr'.

Along with 'Henrietta Marr', three other tales in *Celibate Lives* are reprinted without substantial change from *In Single Strictness* (1922): 'Wilfred Holmes', 'Priscilla and Emily Lofft', and 'Sarah Gwynn'. 'Wilfred Holmes' is actually Julian Moore (b. 1867), the author's youngest brother.[8] Julian failed to make much headway in his attempted professions of novelist, politician, opera composer, or policeman, and settled into hobbies of collecting rare books and prints, while living in London on a small inheritance and allowance from his brother. His sad life is depicted with total familiarity and hopeless honesty.

Wilfred Holmes is a kind of Bartleby the Scrivener, from Herman Melville's famous story, a man who would 'prefer not to', but he is also an extension of another sort of scrivener, George Moore himself. Neither brother, George nor Julian, would just take a job and earn his living; neither could bring themselves to think as others thought. Neither can explain why they are as they are. Each was, as J.B. Yeats said of George Moore, like a man dropped down from Mars, who finds all accepted customs arbitrary.[9] In the case of George Moore, this characteristic became a path to royalties and fame. In Julian's case, it led to poverty and obscurity.

By attributing to Wilfred Holmes something of the psychology of the artist, the story dignifies the pity of his life. Indeed, the author gave a few of his own pet interests to Wilfred Holmes. George Moore himself became obsessed with a blackbird that he heard whistle five or six notes correctly in the Dublin garden of John Eglinton, and he too joined the hunt for the origin of the legend of Tristan and Isolde at one stage of his life.[10] Such pet interests are a typically hobby-horsical side of Tristam Shandyish country-gentlemen, artists, and writers to the editorial pages of newspapers everywhere.

Moore's celibates belong mainly to a single social formation. They are *rentières*, private persons living on income from property or investments, accumulated by an earlier generation and declining ever since. Thus they become case-studies in the collapse of the English and Anglo-Irish aristocracies and the uncertainty of social position in the new age of capitalism and the popular vote. Even the wealthiest – Henrietta Marr – is not totally safe. Her father arose from a lower level of English society through success in a distillery factory, and bought himself and his family status as landed gentry; it was hoped that in future even a title could be arranged. But Henrietta's improvident mother spent much of his fortune on bad paintings and other acquisitions. Neither Henrietta nor her brother look as if they will beget heirs. Wilfred Holmes is the fag end of a gentry family that still contributes to Britain in the colonies and at home. Priscilla and Emily Lofft are the 'old maids' of a spent County family. Albert Nobbs is the bastard offspring of an aristocrat. Only the maidservant, Sarah Gwynn, lacks a familial connection to the upper class in decline (unless one chooses to regard her father's people, the Protestants of Northern Ireland, as such a class). The fact that none of these figures propagate, or show any desire to perpetuate their families, is one of the telltale signs of a dying order.

The mild odour of a wilting class of Irish Victorians characterises the tale of two spinster sisters, 'Priscilla and Emily Lofft'. It is a retrospective narrative from the point of view of Emily Lofft, focusing on the fragmentary last words of Priscilla on her deathbed: 'In the garden.' Searching through a garden shed, Emily finds the secret of Priscilla's tiny but intense private life, the only thing she never shared with her sister. In the late nineteenth and early twentieth century, and sometimes after too, English literature suffered from censorship, often in the name of protecting young women from the dangers of scandalous books. That was the reason cited for banning *Madame Bovary*, *Ulysses*, and nearly all of Zola's novels. Moore's own fiction was often denied circulation. In this story, he plausibly and poignantly investigates the mental world of a 'young woman old', who is exposed to sexual experience only once, and then through the medium of literature. Was it good for her?

'Sarah Gwynn', an oddly sympathetic tale of the Roman Catholic conscience, is narrated from the point of view of a Protestant Dublin doctor with a taste in antique furniture. This character is modelled on Sir Thornley Stoker, the brother of Bram Stoker (author of *Dracula*), and Moore's neighbour during his Dublin years on Ely Place. The representation of the intimate mutualities between Protestants and Catholics in the era is fascinating, similar to the close relationships of African-Americans and Anglo-Americans in the pre-Civil Rights period of US history. In both situations, masters and servants from socially segregated groups frequently lived together in the same house. In spite of the vast power differential between masters and servants, and between different races and faiths, individuals became more personally aware of one another than is common in later ages of legal equality. Such personal awareness is also something with which Moore's narrator – in spite of his egotistical concern with his own comforts – is richly endowed. He accepts that all people have an interior life and a story of their own, and that 'everybody is nonsense to the next one'; there is no normal life.

The master-servant dialectic is cruelly repeated in every sphere of the world of 'Sarah Gwynn'. The factory manager makes the factory girls work long hours for wages that will not pay for food and shelter. The women go on the streets at night just to survive. The men exploit the streetwalkers for prices that never set them free from factory or street. Ostensibly a refuge from the sinful world, the convent merely reproduces the master–slave cruelties. Wealthy choir sisters oppress working lay sisters; the nunnery is a 'sweater's den' too. Sarah Gwynn's efforts to 'pay back' a friend for her charity are a moving protest against such selfish hierarchies and economies.

My favourite story in *Celibate Lives* is 'Albert Nobbs', in my opinion one of the greatest stories of twentieth-century English literature. A dramatisation in French by Simone Benmussa received much critical attention; Moore's original story has gotten little.[11] In 2012, a film of the story starring Glenn Close was released. Had Elaine Showalter's remit extended into the twentieth century, it would have made a good subject for a chapter in her great little work of literary history, *Sexual Anarchy*, along with Gissing's *Odd Women* and Stevenson's *Dr. Jekyll and Mr. Hyde*. 'Albert Nobbs' also embodies the thematics of cross-dressing as explored by Marjorie Garber and others, and of race in African-American narratives of 'passing'.[12]

'Albert Nobbs' was originally published in *A Story-Teller's Holiday* (1918), a sort of imaginary autobiography in which George Moore returns to Ireland after the Easter Rebellion of 1916 and becomes involved in a story-telling competition with a Mayo seanchaí (traditional story-teller), the 'Alec' addressed at the story's beginning and end. Alec tells droll tales of monks and nuns in medieval Ireland, and Moore tells modern stories. 'Albert Nobbs' is one of these modern stories, and 'an attempt to show how pathetic a droll story may be'.[13] I shall not give away the story in this preface; the shocks in its plausible but unforeseeable sequence of events are part of the pleasure it gives. But in addition to that pleasure, 'Albert Nobbs' illustrates vividly the social oppression of females in that period, indeed of all workers, the cruelty of men and women alike, the distinction between love and marriage, the similarities and differences between sexes and sex roles, and the necessity of both passion, compassion, and purpose in life, even for celibates. There is no abstract harping on these matters, and no direct moralising. Indeed, the tone of the story is, as Moore aimed for it to be, created by matching a vision of the sadness of human life with a wondering smile at how strange and queer we all are.

Celibate Lives is one of the great collections of modern short stories. Moore pioneered the concept of a short-story sequence with a premeditated stylistic coherence and interlinked themes. The afore-mentioned *Celibates* (1895) was his first such collection. His most influential, probably, was *The Untilled Field* (1903). That collection depicts an Ireland of ruin and weed, in which the first attempts at cultural revival are crushed by poverty, ignorance, and the over-whelming authority of the Roman Catholic clergy. It is the first great prose work of the Irish Literary Revival, and inspired the second: Joyce's *Dubliners*. An assiduous reader of Moore's books, Joyce developed the theme of cultural paralysis in a comparably naturalistic style but in an urban rather than a rural setting. Joyce also went a good deal further than Moore in the direction of scrupulous mean-ness and daedalian design. By the early 1920s, Joyce had well surpassed Moore and all others as the most advanced novelist; *Ulysses* was the talk of all literary pages, and sometimes the news pages as well. With *Celibate Lives*, Moore, then in his 70s, did not swerve in the direction of the myriad novelties of Joyce, so very like and so far surpassing the stylistic experimentations of his own early career. He cleaved to his own late personal craft, an art that hides art and a narrative fluency that makes the wonderful appear wholly probable, even inevitable.

NOTES

1. This essay was originally composed for a reprint of *Celibate Lives* by the University of Wisconsin Press in 2004. The series of which this volume was to be part was cancelled before the book was printed.
2. Sigmund Freud, *Civilization and Its Discontents*, translated by James Strachey (New York and London: W.W. Norton, 1961), pp.51–2.
3. George Moore, *In Single Strictness* (New York: Boni and Liveright, 1922), p.197.
4. George Moore, *Celibates* (London: Walter Scott, 1895), p.312.
5. For further information about Pearl Craigie and the Curzons, see Stanley Weintraub, *The London Yankees* (London: W. H. Allen, 1979), p.82–3; Vineta Colby, *The Singular Anomaly: Women Novelists of the Nineteenth Century* (New York: New York University Press, 1970), p.221.
6. George Moore, *Hail and Farewell*, edited by Richard Cave (Buckinghamshire: Colin Smythe; Washington, D.C.: Catholic University of America Press, 1985), pp.47–53.
7. George Moore to Will H. Dircks; 21 February 1895; private collection, Mark Samuels Lasner.
8. Julian Moore donated little treasures from his collection to the British Museum in later years; see *The Times*, 'Gifts to the British Museum' (15 October 1934), p.8, col. G; and 'Acquisitions of the Museums' (12 May 1936), p.10, col. E. For further details on Julian Moore, see Adrian Frazier, *George Moore 1852–1933* (London and New Haven: Yale University Press, 2000), pp.382–3.
9. Frazier, *George Moore 1852–1933*, pp.342, 347.
10. George Moore to W.K. Magee [John Eglinton]; [April 1918]; Harry Ransom Humanities Research Center; Austin, Texas. The blackbird leitmotif runs through several of the stories in *Celibate Lives*.
11. See, for instance, Sharon Ammen, 'Transforming George Moore: Simone Benmussa's adaptive art in *The Singular Life of Albert Nobbs*', Text and Performance Quarterly (11:4) 1991, pp.306–12, and Elam Abell, 'Visual representation in *The Singular Life of Albert Nobbs*', *Text and Performance Quarterly* (11:4) 1991, 313–18. (1991).
12. Elaine Showalter, *Sexual Anarchy: Gender and Culture in the Fin de Siècle* (New York: New York, 1990); Marjorie Garber, *Vested Interests: Cross-Dressing and Cultural Anxiety* (New York: HarperPerennial, 1993); Maria C. Sanchez, Linda Scholssberg (eds), *Passing: Identity and Interpretation in Sexuality, Race, and Religion* (New York: New York University Press, 2001).
13. George Moore to W.K. Magee [John Eglinton]; 14 January 1918; Harry Ransom Humanities Research Center, Austin, Texas.

CHAPTER SIXTEEN

On Albert Nobbs

GLENN CLOSE

Thirty years ago, I was introduced to the character, Albert Nobbs. Simone Benmussa of the Théâtre du Rond-Point, in Paris, had successfully mounted a stage adaptation of George Moore's novella in both Paris and London and was in New York to direct a production of the play, which she had titled *The Singular Life of Albert Nobbs*, at The Manhattan Theater Club. It was early in my career; I had just finished appearing in my first movie role – Jenny Fields in *The World According to Garp*. I remember my audition for Ms. Benmussa was far from satisfactory. I was aware of the highly subtle complexity of Albert and found it incredibly challenging to try to play her in one five-minute scene. So much so that I stopped in the middle of my audition and said, 'I am not doing this character justice. I am boring myself, so I must be boring you. I'm sorry, but I think I'll go now.' And I walked out. That evening, I heard from my agent that Simone thought my audition was the most interesting thing that had happened that day and wanted me to come back. I was thrilled, but determined to do better. So, I contacted an acting coach whom I had heard about through friends, went in for a session with him, was able to get a bit more of a handle on Albert, went back to audition and got the part. The truth is that I wouldn't be here writing this today if I hadn't been given that second chance. When I walked back into the audition room and convinced them that I could play Albert, I unknowingly set into motion events that would afford me one of the most fulfilling experiences of my career, even though it would take years to realise. We had a successful run Off-Broadway and then I went on to other things, having been cast in my second movie, *The Big Chill*.

My career started to take off, but the haunting character of Albert Nobbs never left me. In fact, she kept whispering to me, in her tentative, innocent manner, perched in her very own space in my heart. Albert was unforgettable because she embodies for me three human qualities that I find deeply compelling: innocence, a lack of self-pity and the capacity to be compelled by a dream.

Albert's innocence comes from the fact that she has never had any intimate relationships. Once she buries herself in the guise of a waiter, it is too dangerous for her to seek any human contact. In order to survive, she has to stay invisible. Because she is an innocent, Albert wields unconscious power. She does not judge her fellow man. Her face is like a mirror, causing people to react to her direct, unknowing gaze in ways that reveal, to themselves and to others, who they really are. Her innocence is also Chaplinesque – the funny-tragic face of the human comedy in which we are all players.

Albert's lack of self-pity is due to the fact that she doesn't think the world owes her anything. She is thankful to have found a façade that enables her to have gainful employment in an age when nameless, penniless, unmarried women ended up as streetwalkers or in the poor house. She worked hard and saved her money. She will never have to endure the shame and degradation of wretched poverty.

As a dreamer, ignorant of the fact that she lacks the tools to make her dream a reality, Albert gains our love and respect. I think all human beings are fed by dreams. We long to believe. We are moved by individuals who believe against-the-odds because nothing is easy for anyone and we want to believe that the impossible can, upon occasion, be possible.

Having started developing scripts and producing them as movies for television in the early 1990s, thoughts of Albert kept coming to mind. So in 1998, I optioned the rights to the original material – George Moore's novella, *Albert Nobbs* – and my journey began. Little did I know that it would take fourteen years for the movie of *Albert Nobbs* to come to fruition!

The first step was to get a script written, so I pitched Albert's story to practically everyone I worked with in the ensuing years. It wasn't until I was directed by the great István Szabó, in *Meeting Venus*, that Albert started to gain a little traction. István loved the story and asked to write the treatment. He did a masterful job, introducing the fact that everyone in Morrison's Hotel has something to hide, not just Albert. He also introduced the idea of Albert's death at the end of the story. In the novella, Albert becomes obsessively penurious and isolated after Helen leaves her, until one day she just stops – death by broken heart. István's long-time translator, Gabi Prekop, wanted the chance to write the script. She did a great job, but Gabi is Hungarian, not Irish, so I knew I needed someone with a deep knowledge of not only the Irish idiom, but also nineteenth-century Irish idiom. I called my friend, Stephen Frears, who suggested John Banville. Not yet addicted to Google search, I didn't know at the time that John is considered one of the greatest living Irish writers. I'm glad I didn't or I may have gotten cold feet! As it turned out, I called him out-of-the-blue and was immediately entranced by his directness and his wonderfully dry sense of humor. I ended up contracting John to do the usual two versions and a brush-up.

So with a viable script in hand and István, a world-class director, on board the second phase in bringing Albert to the screen began. It turned out to be the longest, most difficult phase of all – finding additional producers and the money! I have come to characterise independent films as films that almost DON'T get made. The process of finding funding sources who will stick with you through thick and thin is a great test of one's commitment, stamina, resilience and creativity. I proceeded to pitch the script to every studio and then every independent film company to which I could gain access. I reached out to certain wealthy individuals who I thought would respond to the themes of the story. I was very good at pitching. I could get people very excited, but when they read the script, they found it very difficult to imagine me as a waiter in nineteenth-century Dublin. Or sometimes they would love the script and then would consult their lawyers who, I imagined said, 'Have you lost your senses! Invest in a movie ... over my dead body!'

I didn't resent it when people didn't 'get it' and turned me down. I knew it was a hard sell. Besides me being dressed as a man, I knew that the humor was very subtle and that it would depend on the casting of actors who could play each part to perfection. I knew that the movie would be sexy, maybe a different kind of sexy – except for Helen and Joe – but sexy nevertheless. And I never stopped believing in the emotional power of Albert's predicament. Every night on stage, I had felt the audience being emotionally blindsided by this seemingly simple tale. I never stopped believing. We finally succeeded in cobbling together enough money to actually start pre-production. We hired a casting agent and started sifting through audition tapes and resumes. István, the inspired Production Designer Patrizia von Brandenstein and I went to Ireland to reconnoiter possible locations.

Everything seemed to be falling into place. We just needed a few final pieces in our carefully constructed house of cards.

I went to the Toronto Film Festival in 2001 in search of our last chunk of funds. Having met with some exciting possibilities, I was in the cab on my way to the airport on September 11, when we heard on the radio that a plane had struck one of the World Trade Center towers. I thought it was a joke – like Orson Welles's *War of the Worlds* – but by the time I'd gotten to the lounge, all of us gathered around the TV screens and saw the second plane hit the second tower. The Toronto airport shut down and it was only through the compassion and generosity of two Canadian friends of mine that I was able to be reunited with my thirteen-year old daughter, who was home just outside the city and who had friends who lost family members on that tragic day. I was driven by my friends across the border and down through the gorgeous Finger Lakes region of New York. It took us ten hours. It was a stunningly beautiful day, in dire contrast to the living hell that had exploded in my city. I got to my child and with her, and millions of others, witnessed the end of the world as we knew it. The funding for Nobbs fell apart and we lost our window of opportunity. I went on to other jobs, as did István and Patrizia.

Last fall, on the tenth anniversary of 9/11, I was back at the Toronto Film Festival, surrounded by Team Nobbs, presenting our movie at a sold-out gala screening. It was an unbelievably moving moment for us all. So much had happened in the intervening ten years. István Szabó was replaced by Rodrigo Garcia. Bonnie Curtis, Julie Lynn and Alan Moloney had come aboard to produce with me. We had finally made our movie in 34 days for just under eight million dollars. Patrizia had come back and worked her magic. Michael McDonough was our Director of Photography and Pierre-Yves Gayraud our Costume Designer. The equally brilliant Matthew Mungle (Make-up) and Martial Corneville (Wig-maker and hair stylist) had worked through rigorous hair and make-up tests in order to come up with the look for me as Albert and Janet McTeer as Hubert. We were joined by a truly inspired ensemble of actors: Brendan Gleeson, Brenda Fricker, Pauline Collins, Mia Wasikowska, Aaron Johnson, Jonathan Rhys Meyers, Mark Williams, John Light, Antonia Campbell-Hughes and others. At Toronto, Albert Nobbs got a standing ovation.

Five years ago, when Albert Nobbs was still an unrealised dream, I asked myself, 'Should I battle on? Is it unrealistic? Have I gotten too old to play Albert? Should I throw in the towel?' I stood in the middle of the room and came to the decision that I was not willing to give up – that there were things in Albert's story that I still felt to be globally relevant – violence against women, poverty, exploitation, people having to live with secrets in order to survive, people feeling disenfranchised and isolated in a rapidly changing world. The most powerful stories for me are the ones that seem simple – even placed in another era – but that stir things in us that are largely unarticulated and buried. A key line in Albert Nobbs is: 'We are all disguised as ourselves.' To feel apart may be part of the human DNA, but it makes us carry internally the need to be safe and connected. Albert's dream of two easy chairs in front of a warm fire is an elemental dream. So I girded my loins and jumped back into the producing fray. On January 27th, all of us on Team Nobbs humbly offered our labour of love to the world. What a journey it has been!

Index